The
ENNEAGRAM
of
PASSIONS
and VIRTUES

ALSO BY SANDRA MAITRI

*The Spiritual Dimension
of the Enneagram*

JEREMY P. TARCHER/PENGUIN

a member of Penguin Group (USA) Inc.

New York

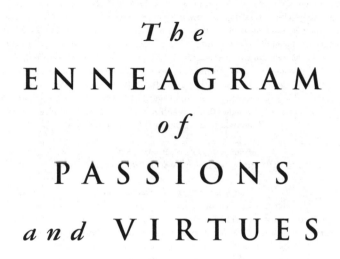

The
ENNEAGRAM
of
PASSIONS
and VIRTUES

FINDING

the

WAY HOME

SANDRA MAITRI

Foreword by A. H. Almaas

JEREMY P. TARCHER/PENGUIN
Published by the Penguin Group
Penguin Group (USA) Inc., 375 Hudson Street, New York, New York 10014, USA •
Penguin Group (Canada), 10 Alcorn Avenue, Toronto, Ontario M4V 3B2, Canada (a division
of Pearson Penguin Canada Inc.) • Penguin Books Ltd, 80 Strand, London WC2R 0RL,
England • Penguin Ireland, 25 St Stephen's Green, Dublin 2, Ireland (a division of
Penguin Books Ltd) • Penguin Group (Australia), 250 Camberwell Road, Camberwell, Victoria 3124,
Australia (a division of Pearson Australia Group Pty Ltd) • Penguin Books India Pvt Ltd,
11 Community Centre, Panchsheel Park, New Delhi–110 017, India • Penguin Group (NZ),
Cnr Airborne and Rosedale Roads, Albany, Auckland 1310, New Zealand (a division of Pearson
New Zealand Ltd) • Penguin Books (South Africa) (Pty) Ltd, 24 Sturdee Avenue,
Rosebank, Johannesburg 2196, South Africa

Penguin Books Ltd, Registered Offices:
80 Strand, London WC2R 0RL, England

Library of Congress Cataloging-in-Publication Data

Maitri, Sandra, date.
The enneagram of passions and virtues : finding the way home /
Sandra Maitri ; foreword by A. H. Almaas
p. cm.
Includes bibliographical references and index.
ISBN 1-58542-406-4
1. Enneagram.   2. Spiritual life.   3. Virtues.   4. Vices.   I. Title.
BL627.57.M34   2005   2004063734
202'.2—dc22

Printed in the United States of America
1   3   5   7   9   10   8   6   4   2

This book is printed on acid-free paper. ∞

Most Tarcher/Penguin books are available at special quantity discounts for bulk
purchase for sales promotions, premiums, fund-raising, and educational needs.
Special books or book excerpts also can be created to fit specific needs.
For details, write Penguin Group (USA) Inc. Special Markets,
375 Hudson Street, New York, NY 10014.

Where indicated, for purposes of analytical treatment, the author makes reference
to terms and concepts associated with Oscar Ichazo and/or the Arica Institute.
The author, however, has no connection with Mr. Ichazo or the Arica
Institute, and her interpretation and methodology are strictly her own.

To my fellow travelers
of all traditions

CONTENTS

Section 1

THE OUTER-DIRECTED CORNER

―∞∞∞―

Section 2

THE IMAGE CORNER

―∞∞∞―

Section 3

THE FEAR CORNER

―∞∞∞―

ACKNOWLEDGMENTS

The idea for this book arose following workshops I led in the fall of 2002 and spring of 2003 for the Ridhwan School in Boulder, Colorado, and the Enneallionce for Inner Work of Hamburg, Germany. I am grateful to Anne Laney for organizing the Boulder workshop and to all who supported it, and to the various organizers in Hamburg, especially my translator, Boris Fittkau.

I am deeply grateful to my very bright and very talented editor at Tarcher, Mitch Horowitz, for his continuing appreciation, support, and understanding of my work. His astute editorial input has once again helped to make a better book. I am also grateful to him for leading me to my wonderful and also very smart agent, Katherine Boyle, to whom I would like to express my gratitude for her ongoing support. Mitch and Katie both understood my vision and saw the importance of this book, and together encouraged me to produce it. I would also like to thank Deborah Miller for her meticulous copyediting of this book and for her astute queries and suggestions, which have helped to make this book, like my first one, stronger.

My profound thanks go to Hameed Ali (A. H. Almaas) for his generosity with his material, for his gracious Foreword to this book and his encouragement for me to write it, for his wisdom, and for being the remarkable light that he is for the planet at this time. And deep gratitude goes to Claudio Naranjo, who introduced me to the enneagram back in 1970, and as my first spiritual teacher, started me on the Path. I feel deeply honored by his support of my writing on the enneagram.

I would also like to thank Sherry Anderson, Mayuri Onerheim, and especially Rosanne Annoni for their reading of the manuscript, helpful comments, and encouragement. Rosanne, in particular, spent hours going over it and making useful suggestions. She is also a member of my painting group, which includes Jeannine Jourdan and Gabi Spina, and to all three I am grateful for the weekly nonverbal respite from writing. Many others contributed directly and indirectly to this book, and I would like to express my gratitude to some of them: to Eugene Cash for his helpful etiological input and Buddhist quotations; to Ralph Sharrett for making the diagrams; to Alia Johnson for showing me the Virginia Woolf passage so many years ago; to Bob Rosenbush for his ceaseless support and encouragement of my writing; to my dear friend Geneen Roth for her interest, enthusiasm, and advice about this book and many other things; to Jeanne and Paul Rosenblum for their friendship, many meals, and sustaining warmth; to Joyce Lyke for being such a good friend during this period, which I am more thankful for than I can express; and finally, to Brian La Forgia for his healing presence, wisdom, generosity of heart, and his love.

My students have taught me much of what is contained within this book, and to all of them, I express my thanks for their sincerity and devotion to the truth. It is an honor to work with them all, and I am grateful that I am able to do this. Decades of witnessing the personal processes of my group-mates and fellow teachers of the Diamond Approach has also contributed to the understanding in these pages. It is also an honor to be on this journey with them, and to watch and be part of their transformation.

And to all those who have made their own inner journey over the centuries, I am grateful. This book would not be here without the legacy they have bequeathed to us in advancing our collective consciousness.

List of
DIAGRAMS

FOREWORD

Being so involved and lost in the details of our lives, we forget that these particulars are actually the outer layer of our real lives. We might not even know, if we have not had the good fortune to have some awakening to true reality or to have encountered some genuine spiritual teaching, that these details merely form the outer layer of what is a much more magnificent reality. We might remain so surface-bound that we view ancient spiritual tools and methods for accessing this magnificent potential of human life only as means to help us deal with such everyday details. This is, to a great extent, how the wisdom of the enneagram has been used—which is why I am happy when I see books about it that remind us of its original and noble intention. Such is the present book.

In this second book on the enneagram by Sandra Maitri, she succeeds again, and in a more effective way, in showing how the enneagram is, more than anything else, a tool for inner transformation. She achieves this in a new way, one that both illuminates the basic and subtle aspects of the path of transformation and that reveals the inner meaning of some important levels of the knowledge of the enneagram. In her first book, *The Spiritual*

Dimension of the Enneagram, Sandra focused on the enneagram of fixations, or the psychological types. Here the focus shifts to the enneagrams of passions and virtues, with a pioneering exposition of such important dimensions of the amazing wisdom inherent in the enneagram.

The map of the enneagram, according to its original sources, reveals the design of reality in all its facets. There exist many enneagrams in this system, each revealing and elucidating the structure of reality in one of its dimensions. The enneagram of fixations, for example, addresses the dimension of ego or personality types, that is to say, the dimension of normal egoic experience. The enneagram of fixations focuses on the mental nature of the ego types, their underlying delusions, and the many character traits that emerge from such delusions. Sandra clearly showed in her first book how the fixations emerge from the loss of the Holy Ideas. This developed and fleshed out, amongst other things, the insights of my book on the enneagram, *Facets of Unity,* in which I primarily focused on the Holy Ideas and how their loss leads to the delusions of each fixation. In her book, Sandra showed how the totality of the fixations develop out of such delusions.

In my work, that of the Diamond Approach, I use the map of the enneagram in three significant places. At the beginning of the inner work of transformation, I frequently use the enneagram of fixations, which can help in recognizing and understanding the patterns of one's ego personality and sense of self in great detail. As the path unfolds and delves deeply into the nature of reality and realization, I use the enneagram of Holy Ideas, which can help, in amazingly clear ways, to reveal the true design of reality, reality as experienced in enlightened consciousness. In the middle of the path, however, where one begins to experience one's essential nature and experiences some integration of this essential presence, I use the enneagrams of passions and virtues, as developed and understood within the view of the Diamond Approach. The passions are the qualities of the heart when under the influence of egoic experience, which manifest as inner attitudes and affective atmospheres that both express the fixations and drive their particular actions. The virtues are the expression of the openness and development of the heart due to the realization of spiritual nature resulting from inner transformation.

Working with these enneagrams helps a great deal in seeing how what are called the passions, such as anger, envy, avarice, and lust, both express the egoic self and function as major obstacles to the path of transformation and realization. The virtues, in turn, reveal how inner realization impacts our soul or individual consciousness by adorning it with the attitudes of serenity, truthfulness, humility, nonattachment, and so on. The virtues turn out to be the visible signs of inner realization in both attitude and action.

In her present book, Sandra skillfully takes what she learned from Dr. Claudio Naranjo about the enneagram in general and about the passions and virtues in particular, weaves it together with the understanding of soul, passions, and virtues in the Diamond Approach, and—using her extensive experience in teaching both the enneagram and the Diamond Approach—develops a way of understanding the inner transformation of the soul within the context of these two enneagrams. The result is a book that is both a clear and deep appreciation of the inner path of transformation, and a detailed teaching about how the enneagram maps the region of the heart. With her characteristic clarity, Sandra shows how the human heart, when limited and constricted by the fixations of the ego personality, cannot but express the passions of anger, pride, deception, envy, and so on, with their attendant psychological suffering. While the book focuses mostly on the enneagram of passions, Sandra provides the teaching of the virtues with clarity and necessary detail, and clearly shows how the heart, when open and matured through the realization of inner transformation, is arrayed with the beautiful and generous virtues of truthfulness, sobriety, equanimity, courage, serenity, nonattachment, humility, true action, and essential innocence.

— A. H. ALMAAS, NOVEMBER 2004

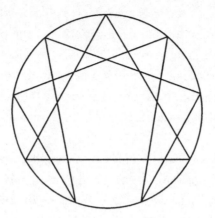

Diagram 1

THE ENNEAGRAM

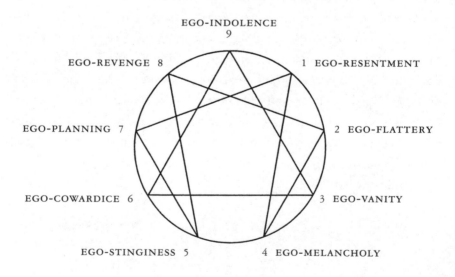

EGO-INDOLENCE
9

EGO-REVENGE 8

1 EGO-RESENTMENT

EGO-PLANNING 7

2 EGO-FLATTERY

EGO-COWARDICE 6

3 EGO-VANITY

EGO-STINGINESS 5

4 EGO-MELANCHOLY

Diagram 2

THE ENNEA-TYPES

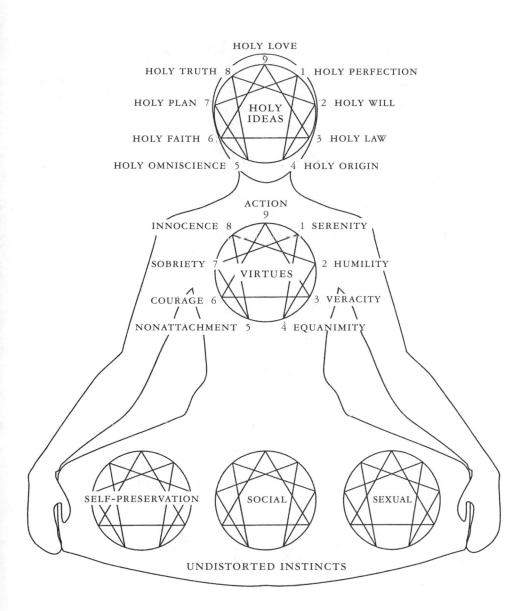

Diagram 3

THE OBJECTIVE ENNEAGRAMS

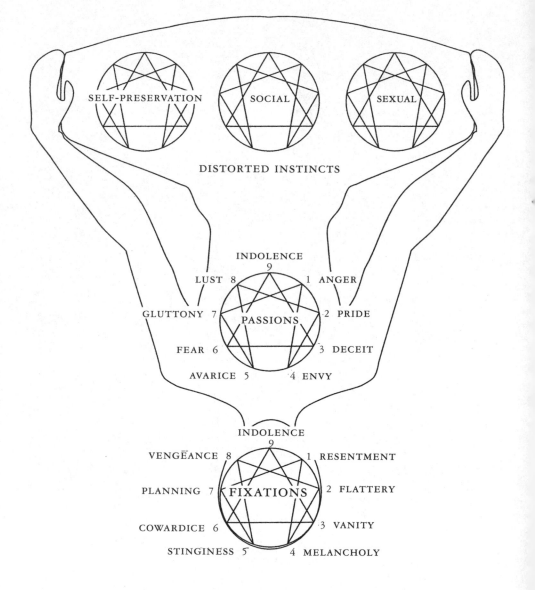

Diagram 4

THE ENNEAGRAM OF PERSONALITY

The
ENNEAGRAM
of
PASSIONS
and VIRTUES

INTRODUCTION

This book is not simply about the enneagram. It is about inner transformation. It is about understanding some of the major characteristics of our consciousness in the state of personality or ego—that of believing and taking ourselves to be the person who is the product of our personal history. It is also about the changes our inner atmosphere undergoes as we become free of that identification. And finally, it is about skillful means, as the Buddhists would say: how to orient ourselves so that this transformation has the possibility of becoming a reality.

Obviously, these aims imply that most of us are living within inner confines of which we are unaware, and that there is much more to us and to our potential experience of reality than we experience within the perimeters of ego. It also implies that it is possible to expand our consciousness beyond these constraints. This has been the endeavor of spiritual seekers throughout the ages, based on an inner intuition, or perhaps direct experience in extraordinary moments of deeper dimensions beyond those of ordinary consciousness.

Since the Age of Enlightenment in the eighteenth century, the collective consciousness of mankind, especially in the West, has progressively come to see the physical dimension of reality as ultimate. As a result, we have lost sight of the numinous. Our modern and postmodern world, based on this materialistic perspective and extolling only reason and scientific objectivity, has produced alienation, depersonalization, and existential meaninglessness experienced in small or gross ways by many. Rebellion against this worldview erupted en masse throughout the Western world in the 1960s, fueled by post–World War II prosperity affording the luxury of introspection, as well as by abundant supplies of psychotropic drugs, opening the doors of perception, to paraphrase Aldous Huxley.

The baby boomers sought in various ways to experience greater meaning and depth in their ongoing experience in those heady years. Finding little meaning in religious dogma or rote observances, many tried to discover if the Divine could be accessed directly, within themselves, and interest in mystical spirituality blossomed. As a result, spirituality—one of the deepest and previously most subterranean currents in the stream of human consciousness—emerged into the mainstream in the decades to follow. While spiritual seekers are found throughout human history, they have existed to a great extent at the fringe of society and of the various religions, and their numbers—at least in the West—have been relatively few. Beginning in the '60s, that situation also changed. This is not to say that spirituality has become a concern to many or even most people, but the numbers have swelled and Eastern traditions like Buddhism, whether of the Zen, Theravadan, or Tibetan variety, and Sufism are no longer foreign to the West. Almost everyone knows someone who meditates or does yoga. And even many of those immersed in corporate culture have heard of the enneagram, which this book is also about.

I was introduced to the map that is the enneagram in 1970 when I first met Claudio Naranjo in the backyard of his house in Berkeley. The transplanted Chilean psychiatrist had risen to the fore of what came to be known as the human potential movement in the '60s and, although I did not know it at the time, Naranjo was one of the people responsible for putting spirituality on the contemporary Western cultural map, so to speak. He also would become the source for almost all of the publicly known information about the system of the enneagram in the years that have followed.

This gathering in Naranjo's garden was the nucleus of the group that he would call SAT, for Seekers After Truth, the same name the Greek-Armenian mystic G. I. Gurdjieff and his fellow seekers called their group at the end of the nineteenth century. The group's focus was on spiritual development, and while Naranjo's teaching embodied a similar spirit to that of Gurdjieff, its most remarkable and innovative feature was its pioneering inclusion of psychological understanding in spiritual work. Traditionally, spiritual practices in all of the traditions were designed to transcend, overcome, or sidestep our psychology—that collection of mental, emotional, and behavioral patterns shaped by our personal history. Working with our psychology head-on was something entirely radical in spiritual work, something that was only becoming possible in the second half of the twentieth century, a century that has been dubbed the psychological century.

While we take psychological understanding for granted even in popular culture these days, knowledge about how our psyche ticks, and the forces that have shaped our behavior patterns, character, and psychological structure, has been extensively explicated only in the last hundred years. The modern field of psychology came into being at the dawn of the last century through the work of Sigmund Freud, and while one of his disciples, Carl G. Jung, took the understanding of the psyche into spiritual realms, it would be another seventy years before the field of psychology would begin to influence spirituality.

This fusion of psychology and spirituality has today become quite widespread. This is because in it lies the potentiality for spiritual development to be possible not simply for the exceptional few. Ultimately, it is out of this orientation, developed and worked with for the last three and a half decades, that this book is grounded. By understanding, and therefore being able to skillfully work with and through, the psychological pitfalls that have bedeviled spiritual seekers throughout the ages, the deeper dimensions of reality can become more readily accessible. To do so, we will use the knowledge about these things charted by the nine-sided figure contained within a circle, called the enneagram. As we shall see, the enneagram can unlock great wisdom about how the personality works and about how to find our way to what lies beyond it. Using it as our guide, we will explore the ins and outs of our personality structure not simply so that we can become more functional and "fixed" but, as in Naranjo's original orientation to this map, so that we can gain deeper access to the full dimensionality of who and what we are.

Let's return for a moment to our story about one of this movement's pioneers. Trained as a psychiatrist, Naranjo had come to the United States in the early '60s and ended up at the forefront of the "consciousness revolution" centered largely in the San Francisco Bay Area and at Esalen Institute in Big Sur, California, the growth center where the human potential movement was more or less born. Abandoning more formal academia, Naranjo worked with Fritz Perls, the founder of Gestalt therapy, and his perspective also began to include spirituality. He worked with Idries Shah, teacher of Sufism, the mystical branch of Islam, while with his astute and adventurous intellect, he familiarized himself with a broad range of other spiritual and psychological ideas. He wove his distillations of these traditions into a teaching that synthesized them and made them into a whole.

The enneagram became the primary framework for the structure of his teaching in our first SAT group. He had learned about the nine-pointed diagram from a Bolivian mystic named Oscar Ichazo, whom he had just returned from working with in the Arica desert of northern Chile. Ichazo's source for the enneagram has variously been ascribed to the same secret Sufi order in what is now Afghanistan as the order from which Gurdjieff is sometimes said to have learned the system; and, more recently, to Ichazo's own channeling of the information. Gurdjieff used the figure of the enneagram, seen in Diagram 1, page xviii—a circle divided into nine points (ennea meaning "nine" in Latin), variously connected with lines—to describe the cosmic order of the universe, from the planets to the musical scale.

Ichazo was the first, at least publicly, to interpret the symbol to describe different aspects of the human experience. Ichazo taught that, among other levels of interpretation, the nine points of the enneagram refer to nine distinct ego or personality types, which we see in Diagram 2, page xviii. This means, in effect, that humanity is divided into nine types of personality structures, each based on estrangement from the spiritual dimension of reality. This disconnection leads to nine different "takes" on reality shorn of its innate depth. These nine distorted and fixed beliefs about how things are—distorted since they are incomplete perceptions— lead to the nine different character types or ennea-types, each with characteristic mental, emotional, and behavioral patterns arising out of this fundamental skewed perspective of reality.

Although I am unfamiliar with Ichazo's original teaching of the enneagram, it seems clear that Naranjo fleshed it out with his own psychological understanding, elaborating the basic descriptions of the ennea-types into psychologically cohesive character patterns. We worked with the enneagram theory intensively in the four years that the first SAT group lasted, finding its truth in our direct experience of ourselves and of one another. As a map of the human psyche, it brought to consciousness aspects of ourselves that would have taken many years of difficult introspection to see without it. Naranjo knew and recognized the power of the enneagram as a psychospiritual tool, and its potential and place as part of serious spiritual work, and so he swore all of his students not to teach the enneagram without his permission.

Given its potency, it was perhaps inevitable that the enneagram would begin to leak out. The enneagram found its way into the Jesuit community and has since become an accepted part of its training; and the enneagram, stripped of its spiritual function, became widely known as a psychological typology as books on it flooded the market, and even corporate institutions began to adopt it. Naranjo, in response, stopped teaching it in the United States.

The enneagram's popularity, however, did not end its use as part of dedicated work on personal transformation. One of my friends and group-mates of the old SAT days was Hameed Ali, who writes under the name of A. H. Almaas. Following the disbanding of the group, Almaas's own development took off, propelling him into the formulation of a new way or path of personal transformation. In the late '70s, he was opening to the understanding that would become formalized as the Diamond Approach to Inner Realization, and began working with a small group of students in Boulder, Colorado. Carrying on and extending Naranjo's synthesis of psychological understanding and spiritual practice, Almaas ended up founding a spiritual school whose teaching and methodology has changed the lives of many hundreds of students throughout the world.

Abandoning the old spiritual model of the ego as an enemy or devil needing to be overcome or extinguished, Almaas saw that direct contact and exploration of our mental constructs opens them up, revealing the psychodynamics that put these self-representations and beliefs in place. Further exploration leads to the core of these psychological structures— loss of contact with one of the qualities that is variously called the Divine, God, Being, or True Nature. To put it a little differently, what he found was that our psychological structures arise as responses and coping strate- gies to deal with estrangement from aspects of our divine nature, a process occurring for the most part in early childhood. Hand in hand with the de- velopment of our ego structure, then, is a gradual diminishment of access to the fullness of our nature.

Key to the Diamond Approach's method is learning to be present to our here-and-now experience, and exploring and inquiring into the inner terrain that we encounter. For this inquiry to be transformative, it must involve more than intellectual insights about ourselves. Rather than us- ing our minds to lead our inner exploration, our understanding needs to arise from our direct experience. We must be in touch with the whole of our present experience, including our emotional life and our physicality. What Almaas found is that if we engage our inner process in this way, things will naturally unfold within ourselves, revealing progressively deeper layers of experience. If we dive into the contents of our conscious- ness in this way, we work through them. Without pushing or pulling at ourselves, we can move effortlessly through layers of our personality struc- ture and into the realm of Being—discovering who and what we are be- yond our historical and familiar sense of self.

Looking at the following example will give a brief sense of the Dia- mond Approach's method. If our sense of reality is that the world is un- supportive of our endeavors and that we lack the capacity to sustain ourselves, whether materially, emotionally, or spiritually, being present to the direct experience of these beliefs will probably lead to memories of instances in childhood in which these assumptions took shape in our psyche. Exploring those memories—entering into them, in other words—will probably lead to a sense of absence of support, and staying with that will in all probability lead to the sense of shaky ground beneath our feet and then perhaps a feeling of falling through space. Letting ourselves fall will most likely result in a sense of floating, of being held and supported by reality. We might then feel the palpable presence of support, something we don't have to generate or sustain but that simply is part of reality, arising seemingly magically through the process of contacting the felt sense of its absence.

Such an approach to our inner world radically shifts spiritual practice, obviating the traditional emphasis on disidentifying with the makeup of our personality. Rather than attempting to separate or move away from our egoic material, the focus changes to actively engaging it. Almaas's discovery was one whose time had come, made possible by the advent of psychological understanding in the twentieth century. Without the psychological knowledge and methodology available to us now, working directly with the personality was too difficult, and so spiritual practitioners of the past had little choice but to treat it as an obstacle—if not an enemy—to unfoldment.

The Diamond Approach informs what you are about to read, as does the enneagram. Some of the information on these pages is rooted in the teaching of Naranjo, and some of it is grounded in that of Almaas. To both, I am deeply appreciative and I feel blessed to have had the opportunity to work with them. The enneagram, as I have said, was part of the fabric of my introduction to spiritual work during my early twenties, and continues to be inseparable from it. This book is the result of the more than three decades that have ensued, in which my life has been devoted to the Path and in which the enneagram has formed a backdrop to my journey.

In the pages that follow, we will use the enneagram as a framework to understand what inner work is all about and how to work with our inner process in such a way that our journey is a fulfilling one, bringing us into direct and sustained contact with our deepest nature. In particular, we will explore the *passions* delineated by the enneagram—the drives, orientations, and emotionally imbued attitudes that characterize us when we are identified with our personality structure—and we will see how the passions transform into the *virtues,* which describe both inner atmospheres that result from moving beyond our personality structure as well as attitudes that assist us in that transformation. (See Diagrams 5 and 6, pages 15 and 19, depicting the enneagrams of the passions and virtues.)

This radical shift of consciousness expressed in the movement from the passions to the virtues necessitates first of all understanding the territory— what forces and motivations propel our ordinary consciousness. And I don't mean simply understanding it intellectually, since it is only by traveling *through* this terrain that we will discover what lies beyond it. By looking deeply into the passions, we will explore how the enneagram elucidates feelings and inner forces that characterize us when we are functioning from our personality structure—not simply for those of a particular ennea-type but for all of us.

It is important to emphasize what I have just noted: one of the basic principles about the enneagram is that it charts universal truths about the nature of reality and the nature of human beings. *Universal* means common to all of us, and it is from this perspective that this book is written. While the issues and conundrums symbolized at each point of the enneagram are stronger for those of that type, they are issues and conundrums that we all share.*

We will also explore how to work through these facets of the personality and how they transform into qualities that form an inseparable part of bona fide spiritual realization. The virtues describe how our inner landscape changes as we become less identified with our personality or ego structure—what happens as the biases and drives of the ego diminish and quiet. We will see how experientially understanding the passions will naturally lead us to the virtues, and we will explore this metamorphosis of each passion to its corresponding virtue. We will see how the felt sense or texture of our inner atmosphere gradually changes as we evolve, how the passions give way to the virtues as flavors of our inner life, and how this shift is reflected in our changing attitudes and feeling tone. We might, for

*For a thorough description of each ennea-type and guidance in figuring out what your type is, I refer the reader to my previous book, *The Spiritual Dimension of the Enneagram: Nine Faces of the Soul.*

example, notice a realized teacher's nonattachment, reflected in his ease in letting go of things (the virtue of Point Five), or we might recognize her openness to whatever arises (the virtue of Point One) or her dedication to truthfulness (the virtue of Point Three).

The virtues also represent attitudes toward our experience, whether inner or outer, that support or set the stage for this transformation. To understand this, we need to remember the truth contained in that old adage that the means determine the end. Translated into spiritual terms, this means that if our practices and our orientation toward our personal process are those congruent with the ways our deepest nature operates and the ways that it affects the human soul, our inner work is likely to bring us closer to our depths. If our practices and orientation are those of the personality, they will only lead us deeper into enmeshment with that structure.

So we are seeing that the virtues depict attitudes and orientations that are not only the expression of our realization of our deepest nature but they are attitudes and orientations that help make that realization possible. Skillful spiritual work, from the perspective of the enneagram, entails opening to and using the attitudes of the virtues as inner bearings.

Let us, then, turn our attention to the enneagram to discover what this ancient spiritual map can reveal to us about our inner terrain. We will see what it can tell us about how to navigate through our inner experience in a way that deepens and enriches us, unlocking access to what lies beyond our familiar territory. It is my sincere hope that what I have understood will assist my fellow travelers in finding their way to that home that, upon reaching, we realize was here all the time.

The ENNEAGRAM, the SOUL, the PASSIONS and the VIRTUES

———◁●/●/●▷———

All things are filled full of signs, and it is a wise man
who can learn about one thing from another.
—PLOTINUS[1]

Before we explore the passions and virtues, a bit of groundwork is in order so that we can understand their place in the overall system of the enneagram. In the enneagram theory as passed down via Claudio Naranjo from the teachings of Oscar Ichazo, there exist two sets of enneagrams. One describes specific characteristics of egoic experience, and the other describes their correlates, equally specific characteristics of human experience beyond the personality or ego structure—enlightened experience, in other words. Implicit is the overarching understanding shared by all spiritual traditions: that our ordinary experience is filtered through the veils of personality, and that it is possible to perceive reality objectively, without this subjective obscuration. We have, then, the set of enneagrams referring to egoic experience, called collectively the *enneagram of personality,* and the set of enneagrams referring to experience when free of the personality, the *objective enneagrams,* which we see represented in Diagrams 3 and 4, pages xix and xx.

Looking at these diagrams, we see that the enneagrams of the *fixations* and of the *Holy Ideas* are located in the head center of both figures. This is because these two enneagrams refer to our beliefs and perceptions of reality—the fixations referring to our mind-set when we see reality through the obscurations of the personality, and the Holy Ideas when our sense of reality is not so occluded. The passions and the virtues are depicted at the heart center of both figures. This indicates that they have to do with our emotional or affective states when we are identified with our personality—the passions—and as we become progressively free of that identification—the virtues. The third set of enneagrams refers to our instinctual drives, of which there are three in the map of the enneagram: self-preservation, social, and sexual. When our consciousness is identified with our personality, these drives become motivated by the passions and are thus distorted. The freer we are of our ego identification, the more these drives are informed by the virtues and function in an undistorted way.

The understanding associated with the enneagram tells us that as we develop a personality structure in early childhood, we gradually lose contact with Being. By the time our psychological structure is solidified, our contact with the depth of ourselves is largely lost to our consciousness. The enneagram of personality dominates our experience. With the loss of experiential contact with what makes life full, rich, and meaningful—our deepest nature—our personality has at its core a gaping absence. We see reality through the occluded lens of our fixation in which this depth dimension is absent, our emotional life is colored by our passion, and our passion drives our instincts in an attempt to fill the emptiness we feel.

Our inner affective state goes hand in hand with our perception of reality, meaning that how we feel is intimately connected with the way we see things. Most of us perceive reality through the filter of our personality structure, and our emotional state corresponds to that. In the language of the enneagram, we are perceiving reality through the fixations, and our emotional life takes on the feeling tone of the passions. As we work on ourselves and progressively perceive reality—both inner and outer—through fewer obscurations, our view becomes more objective and our affective atmosphere becomes clarified and purified. In enneagrammatic terms, as we develop, we increasingly see reality from the vantage point of the Holy Ideas, and our affective atmosphere takes on the qualities of the virtues. The fixations and the passions, then, are interlinked, just as the Holy Ideas and the virtues are intimately connected.

An interesting question arises: does our view of reality shape the way we feel, or is it the other way around? This is another way of asking which is more primary to the formation of our personality structure: the loss of perception of reality as it is (i.e., the loss of the Holy Ideas), or the loss of the felt connection with the realm of Being (i.e., the loss of the virtues)? Does the passion give rise to the fixation, or is it the other way around? Taking a brief look at this question is important for our understanding of the passions and virtues.

As both Almaas and I recall, Naranjo taught us that the origin of our personality structure or ennea-type is rooted in our "sensitivity" to one particular Holy Idea. This means that when we are born, one of the enlightened views of reality—one of the Holy Ideas—is tenuous. Like a sensitive nerve, the impacts of early childhood are filtered through this sensitivity. The effect is that our particular unobstructed view of reality is weakened, diminished, and overshadowed by the vicissitudes of our formative years. We lose sight of this way of perceiving and experiencing ourselves and the world around us, and in its place we develop a fixed and distorted perspective about reality without it. This becomes our *fixation.* Since this perception is inaccurate, it can as easily be called the core delusion of each type. It forms the cognitive basis of our personality structure, and as we were taught, our behavioral, emotional, and psychological patterns arise from it. Claudio refers to our fixation as a cognitive mistake and an ontic obscuration, meaning that our perception of Being is obscured and we form a mental construct of reality without it. He cites Ichazo as defining the fixations as "specific cognitive defects—facets of a delusional system in the ego."[2]

For example, if Holy Perfection is the Holy Idea to which we are born sensitive (meaning that we are predisposed to become an Ennea-type One), as we gradually lose contact with Being and begin developing a personality structure, we likewise gradually lose the perception of the inherent perfection of everyone and everything, including ourselves. In time we come to the conclusion that we are not okay as we are, which solidifies into the conviction that we are fundamentally flawed. This fixed cognitive belief in the not-rightness of things and of ourselves becomes the basis of the perfectionism of the ennea-type at Point One. Ichazo gives *resentment* as the fixation of Point One, but perhaps *imperfection* more fully captures the cognitive distortion of this type.*

Almaas developed the understanding about how disconnection from the Holy Ideas leads to the fixations, and more fully elucidated what the perspectives of the Holy Ideas are. His book, *Facets of Unity: The Enneagram of Holy Ideas,* describes how inevitable early experiences of the absence of complete attunement and the meeting of one's needs leads to the gradual loss of perception of the spiritual or depth dimension of reality. Coemergent with this loss of contact with Being is, obviously, the loss of the nine different perceptions of it—the Holy Ideas. We will explore the process of this diminishment of perception—referred to in traditional spiritual teachings as the fall from paradise—more fully in Chapter 2, in which we explore the passion and the virtue of Point Nine.

In all likelihood, our early reactions to what is traumatic for our infant consciousness are inseparable from our loss of perception of the ultimate goodness of reality. That is, our emotionally reactive patterns, which in time crystallize into our passion, arise concurrently with our distorted view of reality, our fixation. Whatever the causative factor, it is clear that we are predisposed to develop into one particular ennea-type, with its belief structure and its corresponding set of emotional and behavioral patterns.

THE PASSIONS

The passions, as we have seen, are the emotional, affective, and feeling tones or qualities that characterize each ennea-type. As Naranjo describes it, they are also "deficiency-motivated drives that animate the psyche,"[3]

---

*A brief note about terminology: In the early days, we referred to our type on the enneagram as our fixation, but in recent years, Naranjo has introduced the term *ennea-type* to denote the sum total of characteristics discriminating each enneagrammatic type. Although usage of the term *fixation* to denote one's type persists in the enneagram community, I think that the use of *ennea-type* is definitely more accurate due to its inclusivity.

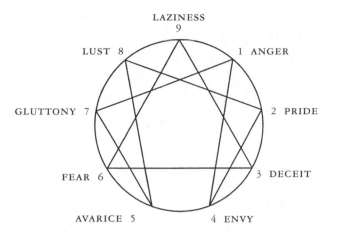

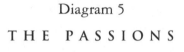

Diagram 5

THE PASSIONS

meaning that the passions arise out of the emptiness of the ego, and seek—while at the same time they obstruct—restoration of fulfillment and contentment. In the absence of contact with the realm of Being, then, we are driven to search out the wholeness we vaguely remember from early childhood. Not consciously understanding that it is our True Nature we experience as absent, our passion drives us to try to fill that void.

In the usual way in which we use the word *passion,* it means primarily intense and consuming emotional energy, as well as amorous drivenness. In the language of the enneagram, the passion is the feeling tone of a person's consciousness when under the sway of their personality or ego structure, the knee-jerk habitual reactive tendency. Just as passion is used to describe the suffering of Jesus during his Crucifixion, while not consciously chosen, our passion is likewise our suffering.

The passions are "passionate" insofar as they are compulsive—as Naranjo says, "we are subject to them as passive agents."[4] We cannot choose to disidentify from our passion, since its whole bias and orientation is basic to our personality structure. Our passion, then, is in operation to the extent that we are identified with our personality.

To refer to our passion simply as an emotion would be misleading. As Kant says in his *Anthropologie*,

> *An emotion is like water that breaks through a dyke, passion like a torrent that makes its bed deeper and deeper. An emotion is like a drunkenness that puts you to sleep; passion is like a disease that results from a faulty constitution or a poison.*[5]

This feeling tone is composed of habitual emotional reactions arising out of our distorted perspective of reality. For example, when we believe that we are ultimately separate from the rest of reality (the deluded perspective of Point Five), it follows that what we possess might be all that we will get, and so we must conserve our resources. Hence the passion of Point Five, avarice or stinginess, and the characteristic constriction, withdrawal, and elusiveness of Fives. We can see from this example how the passions are both feeling states as well as motivating drives, as Naranjo describes. Much more, of course, will be said about this particular passion, but perhaps in this brief example, we can get a sense of what a passion is.

Passion in ordinary usage also has to do with our reason being overcome by strong or violent emotions triggered by something or someone external to us. When seized by passion, we are not ourselves. To the extent that our passion dominates, we are indeed subject to forces external to who we are: we are subject to the pushes and pulls of our personality or ego. We are operating out of a sense of mistaken identity, believing ourselves to be ultimately separate entities. Our sense of who and what we are is grounded in the belief that we are primarily our bodies and that our fundamental nature is devoid of any deeper dimensionality than the physical—which itself we experience through a distorted lens. This is the deepest belief at the core of the general condition of humanity. It is the fundamental belief upon which the personality, regardless of our ennea-type, is based. Since by definition the personality is a sense of self built around the absence of the depth dimension of reality, it is inevitable that when we are identified with it, we experience ourselves as lacking something fundamental. We experience, in other words, a sense of deficiency, which we may ascribe to various causes or character flaws, but which is part and parcel of the territory of the ego.

THE SUBTYPES

We will shortly turn our attention to the virtues, but it is first important to understand a bit more about the *instinctual subtypes*—which can be seen in Diagrams 3 and 4, pages xix and xx—and their relationship to the passions. As noted earlier, in the map of the enneagram, there exist three instincts: self-preservation, social, and sexual. In being one ennea-type, we also experience one of these life arenas as most charged, most salient, and so we have one dominant subtype. Each of the subtypes possesses a characteristic style, and this results in the further differentiation of the nine overarching ennea-types into twenty-seven distinct personality styles. The three subtypes are as follows:

- If the self-preservation instinct is the most pronounced, one is preoccupied with survival and material security in an effort to find happiness and fulfillment.
- If the social instinct dominates, one is oriented toward achieving a sense of belonging, a place and status in community.
- If the sexual instinct is most emphasized, intimate relationship seems to hold the promise of satisfaction.

The inner sense of lack, fundamental to the ground of the personality, is focused and experienced here. In other words, it is in this sphere of life in which we feel the most deficient, in the sense of lacking what it takes, and also the most deprived. Because the glasses through which we view our lives are tinted in this way, we feel lacking in one of these particular life arenas, and because reality has a peculiar way of substantiating such beliefs, we have a hard time experiencing and objectively finding the fulfillment we seek in this sphere.

Since this life arena is the most charged, it is also the area of life in which we most strongly experience the passion of our type. As Naranjo puts it, our passion or motivational drive is "channeled" into that instinctual sphere. Or, to put it differently, one particular instinct becomes the most "passionate" in the sense that our personality is geared around its satisfaction, and this becomes the area of life in which we feel our deepest insecurity and vulnerability. The passions, in turn, bind and distort our instinctual drives so that when we are identified with our personality, our instincts are not functioning freely but are tied up with the concerns arising out of a limited, and thus distorted, self-definition.

Observing where the passion of our type arises most consistently and forcefully is a good indication of which instinctual subtype we belong to. For instance, if we happen to be a Four, we would find our passion of envy arising in instances when either our self-preservation felt threatened, our sense of social standing and belonging felt in question, or when our intimate relationship or our capacity to have one felt in jeopardy. As a Four, we might, for example, feel envious of what another possesses if we were a preservation type; or we might begrudge a friend who seems socially adept and accepted if we were a social type; or covet the sensual allure of another if we were a sexual type. The binding and channeling of the nine passions into three different instinctual arenas produces twenty-seven distinct subtypes, each with a characteristic style reflecting this emphasis. While a complete description of the subtypes is beyond the scope of this book, I refer those interested to my previous book.*

As we can see, the map of the enneagram can be very specific about our fundamental cognitive orientations, our characteristics, behavior, and emotional patterns. But it also describes such patterns that we all share. As seen in the introduction, one of the basic principles about the enneagram is that it refers to universal truths about all human beings and the nature of reality. This means that while we each have one passion that is the most highlighted in our experience, we also have the other eight. Taken together, the passions elucidate nine primary tendencies that characterize egoic existence. It is primarily from this perspective in which we

---

*The Spiritual Dimension of the Enneagram: Nine Faces of the Soul, Chapter 12.

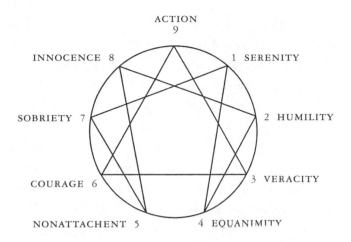

ACTION
9

INNOCENCE 8   1 SERENITY

SOBRIETY 7   2 HUMILITY

COURAGE 6   3 VERACITY

NONATTACHENT 5   4 EQUANIMITY

Diagram 6

THE VIRTUES

see that all of us have and contend with all nine passions that we will explore them in the chapters that follow. Likewise, the virtues describe nine universal attitudes that arise as we work through our personality structure and that also orient this transformation.

THE VIRTUES

As we evolve—as we become less identified with our personality—our instincts function in an increasingly undistorted way, as we have discussed. The more complete we feel, the less we are driven to seek satisfaction or fulfillment in these life arenas, and so we can relate to them without the distortion of deficiency and the drive to fill it. Our particular passion becomes less of a motivational and driving force, and our inner atmosphere progressively loses the feeling quality of our passion. In its place, we are motivated by and take on the affective quality of the virtue of our particular ennea-type.

Perhaps the best way to think of the virtues is as inner attitudes and orientations that are expressed as qualities of action, both inner and outer, reflecting the soul's alignment with Being. Rather than arising from the sense of scarcity characteristic of the soul when structured by the personality, the virtues as a group express an inherent plentitude and spaciousness, an underlying goodness and abundance implicit in life. The virtues cannot really be accurately called emotions, although some people, like Naranjo, refer to them as the higher emotions. Emotions, technically speaking, are the reactive affects of the personality—responses that are habitual and compulsive. The more that our souls are informed by True Nature or Being, the less emotional reactivity we possess. This lack of reactivity is one of the overriding characteristics of the virtues.

So, as we progress spiritually, the virtue of our point on the enneagram increasingly informs our inner experience and is reflected in our outer actions. This is the theory taught by Naranjo. As part of Almaas's teaching, as well as what I've seen in my years of working with the enneagram, it has become clear to me that the virtues are also, and perhaps more importantly, guidelines for bringing our souls into progressively closer alignment with Being. It is the better part of wisdom, then, to understand the attitudes that the virtues represent and to use them as guidance in finding an appropriate relationship to our inner process and appropriate behaviors in response to outer situations. This is not a matter of changing our experience, and this is something I can't underline strongly enough, but of incorporating the *perspective* of the virtues in our approach to what we encounter both inwardly and outwardly. Such an approach can radically shift the state of our soul.

If, for instance, we understand that our development depends upon the consistency of the practices that support our unfoldment—Point Nine's virtue of *action*—we are more inclined to meditate every day. If we include *humility*—the virtue of Point Two—as a guiding principle, we will attempt to be realistic about what we can and cannot do rather than trying to be a superman or -woman in life. Or, if we understand the teaching of *sobriety*, the virtue of Point Seven, we see that development only happens if we are willing to be present to the truth of our experience, regardless of whether it is painful or pleasurable.

THE SOUL AND OUR SENSE OF SELF

Before continuing our discussion of the virtues, it is important to talk a bit further about this term I have just used—*soul.* Insofar as we are discussing transformation, we must understand what it *is* that undergoes a metamorphosis as we develop—what it is, in other words, that is informed by either the passions or the virtues. When I use the word *soul,* I mean our personal consciousness, what we are referring to when we say "I" or "me." It is our soul, then, our alive consciousness, our particular locus of awareness and experience, that takes itself to be either the personality or Being; in other words, I experience myself as my personality or as Being. The personality structure is simply a mental construct, a set of beliefs and internal representations, and this structure shapes the raw material of our soul much like a plaster mold into which fluid is poured and thus shaped. Our soul takes the shape of our personality structure.

As our soul becomes less contained by that structure, it becomes more fluid and dynamic, and without the confines of the fixedness of the personality, it is able to perceive its inner nature, Being. Like the Platonic forms, Being is impersonal and timeless, and it is our human soul that comes into contact with and knows these eternal qualities. It is our soul that experiences and in time embodies the universal principles of Being, such as compassion, clarity, support, and so on. Our alive consciousness, then, is what is informed by the personality and by Being, and implicitly by the passions and the virtues.

One of the principal characteristics of our personal consciousness or soul is that it is highly malleable and impressionable. We are shaped by what happens to us, most dramatically, as psychology has showed us, in the early years of life. Following roughly the age of seven to nine years, the period during which our capacity to self-reflect is fully developed and thus our sense of self coalesces, what occurs is in most cases less pivotal and formative. Our defense mechanisms solidify, and, while we are still impacted by life, our central sense of self—the *central ego* in the Scottish psychoanalyst W. R. D. Fairbairn's formulation—remains constant. This central ego is the part of our personality structure with which we identify—that is, that which we take to be ourselves. There are other parts of our personality, which we split off from consciousness and tend to project onto others, and there are primitive, instinctual facets of it as well that we don't readily identify as ourselves. It is our central self that transforms as we open to these unconscious parts of our personality as well as beyond them, to the realm of Being. Another way of putting it is that who we take ourselves to be changes as our experience of reality expands beyond the perimeters that demarcate our personality.

By way of orientation, we need to understand something further about our sense of self: it is inseparable from our sense of what is *not* ourselves. As the psychological understanding of object relations theory has shown us, our sense of who we are develops in relationship to an "other," originally our mother or the mothering person of early childhood. Our sense of ourselves, then, does not exist in a vacuum but always in relationship. Linking our sense of self and our sense of other is an affect, or, to put it another way, this relationship of self and other is characterized by a particular emotion. Our personality is composed of numerous object relations—units of self and other, linked by a particular affect. Some of these are conscious, coalescing into our central sense of self, while others are unconscious but nonetheless pivotal to our sense of reality.

Although our personality is made up of many object relations, from the perspective of the enneagram, each ennea-type has one that is primary. The affect or emotional tone in this primary object relation is the passion of that type. Each ennea-type, then, has a core object relation composed of a characteristic sense of self and of other, and the passion is the feeling tone of the relationship between these two internal images. In some individuals, this object relation forms part of their conscious sense of self—their central object relation. But this basic sense of self and other is usually not conscious, nor is the passion, and it takes a good bit of inner work to expose it. A Three, for instance, might not consciously realize that he believes he is beyond the rules the rest of us follow, that he sees others as incompetent, and that he lies and is deceptive. To use another example, a Nine might have a difficult time acknowledging that she sees others as being of paramount importance, sees herself as unimportant, and that she is lazy, especially if she is constantly busy with make-work type tasks. It might take some serious introspection for her to see that her "busy-ness" has little to do with herself or her real needs.

Many of us do not encompass the passion of our type in our conscious sense of self, since acknowledging it often feels shameful and bad. To a One, for example, the other typically appears as someone who is imperfect and is in need of correction, while the sense of self is as someone who knows what is wrong and can point it out. The affective tone is the passion of *anger,* which must be understood, as Naranjo says, as "a more inward and basic antagonism in the face of reality than an explosive irritation."[6] For some Ones, this perception of others as imperfect is difficult to acknowledge, as is their resentment about it, and so this object relation functions unconsciously. Other Ones, especially those who have worked on themselves, have no difficulty recognizing their anger, even though they might feel ashamed of it. Regardless, this sense of self and other, and the passion linking them, is basic to a One's psyche.

For a Two, the other appears as someone in need of help and the self as one uniquely fitted to provide what is needed. The passion of *pride,* again understood in the broader sense in which all of the passions are understood in the somewhat cryptic language of the enneagram, is the felt sense of overinflation, an exaggeration of self-importance as well as of self-diminishment. While it is often difficult for a Two to consciously acknowledge his sense of superiority and specialness, pride nonetheless is the primary affect with which Twos must contend.

One of the features of our internal object relations is that the sides can switch. In other words, our sense of self and our sense of the other can trade places, as it were. So, in our examples above, a One can just as easily experience herself as imperfect and the other as critical—which is, in fact, a frequent projection of Ones. Or a Two can and often does experience himself as needy and dependent upon the other, who appears as the unique filler of his needs. The most useful way, then, to conceive of the fundamental object relation that distinguishes each ennea-type is as a unit of self, other, and affect. Different individuals of a particular ennea-type tend to identify with the self side of the object relation characteristic of their type, while others find themselves identifying with the other side of it, and yet others move back and forth in their identification. This is to say that some Ones feel themselves to be imperfect, and see others as better than they are and experience them as fault-finding; while others feel righteous and good, and perceive others as flawed; and yet others flip back and forth.

Our internal pictures of ourselves and of others, then, form a unit and the sides we find ourselves on are interchangeable. Because these internal images are in our own minds, we tend to filter our experience of others through them; and so only to the extent that we are free of our personality is our vision of others unobscured by these veils. We project our object relations onto others and the world itself, and so what we expect to find—albeit unconsciously—is what we in fact experience, forming a self-fulfilling prophecy and reinforcing our personality's picture of reality. Another interesting by-product is that because we are carrying both sides of our object relations within us, the way we see the other in these internal images is often what we disavow within ourselves, yet these same qualities are often what others perceive to be quite central to their experience of *us*.

As our sense of self changes, our personality becomes a progressively thinner veil in our consciousness. Generally, at the beginning of inner work, this veil is more like a curtain, and our sense of objective reality beyond our internal constructs about it, be they conscious or not, is very limited. As we develop, we see things more as they actually are—including ourselves. We get more in touch with our *true* nature, rather than our mental constructs. Our soul, then, becomes progressively more clarified or purified, unclouded by our subjective beliefs about reality. It becomes more and more like a settled, still, and pure body of water, through which you can see the bottom very clearly.

Likewise, our psychological baggage, which at some point we recognize to be very clunky, becomes lighter and lighter. Our ego becomes increasingly less of a dominant force shaping and coloring the texture of our soul, and that texture reveals itself to be one of transparency. As our soul loses its obscurations, its egoic encumbrances, we start experiencing its underlying pristineness, and our sense of self changes. As this gradual transformation occurs within our soul or consciousness, the enneagram of personality becomes less relevant to our experience, and the objective enneagrams become more pertinent. The basic nature of our soul is then expressed in the nine different virtues. We become, in other words, more fully who we really are, and our feeling tone and attitudes then correspond to the virtues.

How does this kind of transformation come about? One fundamental law of the soul is that our beliefs determine our experience. We can see this in the object relations that were described above: if we hold reality to be a certain way, we tend to experience it in that way. What does not fit into our preconceived ideas of how things are might momentarily open our inner doors of perception, revealing more of the real nature of things, but the inertia of the personality will cause us to attempt to restore the status quo. Those who have had peak experiences of one form or another know that they seldom lastingly change our sense of reality. How things were before inevitably reasserts itself in our consciousness. Simply trying to change our beliefs doesn't work, unfortunately. Real change is far more complicated than trying to change how we think, since it involves change in how we experience reality. All successful spiritual practice is a matter of orienting our sense of possibilities, our conceptual framework, and our understanding of the nature of ourselves and the universe in accordance with how things actually are—not how they look through the veil of the personality. In the language of the enneagram, these attitudes are those of the virtues. Understanding them in an experiential way moves our experience progressively more in alignment with Being.

—⁓— Before turning to each of the nine passions and virtues separately, a few final words about their organization. Those familiar with the diagram of the enneagram know that it is formed by dividing a circle into nine equidistant points, and that these points are linked by internal lines forming two figures: a triangle linking points nine, six, and three, and another figure linking points one, four, two, eight, five, and seven (see Diagram 1, page xviii). In periods prior to ours, numbers held a symbolic and often mystical meaning. According to Gurdjieff's student J. G. Bennett, the enneagram was developed in the fifteenth century by mathematicians

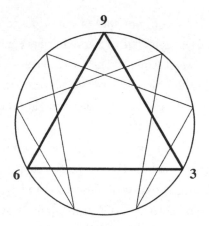

Diagram 7

THE INNER TRIANGLE

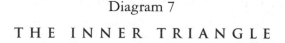

in the Sarmoun mystery school to express the principles symbolized by the newly discovered decimal point. From the Gurdjieffian approach to the enneagram, the figure itself represents numerical symbolism reflecting natural laws about how all processes occur. The so-called *inner triangle,* which we see above, is said to express the "law of three," that of an active, passive, and neutralizing force—a universal three-foldness in all that exists. Or, the notion of thesis, antithesis, and synthesis.

As Bennett points out,

> *When one is divided by three an endless succession of threes is obtained, thus*
> $1/3 = .33333 \ldots$ *written* $.3$
> *The addition of another third part to this produces endless sixes, thus*
> $1/3 + 1/3 = 2/3 = .66666 \ldots$ *or* $.6$
> *When the final third part is added also, endless nines result, thus*
> $1/3 + 1/3 + 1/3 = .99999 \ldots$ *or.* 9
> *Hence we obtain a symbolism for one as an endless recurrence of the number nine.*[7]

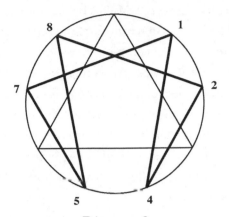

Diagram 8

THE POINTS ON THE RIM

The other figure, composed of the remaining points, has no name in the enneagram tradition, but I have taken to calling these points the *points on the rim*, which we see in the diagram above. This figure reflects the "law of seven" according to this tradition.

Numerically, as Bennett goes on to tell us,

When one is divided by seven, however, another and more complex pattern of numbers appears, which contains no threes, sixes, or nines. Thus

$$1/7 = .142857142857 \ldots or .142857$$

and successive additions of seventh parts reproduce this pattern, but start from different digits, thus

$$2/7 = .285714$$
$$3/7 = .428571$$
$$4/7 = .571428$$
$$5/7 = .714285$$
$$6/7 = .857142$$

When the final seventh part is added, this sequence disappears and is replaced by the recurring nines once again. Thus $7/7 = .9$ [8]

As the mathematical theorist Michael Schneider says in his book on the mathematical archetypes of nature, art, and science, this repeating numerical pattern refers to "a complete yet *ongoing* process, a periodic rhythm of internal relationships. All configured efforts are led in seven stages to perfection."[9] The seventh point is nine, and in the Gurdjieff work, creative processes are represented by the movement from Point Nine clockwise around the circle, with Points Three and Six being "shock points," in which is formed, as Naranjo says, "a link between the realms of being and becoming, an influence from a higher level than that in which a given process unfolds."[10]

With this background, we can understand something further about the passions. One is that they correspond to what have come to be known as the seven deadly sins, those transgressions of moral law designated as primary or capital sins by Gregory the Great, pope from A.D. 590–604. Moving around the enneagram beginning at Point Nine, these are sloth, anger, pride, envy, avarice, gluttony, and lust. Significant is that the passions at the shock points—vanity and fear, the passions of Points Three and Six—are missing from this lineup. Naranjo points out that the shock points are traditionally invisible.

This, however, does not mean that they are peripheral, Pope Gregory aside. In fact, the three passions—indolence, fear, and deceit—on the inner triangle are the most fundamental of all. Beginning with Point Nine, all of the passions can be seen as differentiations of a fundamental indolence or laziness about what is essential—our true nature. This, then, is the primary passion. Along with fear and vanity, these passions at the three "corners" of the enneagram, as they are called, convey, as Naranjo puts it,

> *a statement to the effect that these are cornerstones of the whole emotional edifice, and the ones mapped between them can be explained as interactions in different proportions of the same. Anger, for instance, is a hybrid of psychological inertia with pretending, as is also pride, though with a predominance of inertia or vanity respectively.*[11]

Expanding on what Naranjo alludes to in the above excerpt, the passion of each point is the interaction or synthesis of those of its wings—the points

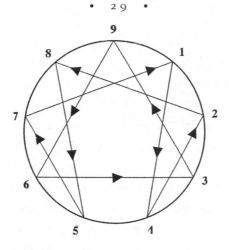

Diagram 9

THE INNER FLOW

on either side. Our fear, for example, the passion of Point Six, is a mix of the contracting pull—avarice—of Point Five, and the expansionistic pull—gluttony—of Point Seven, resulting in doubt, insecurity, and uncertainty.

In terms of the inner flow of the enneagram, the dynamic movement connecting one point to another, we can see that the passion of the point preceding another moving with the direction of the arrows, which is called its heart point, psychodynamically underlies it.

As discussed in my previous book on the enneagram, the movement from one point to that following it in the direction the arrows point represents a movement from one character style to another as a form of reaction formation—an attempt to do the opposite. This means that the qualities of our own particular ennea-type develop psychodynamically in counterpoint to, or as a reaction against, the qualities of the type of the heart point of our type.

Likewise, we can see that the passion of each type is grounded in the passion of that type's heart point. For instance, our envy of others—the passion of Point Four—is rooted in our assumption that what we have and who we are is imperfect—the passion of Point One.

⟶⟋⟍⟍⟋⟍⟍ We will explore the passions and the virtues grouped by corner and, in the process, hopefully understand something further about what the corners of the enneagram represent. We will begin with the outer-directed corner, discussing the passion and virtue of Point Nine and its wings, Points Eight and One. We will then explore the image corner, beginning with Point Three and then its wings, Points Two and Four. Finally, we will explore the fear corner, starting with Point Six and then exploring Points Seven and Five. In each of the corners, we will begin with the points on the inner triangle, reflecting their centrality, and then explore the wings, which can be described as differentiations of what is represented by their neighboring point on the inner triangle. At each of the points, we will explore the passion in depth, and we will see how this understanding leads us to the virtue.

Let us now turn to the passions and the virtues.

THE OUTER-DIRECTED CORNER

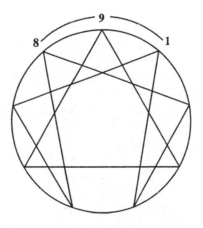

DIAGRAM 10

POINT NINE—

LAZINESS *and*

ACTION

—————

But there are a thousand things which prevent a man from awakening,
which keep him in the power of his dreams. In order to act consciously with
the intention of awakening, it is necessary to know the nature of the
forces which keep man in a state of sleep.

—G. I. GURDJIEFF[1]

Man is asleep. This is the fundamental tenet of all spiritual traditions. Realization is often called awakening. We may experience ourselves as very alert and alive, but as the great spiritual teachers throughout the centuries have taught, we are walking around in a kind of stupor or dream. Our attention is directed outside of ourselves—toward our work or relationships or the myriad of other details that go into our lives—and most of us neglect our inner lives. The top corner of the enneagram—Point Nine and its two wings, Points Eight and One—speaks to this tendency to go to sleep on ourselves, to operate in a mechanical way, as Gurdjieff would say, following the blueprint of our conditioning. As we will see, each of these points addresses different aspects of this trance. Point Nine, as the central point of this corner, addresses this issue most directly.

Not realizing that we are in a slumber of sorts and not doing what it takes to awaken is what the passion of Point

Nine—*laziness*—refers to. Laziness here is not simply a matter of laziness in the usual way we understand that word—being generally reluctant to do things or to bestir ourselves—although this can certainly be one of the superficial symptoms of the deeper laziness that this passion signifies.

Ennea-type Nines who have done some inner work are usually all too familiar with how the passion of laziness manifests in their personalities. It is a drive, if we can call it that, toward inattention to self, self-neglect, and heedlessness. It is a muffling and damping-down of a Nine's inner life, which may feel dull and uninteresting to him. His attention is elsewhere, outside of himself, since his inner life seems of little importance or value to himself or anyone else. Naranjo uses the expression "the defensive loss of inwardness"[2] to describe this deadening to his emotions, his preferences, wishes, and desires and even to his thoughts, which tend to be rigid, literal, and concrete—what Gurdjieff called "formatory thinking." Even though he might be outwardly and even inwardly very busy with things, he is lazy about paying attention to himself.

Because of this, his laziness shows up as a difficulty in discernment and discrimination, since he has stopped attuning to his inner gyroscope. He often has trouble sorting out what needs doing or requires attention; and if he ascertains it, he has difficulty getting to it. There are so many other things distracting him, and he loses the thread of what is most important. He may get mired in a hundred projects—mostly for others—all of which seem equally pressing and consequential, or the many pulls in different directions may overwhelm him and he gives up, resigning himself to inactivity.

Going with the path of least resistance, he is lazy about questioning things, preferring things to be easy, nonconflictual, and not demanding too much self-assertion. His unconscious motivation is to stay on the surface of things, himself most fundamentally.

All of these ways that a Nine's laziness expresses itself point to a much more fundamental issue that permeates the layers of his soul. At the core, his laziness is grounded in a universal issue—a basic inattention shared by most of humanity. This laziness is about our state of consciousness as unenlightened human beings. It is about our human proclivity to not recognize that much of the world we inhabit is our own self-imposed reality, often having little to do with how things really are. The way that we experience the world, others, and ourselves is through the thick filter of our conditioning—how we adapted, were shaped, and conformed to our early childhood environment. Our present sense of reality is largely a product of that distant past—primarily the first few years of our lives—with an adult veneer laid on top. We are indeed sleepwalkers to a great extent, moving through our lives in a trance, unaware that there is more to life than we experience.

Just as Point Nine is considered to be the primary point on the enneagram out of which all of the others are refracted, so too is this passion the most central. From a spiritual perspective, the fact of our asleepness and our inertia in remaining so is *the* principal and fundamental issue. It is at the heart of our discontent and of much of human suffering. The different schools and methods of awakening are all geared toward contending with this universal reality.

It is not that we are purposely lazy, nor are we consciously refusing to wake up. This is not a matter of stubbornness or even reluctance, since those reactions imply awareness of our situation. This aspect of the laziness is such that we don't even *know* that there is a problem. Our sleep is so deep that we can't conceive of any other possibility. This is the condition of most of humanity, and the reason that the majority of people think that spirituality is a lot of wishful thinking and a waste of time, not to mention something they can't relate to. As Naranjo puts it,

> *this degradation of consciousness is such that in the end the affected individual does not know the difference, i.e., does not know that there has been such a thing as a loss, a limitation, or a failure to develop his full potential. The fall is such that awareness comes to be blind in regard to its own blindness, and limited to the point of believing itself free. It is in view of this that Oriental traditions frequently use, in connection with the ordinary condition of humankind, the analogy that invites us to conceive that the difference between our potential condition and our present state is as great as the condition between ordinary wakefulness and dreaming.*[3]

What, then, is the nature of this sleep? Perhaps the best way to express it is that by the time most of us reach psychological maturity—when we have attained the capacity to know and reflect on what we are experiencing and recognize ourselves as particular individuals—our consciousness has become severely limited. By that time, when our capacity for self-reflection has solidified—generally around the age of seven to nine years old—we are aware of just a small fraction of the full dimensionality of our reality, both within and outside of ourselves. As far as we know, human beings are the only creatures with this remarkable capacity for self-reflection, self-awareness, and self-knowledge. Ironically, just as we reach this pinnacle of development of our highly developed brains, a diminishment of perception comes hand in hand with that achievement.

Our awareness has become focused primarily on the physical dimension of reality, and the other dimensions have receded into the background of our consciousness. We take ourselves to be individuals whose edges end at the surface of our bodies, persons separate from all others, just as our body is discrete from other bodies. We also take ourselves to be beings whose lives will end when our bodies die. We have, in short, become identified with our physical forms, believing them to be the whole of who and what we are.

Generally, this identification is not fully conscious. The more sophisticated we are, the more we may consciously identify with our minds and in fact distance ourselves from our "animalistic" bodies. Or, if we are emotionally oriented, we may identify more with our feeling states. If we are spiritually inclined, we might conceptually "know" that we are not our bodies, but when push comes to shove and we are in some kind of physical peril or when our survival appears to be in question, our deep and primary identification with our material form is obvious. For many, the fear of death of the body is the source of greatest anxiety. In many spiritual traditions, inner work is considered the preparation for death, and the moment of the soul leaving the body is the proof of the pudding, so to speak. The goal of inner work, then, can be seen as discovering that who we are transcends the life of the body, and integrating this knowing in an experiential way, which percolates down to the depths of our soul.

How did we become so identified with the material dimension to begin with? Understanding this process is part of helping ourselves open to the possibility of life beyond it. It is the story told in fairy tales and myths of all cultures about our fall from paradise, described allegorically in the Bible as our expulsion from the Garden of Eden. For this reason, in spiritual traditions, it is referred to as the story of the *fall,* the understanding of how we arrived in a fallen state of consciousness, alluded to by Naranjo in the quote above.

It appears that during the first few weeks and months of life, our state of consciousness is characterized by a sense of oneness or wholeness. I say that it appears this way based on the experiential memories of that time of life of myself, my colleagues, and those I have worked with. Obviously, it is almost impossible to know what an infant is experiencing, and our best stab at it is through revisiting our own recollections stored in our nervous system. In those early months, then, everything we experience is part of a unity that we are also part of—all experience is one whole thing, with no sense of an experiencer, nor of discrimination or recognition of what we are experiencing. Our nervous systems have not formed to the point at which we can conceptually distinguish one thing from another or reflect on what we are in touch with. It is not that everything we perceive is merged together—we probably have a sense of differentiation in which the yellow of our rubber duck is different from the wetness of the water in our bath, but none of it is conceptual. The mental knowing, the thought that one is different from the other, is not yet able to form.

All of the dimensions of life coexist and interpenetrate—physical sensation both within the body and on its surface, the sights and sounds around us, the presence of Being, feeling states, our perception of others— all undiscriminated from each other in our consciousness. While we may recognize our mother or mothering person in some dim way, as Daniel Stern, the psychoanalyst whose work is seminal in the intersubjective psychological movement, asserts, since we do not have the mental apparatus formed yet to know what we perceive, she remains nonetheless part of this primordial soup of existence.

Evidence to support this arises from our adult experiences of oneness, considered in the spiritual traditions to be glimpses of how things really are. In such peak moments, we perceive everything as one whole thing, everything made out of the same substance or being a manifestation of a wholeness. We might lose the conceptual labels that we have for things, and experience them directly, as they are, without our names for them, our reifications or concepts. Those who have had such experiences of cosmic oneness often believe that they will not be able to function, that they will simply become a blob, dependent on others to be taken care of. Inquiring into this belief more often than not leads to the recognition that the last time they experienced this sense of unity was when they were babies, too young to function very well and certainly not on their own.

Linking the state of consciousness of early childhood with deep states of spiritual realization has been criticized by the prolific and influential mapper of consciousness, Ken Wilber, who has in my opinion misunderstood this view of development as postulating a regression to the state of infancy. He appears to see Being as something that develops, so that when we experience it, we are experiencing something that has just come into existence. From the perspective out of which I come, what develops is not Being itself, but our consciousness. As I see it, our consciousness develops to the point where we can once again experience the primordial and unchanging nature of everything—which is why we call it True Nature. Spiritual development from this perspective is the gradual thinning of the veils of the personality so that we can access what these veils have been shrouding. And what we experience is what we experienced as young children before our personality structure formed—reality as it is. The crucial difference between adult realization and the infant's contact with the realm of Being is the all-important matter of self-reflective consciousness, which the infant does not have. An infant, having not yet developed the filter of the personality, cannot *but* be experiencing reality as it is in all of its dimensionality, but does so without *knowing* that this is her experience. So we are not regressing to an earlier state of consciousness when we experience spiritual states—we are experiencing what is present all the time, i.e., the True Nature of everything—as we once did without being aware of it as infants.

In moments in which our focus of attention as infants is overshadowed by physical need and distress, like hunger, a wet diaper, or aches and pains, we are pulled out of the primordial oneness, and our sense of self eventually coalesces around such moments. Discrimination between pain and pleasure gradually begins to register in the infant's consciousness and, as it does so, cognition begins to take shape. Prior to this, we obviously experience the difference between pleasure and pain, but such experiences do not register in our minds as such. We simply have an organismic or instinctual reaction to move away from what is painful and toward what is pleasurable, without *recognizing* it as such. Gradually, further discernment takes place between inner and outer, leading to the distinction between self and what is not self: other. Little by little, we take ourselves to be these small bodies that we are learning to operate, and as we identify with the physical dimension, our sense of reality begins to narrow. We slowly take ourselves to be bounded by the edges of our body, and in time come to believe that we are an ultimately separate entity.

Another major factor in the formation of our personality and loss of contact with the depth dimension has to do with our initial lack of differentiated consciousness. To a great extent—completely, if you are of the Margaret Mahler school, or to a limited degree, if you are of the Daniel Stern school*—our consciousness in early infancy is merged with mother or our mothering person. Many people involved in inner exploration recover memories of experiencing their mother's emotional states during pregnancy and early childhood, and in these memories there is little or no discrimination about whose experience it is—hers or theirs. Likewise, her sense of reality, with all of its implicit assumptions about what exists and what doesn't, becomes ours. To the extent that our mother's reality excludes the realm of Being, we likewise learn to eliminate it from our consciousness. This is how the narrowed experience of the world and of ourselves that is the reality of the personality is passed down through society from one generation to another. We absorb it with our mother's milk, so to speak.

This lack of mirroring of all of the dimensions of reality is part of the insufficiency of what the British object relations psychologist D. W. Winnicott has called our early holding environment,** our initial milieu. The

---

*Margaret Mahler (1897–1985) was a child analyst and former pediatrician trained in Vienna, whose work charted the developmental phases and subphases of the ego in early childhood, and was pivotal in understanding ego development. Her notion of a symbiotic or merged sense of self and mother in the first few months of life recently came under attack by Daniel Stern, a contemporary researcher of child development, who postulates that self-differentiation is present from birth.

**For further reading on the process of the fall, readers are referred to Almaas's *Facets of Unity,* and my book *The Spiritual Dimension of the Enneagram: Nine Faces of the Soul,* Chapter 1.

cumulative result of these conditioning factors is that the unquestioned sense of trust that seems implicit in the infant's consciousness begins to change, as the experience of the holding environment becomes not so continuously supportive and sustaining in the baby's experience. These moments occur over and over again, since as infants we are unable to articulate or communicate our needs, and perfect attunement is impossible for even the best of mothers. As our basic trust, as Almaas terms it— our fundamental, unquestioned, and preconceptual confidence in the beneficence of our holding environment—slowly erodes, so too does our fundamental faith in the goodness of the whole universe and of life itself. Naturally, the degree of trauma in our early holding environment determines the extent to which we lose our inherent trust and our contact with True Nature in its manifestation as a loving, supportive, and benevolent foundation of life.

We gradually, then, lose contact with the ground of Being. As our consciousness forms, so does our personality, developing in counterpoint to this loss of contact with Being. As our sense of self becomes limited, we lose consciousness of the oneness of Being pervading all forms. As our capacity to reflect upon and know what our experience is takes shape, the delusion that we are ultimately separate little creatures and that it is up to us to get our needs met and to survive also coalesces, since our fundamental confidence in how things work out has largely been lost. The ground of Being, which we no longer perceive, has not gone anywhere in reality but has receded into the background of our consciousness till we are no longer paying attention to it.

As Almaas describes below, the nine ennea-types arise out of reaction to the loss of our basic trust and concomitant disconnection from Being. I am quoting him at length here, since he captures the ego activity of the types so beautifully and succinctly:

> Implicit in the ego, then, is a fundamental distrust of reality. The failure of the holding environment leads to the absence of basic trust, which then becomes disconnection from Being, which leads to reactivity, which is ego activity. The Enneagram maps the various ways the ego develops to deal with the absence, disruptions, ruptures, and discontinuities of holding. The reac-

tion for Point One is to try to make the holding happen by improving one-self. For Point Two, it is to deny the need for holding but, nonetheless, be manipulating and seducing the environment to provide it. For Point Three, it is to deny the need for holding but pretend to oneself, "I can do it on my own. I know how reality can be and how I'm going to develop and I'll make it happen." For Point Four, the loss or absence of holding is counteracted by denying that there is a disconnection from Being, while at the same time trying to make the environment be holding through attempting to control it and oneself. For Point Five, the reaction is to not deal with the actual sense of loss and not feel the impingement directly through withdrawing and iso-lating oneself, avoiding the whole situation. For Point Six, the strategy is to be more in touch with the fear and distrust, being defensive and paranoid about the environment. For Point Seven, it is by planning how to make it good, and fantasizing what it will feel like, rather than feeling the pain of the loss of holding. For Point Eight, it is to get angry about the loss of hold-ing and to fight the environment to get it back, to try to get justice, and to get revenge for the hurt. For Point Nine, the reaction is to smooth the whole thing over and act as through everything is fine, living one's life in a me-chanical and dead way.[4]

While the realm of Being fades into the obscurity of our unconscious, for some it is not too far away. A faint recollection in the soul remains, al-though to speak of it in these terms is far too conceptual. Let us say that a flavor of it remains present in the soul, a whiff, a preconscious knowing that there is more to reality than what we consciously experience. It is these people who become spiritual seekers, following the trail of an al-most cold scent.

Regardless how removed from consciousness our experience of the deeper dimension of reality becomes, if all goes well, we develop a func-tional personality structure. This might not, at first glance, sound like a such good thing, especially to those who have spent many years meditating or doing other forms of spiritual practice only to encounter their ego at every turn. Nor does it sound like a positive development if your orienta-tion toward inner work is one of seeing the ego as the enemy, to be overcome or eradicated. I think that it is both more constructive and more accurate to

see the formation of our ego structure as part of a continuum of human potentiality. A necessary evolution, in other words. As we have seen, the personality develops conjointly with the capacity for self-reflection. After the
scaffolding of the ego structure is formed, it becomes possible to work
through it while retaining its by-product, our capacity for self-knowing. If
our ego structure is too unstable, it is difficult for it to relax or for us to let
go of it, depending on your point of view. Since it is vulnerable, it is also
brittle, and so experiences of moving beyond it are threatening and can be
traumatic. This is the reason that it is important to have a well-developed
personality structure before beginning spiritual work.

It appears—since this is how we are designed—that developing a personality structure is part of our human journey, and the next stage of it is
moving beyond it. It is likely that we are wired in this way so that we can
consciously know Being, so that we can know the Divine as our nature. So
rather than simply being the embodiment of and being made up of Being,
which is what all of manifest reality is, we have the unique opportunity to
know ourselves as such. It may be that this is how the Divine can know
Itself, through our human soul's experience.

Whether we believe that this is our purpose as human beings or not,
what is certain is that it is possible to move beyond our personality structure. There are volumes upon volumes recounting the stories of those
souls over the centuries who have not only glimpsed objective reality but
have learned to abide there. All of the spiritual traditions were founded by
one such individual, whose view of objective reality became the logos of
that teaching, and whose way of getting beyond the veil of the ego became the methodology of that path. And there are lineages of such individuals in many of the traditions.

This Journey, as it is called, beyond the personality is not easy, nor is it
a rapid one in most cases. As discussed earlier, it requires an inward
change in who and what we take ourselves to be, and in who and what we
take others and the world outside of us to be. This means moving beyond
our past and our conditioning—beyond how our soul adapted, was
shaped, and conformed to our early holding environment—and experiencing reality as it is right now, in the present moment. The biggest obstacle is the passion of laziness that we are discussing.

The passion of Point Nine was originally called *laziness* by Ichazo, and he referred to the fixation, the fixed cognitive distortion, as *indolence*. Naranjo, in recent years,[5] thinks that the most accurate term to describe this passion is the Latin word, *accidia,* which was replaced by the word *sloth* in Christian theology. *Accidia* means laziness of the psyche and the spirit, a spiritual indolence, and does seem to encompass the broader context of a fundamental inertia and heedlessness about the state of one's soul. Laziness literally means the state of being resistant to physical or mental exertion, of not being vigorous or energetic, and that is not exactly the sense of this passion. One can be very active, work exceedingly diligently, and accomplish masses of things—not be lazy at all in the sense that we use that word—and still be completely neglectful of the state of one's soul.

This is the normal condition of most of humanity. One might argue that the majority of humanity is deeply religious, but that is not what we are talking about. We are not talking about going through the motions of religious forms, nor about devotional worship to a divinity that we believe in our minds is present somewhere. What we are talking about is radical personal transformation, such that we know ourselves to *be* the Absolute, the Divine Itself. Again, as mentioned earlier, it is not that most people envision this possibility and stubbornly resist it. Because of the thick blanket of conditioned sleep, they are not even aware that they are sleepwalking and when they are told, they don't believe it.

We have seen that this sleep can best be described as a diminishment of awareness, such that we are blind to ourselves and the universe in all of its dimensionality. The situation is like that of prisoners who have become so used to the four walls of their cell that they think these walls are the actual edges of the universe rather than all they can see. Describing to them a world beyond these walls would sound like a fantasy. This is the predicament in attempting to describe what the realm of Being is like to those who have not experienced it consciously.

To know reality as it is means waking up, and doing what it takes to awaken to our true state of affairs is what the virtue of Point Nine is all about—*action.* Just as we have seen that the passion of laziness does not simply mean being unindustrious or inactive, likewise the virtue of action refers to far more than just being busy. It signifies being involved in the most important kind of endeavor—that of overcoming the inertia of the personality to remain asleep. Real action, then, is a matter of shifting the habitual orientation of our own consciousness. We have seen that the state of asleepness is one of a diminishment or curtailment of what we are aware of. It is a constriction of apprehension, and so for our consciousness to expand in order to include more of reality, we must do what it takes to expand our awareness. This is essential action, and is the basis of most spiritual practices.

Deepening and broadening our awareness requires understanding the habitual orientation of our souls. Most of humanity lives in a state in which their attention is directed outward, focusing on the thing that they are doing or on the person they are engaged with. This state might be called one of automatic pilot, living and operating mechanically in response to the external with little or no inner awareness. This is the nature of our sleep, and to awaken requires expanding our consciousness to include ourselves and all the dimensions of reality that are a part of us and that we are part of.

There are many types of true action—spiritual practices that open us up to more of reality. Spiritual practices are only successful in bringing us closer to our depths if they are expressions of the characteristics of that depth. One of our ultimate nature's central characteristics is that of presence—the fact that it is substantial and immediate, a here-ness. This is why it is called Being. In fact, we can only be in touch with Being when we are fully in the moment. This is why one of the most powerful practices I know, if we work at it consistently, is what Gurdjieff called self-remembering. It is a matter of being fully present in our direct experience and dividing our attention between the external and the internal. As one of Gurdjieff's most well-known followers, P. D. Ouspensky, says about self-remembering,

> *I said that European and Western psychology in general had overlooked a fact of tremendous importance, namely, that* we do not remember our-selves; *that we live and act and reason in deep sleep, not metaphorically but*

in absolute reality. And also that, at the same time, we can remember our-
selves if we make sufficient efforts, that we can awaken.[6]

Effort, as Ouspensky notes, is required since outer-directedness is one
of the primary characteristics of our personality structure—it cannot exist without it, and we have to exert ourselves to overcome the inertia of
this tendency.

This inertial pull to maintain our status quo with its outer orientation
is one of the deepest and most insidious barriers in spiritual work, and is
laziness in action once we are aware that we are asleep. It is the reason that
deep and profound experiences of True Nature do not instantly change
most people, despite all the stories we read about such occurrences. These
stories are usually about those in the East, and most Western seekers have
the disappointing experience of knowing utterly sublime states, only to
find themselves shortly back in the same old familiar reality. One of the
major characteristics of our personality structure is its tendency to hang
on to and quickly reassert the familiar, despite it being an unsatisfying or
even a miserable one.

Many nondual spiritual teachings and enlightened teachers, speaking
from the perspective of Being, say that there is nothing to do to awaken,
since that is our nature. This is all well and good if you are abiding in a
state of consciousness in which you experience that, but for those who are
not, this can only be wishful thinking and empty words. Effort is needed
if we are to overcome the undertow of the personality, lulling us back into
the sleep of our conditioning. Adopting a so-called nondualistic attitude
that there is nothing we really need to do to awaken is, for most people, a
spiritually sophisticated way of succumbing to their laziness.

Those who follow devotional paths centered around an enlightened
teacher often maintain the outer-directed orientation of the personality in
the sense of waiting for a transmission to open up their consciousness.
This does, of course, happen. In the presence of someone in a deep state of
realization, if we are receptive to it, our consciousness cannot *but* expand,
since the depth such a person embodies and is in touch with exerts a pull
on our consciousness. It does this because this depth is what is most real.

And attuning ourselves to and emulating such an individual is one way of orienting our consciousness toward the reality they inhabit. But for many who have followed a guru, the "hit" of that deeper dimension they receive from time to time is often insufficient to transform their ongoing sense of self and of reality. Such a metamorphosis is, for most of us, impossible without diligent inner work designed to counteract the powerful pull of our habitual state of sleep—the work of self-remembering.

Nor can we simply go through the motions of inner work. That is merely another form of laziness. Sitting in meditation, even for an extremely long time, will get us nowhere if we are daydreaming, planning our day, or going over our shopping list. Action means applying ourselves to the practice, regardless of which one we are doing. This is the reason spiritual methodologies are called practices—we must continually work at them. The occasional retreat, workshop, or weekend may put us momentarily in touch with our depth dimension, but it takes steady, moment-to-moment practice for real transformation to become possible. Our self-remembering cannot be sporadic or practiced only when we feel like it. To truly have a lasting effect on our consciousness, we must work with it continuously.

What is it that we are becoming conscious of when we remember ourselves? At the beginning, it is a matter of becoming present within our bodies. This means *feeling* our bodies, not simply occupying them, as most people do. It means experiencing them from inside. Turning our attention to the actual sensations both at the edges and in the interior parts of the body. The more consistently we practice self-remembering in this way, our sense of what it is that we are paying attention to changes. In time, our awareness deepens so that it includes the fabric of our whole field of consciousness—our soul, in other words. What we are contacting then doesn't end at the edges of our body, but instead extends sometimes a few inches and at others, infinitely. We understand when we experience this that who we are cannot be limited to or contained within the body, and so the body cannot be who and what we are. Our sense of who we are can then shift from our deepest identification with the body to knowing that we are something beyond it. Eventually, we may come to see that the body is animated by the soul and is its vehicle.

Our sense of what the body itself is changes of necessity in the course of our development. With our deepest identification being on our materiality—the physical matter of our bodies—and our consequent focus on that level of reality to the exclusion of the others, our sense and experience of the material world itself is distorted. We might think that we experience our body as it is, but we are actually experiencing it through a thick cloud of assumptions. If we were to contact it directly, without our ideas and inner pictures of it obscuring and informing our perception, we would experience it completely differently—as pure luminosity, for instance. With our outer-directedness and narrowing of experience to the surface of things, we are likewise eliminating from our awareness perception of energetic fields, as described in the chakra system of the body, in acupuncture, and perceived by those who see auric fields. We also have hardwired into our human organism the perceptual barrier that prevents us from perceiving the space that forms the major part of all matter. We know from subatomic physics that matter is mostly composed of space, with the tiny components—electrons, photons, quarks, muons, etc.—forming the smallest part of atoms. Looking at an atom under extreme magnification is a bit like looking at the solar system or distant galaxies, with vast amounts of space between dots of matter, and the laws and structures of the macrocosm and the microcosm mirror each other, as seen in subatomic physics and astrophysics. These are just a few examples of aspects of the material world that we do not perceive directly most of the time—not to mention the dimensions of Being that by the time we reach adulthood are screened from consciousness.

As our consciousness deepens, so does our sensitivity to the nonphysical dimensions of things. We might at times experience the body as transparent, or as made up of light. In such experiences, we are having a more complete experience of these forms we inhabit and the forms we see around us. We discover that our perceptual capacity itself is far broader than it was, as we find ourselves perhaps feeling another's state of consciousness or sensing what is going on in her body. As we sense our own body with increasing acuity, we will probably find tension patterns that have a particular shape, color, and feel to them, and when we continue to explore them by making direct contact with them in our experience, we might remember repeated moments of feeling the emotions that seem one and the same as these knots. They may open up and reveal memories of the original events that began to structure this twist in our consciousness initially, and then we see that all subsequent related incidents were a telescoping of these sources.

As we continue with this type of exploration, an extremely interesting thing happens: our experience starts to open up, revealing deeper and deeper layers within ourselves. The outermost layer is, of course, the body, and as we move deeper, we are moving into our soul. Then in time, we start to experience the nature of our soul, which is the reason it is called our True Nature. One law of our souls is that if we are present to our here-and-now experience with an open and fresh attitude of curiosity and inquiry into the contents of our consciousness, our experience will rapidly deepen.

A complete description of what we call True Nature or Being is beyond our focus in this book, but a brief overview might be helpful. Our ultimate nature is who we are without our history, without our mental constructs defining, albeit unconsciously, our experience both of ourselves and of the world around us. It is who and what we truly are, stripped of all conditioning. It is our beingness, the substance and nature of our soul. Rather than being one static state, it arises in different qualities, many of which are familiar to most of us, like compassion, fulfillment, contentment, a sense of indestructibility, peacefulness, silence, to name just a few. All of the ways it appears in our consciousness are simply different facets of one thing, arising out of its intelligence as needed in the moment. If we are in the presence of someone who has just suffered a big loss, for instance, the wisdom of Being will manifest compassion in our soul if we are open to it. Or, if we are faced with a huge challenge of some sort, Being will respond as courage, if we are not blocking it. Receptivity to Being requires that our soul must be permeable enough for the qualities of Being to reach our consciousness. This means having some degree of freedom from our personality, and this develops as we do our practices—as we practice the virtue of action, in other words.

In time, as our consciousness deepens, we see that the True Nature of our soul is the True Nature of everything. We experience Being, then, in its boundlessness—unlimited by any form, even that of our own soul.

There are a number of dimensions of Being that it is possible to experience, each progressively freer of conceptual veils, until we reach a state beyond all concepts, even those of being and nonbeing, existence and nonexistence—beyond even consciousness—which is called the Absolute in a number of traditions.*

As we assiduously practice the virtue of action, doing what it takes to become more present and conscious, we are setting the stage for this gradual shift of our inner sense of gravity from the personality to Being. Our souls are highly impressionable, as noted earlier, and we learn by repeated experiences. This is not simply how we become conditioned but is also how we become liberated. We apprehend something more about the truth of how things are each time a veil of the personality parts a bit, revealing deeper layers within our soul, and we remember. In time, with repeated experiences that offset our historical sense of who we are, that sense of self changes. After experiencing over and over again, for instance, that the basic nature of our soul is something fluid, changing, and has a sense of purity and goodness to it, we can no longer sustain the old belief that we are fundamentally stuck or bad, for instance.

We cannot make this shift from personality to Being happen for the simple reason that the very one who wants to make that shift is the personality. Or, more accurately, our soul informed by our personality, since the personality is a mental construct and our soul is what gives it life. We cannot make ourselves change, just as we cannot make ourselves feel love for someone we don't care about. Change does not happen through our own efforts. No one has ever made themselves or anyone else change—our parents know that! But our efforts can orient our consciousness in such a way that transformation is more likely. This is one of the meanings of true action.

There is inner action: doing what it takes to realize our True Nature. There is also outer action: behaving in accordance with the principles and characteristics of True Nature, which the Buddhists call right action. This is another nuance of the virtue of action. Basing our conduct on the deepest principles we know is a practice that helps to bring our soul into

*For more on our essential nature and the dimensions of Being, see the works of Almaas, in particular *Essence: The Diamond Approach to Inner Realization, The Pearl Beyond Price, The Point of Existence,* and *The Inner Journey Home.*

alignment with the enlightened state, and supports our consciousness opening to Being. While such a practice may seem like a pretense and can become one if it becomes an empty form, it is really an evocation of the truth of our depths. Acting out of our reactivity is the real make-believe, since such actions do not express who and what we truly are. Right action is an assertion of our will in doing what is most authentic, functioning in accordance with the truth of our depths, and such right action helps us contact that depth. Functioning according to our deepest truth, not that of the personality's reactivity, actually reinforces our embodiment, our living of True Nature.

As we practice the virtue of action both inwardly and outwardly, our soul transforms, our consciousness changes. Instead of having to exert enormous effort to overcome the leaden inertia of our personality, in time self-remembering becomes the norm, and right action is simply how we live. At this point, the virtue of action is no longer in the service of our realization, supporting our endeavor, but becomes an expression of that realization, that knowing of what our nature truly is. At this stage, Ichazo's definition of this virtue is relevant:

> *It is essential movement without interference from the mind, arising naturally from the body's need to function in harmony with its environment. Action is the normal attitude of a being in tune with his own energy and with the energy of the planet.*[7]

We can translate "mind" here as the mentality of the personality, and I think replacing the word "body" with "soul" gets closer to the heart of things. The last sentence refers to living realistically, in touch with one's self and the world, which is a prerequisite for right action.

When our center of gravity and our sense of who we are is grounded in Being, the distinction between inner action and outer action evaporates. It is more appropriate at that point to conceive of our inner state as one of transparency, an openness to our depths, with progressively less of a self present to interfere with our direct expression and embodiment of Being. To speak of alignment with Being at this stage ceases to be accurate, since we know ourselves to *be* Being, living a human life. Veils and obscurations in our consciousness still present themselves, but working through them no longer requires effort. It is a spontaneous process of digesting them as they are perceived. At this stage, our life is the virtue of action in active manifestation.

CHAPTER 3

POINT EIGHT—
LUST *and*
INNOCENCE

———◦/◦/◦———

And they brought young children to him, that he should touch them: and his
disciples rebuked those that brought them. But when Jesus saw it, he was much
displeased, and said unto them, Suffer the little children to come unto me, and
forbid them not: for of such is the kingdom of God. Verily I say unto you,
Whosoever shall not receive the kingdom of God as a little child, he
shall not enter therein. And he took them up in his arms,
put his hands upon them, and blessed them.
—MARK 10:13–16[1]

The most intractable aspect of ourselves to deal with—
regardless of what life arena we are involved in—is the part
of our psyche that is animal-like, concerned primarily
with our physical survival. Here we are slaves to our desires, and we are driven to satisfy our various hungers—
for physical well-being and pleasure, for sustenance,
shelter, sexuality, and a sense of belonging to what appears as our tribe or our pack. Our appetites in this area
seem endless and insatiable, voracious, huge, and primitive. This side of us is interested only in pleasure and the
gratification of our drives and desires, irrespective of the
consequences to others or even to ourselves. When this
aspect of our psyche comes to the fore, we want what
we want, and we want it *now.* It doesn't matter if what we
want belongs to someone else—another's partner, for in-

stance—or if what we want is not good for us—a second dessert, perhaps, if we are already physically full and corpulent anyway. Although we may be loath to admit it, we all have such a side of ourselves, which our reason and civilized sensibilities do not touch.

This aspect of us is the core of our ego structure, and it is the hidden and usually unacknowledged driving force in most people's lives. It is where our earliest identification—with our physical bodies—resides and continues to inform our psyche. We have seen that our ego, or sense of self, was shaped by our very early and primitive experiences of what was inside the edges of our skin and what was outside of it. As Sigmund Freud noted, "The ego is first and foremost a body ego."[2] Our sense of who and what we are, then, becomes the body and the rest of what we are, as we have discussed, fades into the background of our consciousness, until by adulthood it is completely forgotten. We become identified with the outer surface of ourselves—our physical form—and the inner dimension of our soul is lost in the unconscious. So our deepest identification is with the body and with its drives and biological imperatives.

With our sense of self grounded in the physical, our sense of reality is far more skewed than most of us realize. When the physical is the only dimension of reality that we are perceiving, we may believe that we are seeing things as they are, but in fact we are seeing through a distorted lens. We see the surface of things, including ourselves, and this lack of dimensionality alters our very perception of that surface and we do not even see the physical dimension as it truly is. This materialistic orientation is what we consider normal, the legacy of centuries of progressive dissociation of matter and spirit. In science, that most revered of modern disciplines, to be considered objective—seeing things as they are—means only giving credence to what can be perceived and measured using our physical senses. This remains so, despite scientific findings that the observer of an experiment affects the results of it. No wonder, with our value and awareness being firmly invested in matter, the surface of things, emptiness and meaninglessness are endemic in our most modern of cultures.

Our sense of who we are being decidedly rooted in the body and the inner experience of emptiness to which it gives rise leads us to our next passion, that of *lust*. Simply put, it is the drive and orientation to fill that emptiness through physical gratification—and a lot of it. One of the meanings of the word *lust* is an unquenchable craving and yearning, and as we shall see, this emptiness is one that we can never fill. While the word *lust* carries a sexual connotation, as Naranjo says, lust is "a passion for excess or an excessive passionateness to which sexual gratification is only one possible source of gratification."[3] This is a drive to have, to consume, to satiate and saturate ourselves with physical sensation, and, while Ennea-type Eights' personality structures are driven by this urge, it isn't hard to see that looking to the physical for satisfaction is an orientation common to us all.

Perhaps the most complete way of understanding the meaning of the passion of lust as it is used in the map of the enneagram is as an orientation excessively tipped toward the physical. Fulfillment is sought through the senses. The irony, as Almaas has noted, is that an excessively materialistic orientation is part of our postmodern way of life—and so the passion of lust may not at first glance seem like any sort of problem. In former times, however, an excessively physical orientation was considered sinful, and in religious and spiritual traditions throughout the ages, lust was considered the greatest of obstacles. If we believe deep down that fulfillment can be found only through sensual gratification, obviously our attention is diverted from what is beyond the body. This is the basis of asceticism—renouncing physical gratification as a way of connecting with what is beyond the body.

Indeed, renunciation is a time-honored approach to this deepest orientation in the soul—but hair shirts and celibacy are not very appealing to most of us these days, nor is such a path well suited to a life lived in the world. Another way to go is *through* our physically based orientation. This is the tantric route—engaging this side of ourselves, understanding it, and working through it.* Such an approach takes us into the heart of a very primitive sense of self—to the deepest and most primary structuralization of our soul—where we are completely identified with ourselves as organisms.

Before turning directly toward this structure, let's explore for a moment those whose personality style is organized around Point Eight. They

---

*When using the term *tantric,* I am referring to the Buddhist and Hindu orientation toward physical drives and emotions of going through them to contact and release the underlying spiritual energies—not the way the use of the term *tantra* has been debased to mean achieving greater sexual satisfaction.

constantly deal with their proclivity for excess, for living large, as it were. They seem to lack restraint and fly in the face of prudence, overindulging and seemingly knowing no limits. They appear driven to immerse themselves in whatever they encounter in life, engaging in it to the full. While Eights may seem unburdened by the usual constraints other types are subject to, this very tendency toward overdoing everything is part of an Eight's inner struggle.

There is the sense of being compelled by one's desires, unable to stem the powerful inner force toward pleasure and satisfaction, toward consuming and acquiring. Eights often feel dragged around by the sheer force of their desire, and their ability to control their impetuosity and headlong lunge toward gratification of their urges often feels like a losing battle. In their emotional life as well, things tend to be hot and volatile, regardless of whether the feeling is positive or negative. While some Eights have a cool and withdrawn veneer, this is often to conceal from themselves and others the passionate nature of their drives and emotions beneath the surface.

Their appetites are typically huge—*moderation* is not a word in their vocabulary—and in direct proportion to the degree their soul is oriented toward the physical, to that same degree is their hunger for what feels most tangible and palpable. It takes a great deal of sensation to penetrate the thickness their souls can take on, so there is little place here for the refined and subtle. On top of their struggles with the power of their inner drives, there is an assumption that these forces are not acceptable, adding a defiant and contentious cast to their expression.

Eights, then, contend with the primitive, the instinctual, the animalistic; but while this aspect of the human psyche is highlighted in their process, it is, as are all the passions of the enneagram, universal. Although it may be more camouflaged than it typically is in Eights, we all have such a side to ourselves. While we may know that this aspect of us exists, by the time most of us reach adulthood it has been suppressed to a great extent through the conditioning process we discussed in the previous chapter. We no longer throw our food or grab someone else's piece of chocolate, but this element of us has not been socialized out of existence. We have simply found more sophisticated, circuitous, and socially acceptable ways of satisfying the drives of this part of us.

It is alive and well in the background of our psyche, running the show in our lives both individually and collectively more than most of us care to realize. We see it whenever acquisitiveness and power grabbing predominate, and we see that just about every time we look around. We see it collectively in instances of corporate greed, in which the bottom line justifies clever concealment of shady business practices. We see it at work in the Middle East, with modern "tribes" killing each other to grab what each considers their turf. We see it in the taken-for-granted form of nationalism. To a great extent, the laws and conventions of society are designed to contain and protect us from this aspect of ourselves.

On a more personal level, we are concerned with our physical and emotional appetites and desires here, in a completely self-centered way. Others are seen only as the objects of our desire, as obstacles to what we desire, or as helpers in getting our desires filled. This part of us has no capacity for delayed gratification, the very adult ability to patiently wait until the table is set, for instance, and others have been seated before launching into a meal. This part wants to grab the best morsels for ourselves and to hell with manners!

Our love for what we desire and fully taking it in—devouring it—are indistinguishable here. Here, we are like a lion stalking our prey, filled with a primitive kind of love that seeks to immerse our teeth and tear into that lovely gazelle over there that so excites us, filling us with a burning, raw passion. We are indeed driven, and cannot turn away from the object of our desire any more than our lion can. Here, everything and everyone is just food to us. Even the most sublime spiritual experiences are just something yummy to be consumed, and if they aren't clearly going to give us some sort of gratification, who cares about them—this part of us is not interested. Altruism and self-sacrifice be damned.

For this reason, dealing with this animalistic aspect of our soul is crucial if our inner work is not to be derailed or usurped by this primitive and usually semiconscious force. The Sufis have graphically dubbed this part of us the animal soul—*nafs-i-ammara* in Arabic—and Almaas has elaborated its understanding. Our animal soul is precivilization and prehuman. It is the part of our soul at the interface of our biology and our consciousness, shaped and fixed as a sense of self. It is an earlier and more primitive structure than that of the rejected aspects of ourselves as a very young child—a structure which Almaas has called our soul child.

Our soul child is a sense of ourselves as we were when we were quite young, crystallized and frozen in time within our psyche. This structure is not simply a younger version of ourselves but encompasses qualities that were, for one reason or another, not ones that we experienced as encouraged or supported in our early environment. These aspects of ourselves, then, we suppressed and sealed off from consciousness, and our sense of self developed both in reaction to and without them.*

Experientially, we find the animal soul contained within the soul child. The animal soul was structured prior to having the concept of ourselves as children, and so is a younger and more primitive structure. It carries with it the legacy of the whole of our evolutionary past, and we may experience it as having the felt sense of being an animalistic creature, or at deeper levels as simply worm- or tubelike.

The author Virginia Woolf gives a beautiful description of this aspect of ourselves in her novel *The Waves*:

> There is the old brute, too, the savage, the hairy man who dabbles his fingers in ropes of entrails; and gobbles and belches; whose speech is guttural, visceral—well, he is here. He squats in me. Tonight he has been feasted on quails, salad, and sweetbread. He now holds a glass of fine old brandy in his paw. He brindles, purrs and shoots warm thrills all down my spine as I sip. It is true, he washes his hands before dinner, but they are still hairy. He buttons on trousers and waistcoats, but they contain the same organs. He jibs if I keep him waiting for dinner. He mops and mows perpetually pointing with his half-idiot gestures of greed and covetousness at what he desires. I assure you, I have had great difficulty sometimes in controlling him. That man, the hairy, the ape-like, has contributed his part to my life. He has given a greener glow to green things, has held his torch with its red flames, its thick and smarting smoke, behind every leaf. He has lit up the cool garden even. He has brandished his torch in murky by-streets where girls sud-

---

*For more on the soul child, see Chapter 11 of my book *The Spiritual Dimension of the Enneagram: Nine Faces of the Soul*.

denly seem to shine with a red and intoxicating translucency. Oh, he has tossed his torch high! He has led me wild dances![4]

As Woolf describes, while the animal soul is bestial, it also is the repository of our aliveness, our vibrancy, and our capacity to fully engage in life. We will discuss this more fully later on.

When we look closely at this sector of our consciousness, what we see is very crude. It feels beastlike—savage, brutal, coarse—a remnant of our evolutionary past, prior to civilization. Its needs and interests are entirely physical and sensual, and at this level of our psyches, we are pure organism. Here we are driven by our survival instinct, the force within us geared toward preserving ourselves at all costs. Our identification with our body is firm and irrefutable here, despite all the fancy talk that we might fundamentally be something else. We are speaking here of pure instinctual drive directed toward sustaining life, and we cannot discuss this force without also discussing the understanding of Freud, who was perhaps the first to conceptualize this aspect of the human psyche and to perceive its driving force in our lives and civilization. Although Freud has fallen out of favor in some circles, he is nonetheless quite relevant to understanding many aspects of the psyche, which are the same now as they were in his time.

While Freud's thinking evolved over time, central to his unchanging observation about what makes humans tick is the notion that we are subject to drives (*Trieb* in German),* which activate our psychic structures. Ambiguity has remained in psychoanalytic thought about whether the drives are biologically based or of a purely psychological nature, and to Freud they exist at the interface of the two. While perceiving that there are numerous drives, he postulated two primal ones in 1915: the self-preservative and the sexual instincts. In his initial formulation of the drives, he saw that of self-preservation being at odds with the sexual drive, in that responding to the latter's urgings might bring social alienation and thus threaten one's well-being. Over time, his sense of the pri-

---

*This term was mistranslated in the *Standard Edition* as *instinct*, perhaps in an attempt to establish a more physiological/medical footing for the nascent field of psychoanalysis. Instinct refers to the inborn instincts of animals, and Freud did not use the German *Instinckt* in relation to humans—only when discussing animals.

mary drives changed to the sexual drive (*libido*) and the aggressive drive (*eros*), and then later (perhaps in reaction to his former disciple Carl Jung's criticism of his focus on sexuality) he saw the two primary drives as that toward life and that toward death.*

He believed that the root of all human activities was the demands of our drives, mitigated by our defenses against them. The passion of lust, then, is primary. In his model, the function and importance of others is based on their ability to help us discharge our drives. Thus Freud saw humans as primarily isolates attempting to satisfy their individual needs, in contrast to the current trend in psychoanalysis toward a relational model in which humans are seen as inherently social creatures. For this reason, he saw society as an imposition and a safeguard against the acting-out of the individual drives of its members.

This is certainly the perspective of Eights, in which deep down their own drives are primary, social conventions and niceties often feel flimsy and extraneous, and others are often seen as either challengers or sources of gratification. So although this Freudian model is currently unfashionable in psychological thought, we see that for this character type, it fits. This suggests that the numerous and often contentious psychological schools with their differing theories about how we are wired up may all have some degree of accuracy, reflecting different experiences of the human journey from different angles. Freud's perspective also adds weight to the view of many that he was an Ennea-type Five, since Eight is the underlying core of that personality style. Eight is Five's heart point—the one directly before, moving backward along the lines of inner flow shown in Diagram 9, page 29. The heart point, as discussed briefly in Chapter 1, is the heart or core of one's ennea-type. Its characteristics are those of one's soul child, mentioned above, and it forms psychodynamically an underlying layer in one's psyche. The passion of an ennea-type's heart point likewise forms the basis for its passion.** To Freud, then, the passion of Point Eight—lust—was foundational.

---

*Many speculate that Freud's initial focus on sexuality as a primary drive may have been because the population he worked with was primarily hysterics, whose neurotic symptoms did indeed originate in dammed-up sexual energy.

**For more on the heart point, see *The Spiritual Dimension of the Enneagram,* Chapter 11.

With the publication of *The Ego and the Id* in 1923, Freud introduced the tripartite model of the psyche.* In it, there are three major structures or systems in our personality: *das Ich* (literally, "I"), *das Es* ("it"), and the *Über-Ich* ("above-I"). These were unfortunately translated into English editions of Freud's work as the *id,* the *ego,* and the *superego,*** losing the immediacy of the original German. The drives, which we have been discussing, reside in *das Es,* or the id. In naming it "the it," Freud sought to convey how this part of our psychic structure feels like something other than ourselves. We do not readily identify with it—with the exception perhaps of Ennea-type Eights—and we often feel led around by its promptings. He saw the id as the repository of the drives, and the source of the energy in our psyche.

The id is run by what Freud called the "pleasure principle": avoiding pain and finding pleasure. He theorized that we, like all other organisms, attempt to maintain a state of homeostasis, and so we try to discharge any internal pressure, which is experienced as tension and thus "unpleasure." Pleasure, then, especially in the early Freudian model, is lack of internal tension or stimulation. We seek, then, to find gratification for our drives so that we are not subject to the pressure of them, rather than purely to experience enjoyment. Although, as the psychoanalytic writers Greenberg and Mitchell note in their sweeping overview of psychoanalytic thought, Freud never seemed fully comfortable with this theory, he never fully discarded it, either; and in later years he reworked it leaving the understanding of what pleasure and unpleasure are quite open.[5] No longer defining pleasure as simply the absence of internal tension, he pointed toward the possibility that the sense of pleasure has a qualitative source and perhaps lies in the alternation of quantities of stimulus. We will discuss the pleasure principle more fully in Chapter 9.

Freud saw the id as our primary subjective reality, historically existing

*As noted by Bruno Bettelheim in his very interesting book, *Freud and Man's Soul,* when Freud used the term *psyche,* as in psychoanalysis and psychic structure, he was referring to the soul (*die Seele*), which, as Bettleheim notes, has in German an even more exclusively spiritual connotation than it does in English. All references to the soul have been expunged from English translations, with *psyche* being translated as *mind.*

**Strachey's translation of these terms into Latin in the *Standard Edition* loses the original connotations Freud sought to give to them, as noted by Bettleheim and Ornston in an article in the *International Journal of Psycho-Analysis.*

prior to any interaction with the world and remaining throughout our lives out of contact with what is external to us. It is that part of our structure residing beneath the surface of consciousness, thus not making direct and conscious contact with what is beyond our own body. Because it is a part of our soul that is sealed off from the outside, there is only self and no sense of other. Everything here is about ourselves, without any concept of a self, since that can only exist if there is a sense of what is not ourselves. Likewise, there is no self-reflection, since that requires the capacity to move beyond our immediate felt experience and view it from a degree of distance.

It is the part of us that is primitive, in which we are mostly wild animal and very young child. Everything is elemental, chaotic, and untamed—the part of our soul caught up in bodily functions, energies, and impulses at the borderline of biological imperatives and psychological wants. Body and psyche are indistinguishable here. Nothing is thought out here since the id is preconceptual, so there is no logic or reasoning—and these more sophisticated functions, which belong to the ego, do not affect it. Neither is it ethical nor moral—these are the domain of the superego. The id either wishes or it acts, propelled by its raw forces, and self-restraint and patience have no place here. We are driven by the pleasure principle to satisfy and discharge our drives, and like a child, the id will not tolerate delay.

The wish-fulfilling impulse just mentioned of the id requires a little explanation. Freud believed that the id cannot distinguish between an outer object of gratification and the internal image of it, so the id fulfills its urges by either taking action to get what it needs and wants or it dreams and fantasizes about getting it. He believed that our dreams are wish fulfillments, one of the ways that the id discharges its drive energy. We might, for instance, see the id in action when we dream about having an affair with a friend's husband or wife, or when we dream about eating endless amounts of chocolate cake—especially if we are on a diet. Or when we find ourselves daydreaming about being on the beach in Hawaii as we sit in our cubicle at work. The realm of fantasy and dreams, then, are its domain, and the id's only goal is to get rid of internal tension, moving away from what it experiences as unpleasurable and toward what is pleasurable.

As Calvin Hall, professor of psychology, writes of the id in his over-view of Freudian psychology, it is the repository of inherited tendencies and is thus "archaic"; and,

> *it is also archaic in the life of the individual. It is the foundation upon which the personality is built. The id retains its infantile character throughout life. It cannot tolerate tension. It wants immediate gratification. It is demanding, impulsive, irrational, asocial, selfish, and pleasure-loving. It is the spoiled child of the personality. It is omnipotent because it has the magical power of fulfilling its wishes by imagination, fantasy, hal-lucinations, and dreams. It is said to be oceanic because, like the sea, it con-tains everything. It recognizes nothing external to itself. The id is the world of subjective reality in which the pursuit of pleasure and the avoidance of pain are the only functions that count.*[6]

As Freud described it in his *New Introductory Lectures on Psychoanalysis,* the id is "the dark inaccessible part of our personality. . . . We approach the id with analogies: we call it chaos, a cauldron full of seething excitation."[7] He believed that we could only contact it indirectly via dreams and neu-rotic symptoms, such as anxiety, depression, uncontrollable repetitive be-haviors or thoughts, irrational fears and phobias, and so on. After introducing the concept of the id, Freud in fact used the term inter-changeably with the *unconscious* of his earlier topographic model, in which the psyche was composed of the *conscious* (what is present in our awareness), the *preconscious* (what we are unaware of but can bring to consciousness), and the *unconscious* (what we are unaware of and cannot readily contact, and also referred to as the *subconscious*). Aspects of the ego and superego may also be unconscious, so it might be most accurate to say that the id occu-pies a large—and perhaps the largest—sector of our unconscious.

And while we get in touch with it in a roundabout way via the con-tents of our dreams, fantasies, and neurotic symptoms—as Freud so in-sultingly put such behaviors and characteristics of our personality—we also get in touch with our id when we act out impulsively. For example, when we have reached the limits of our monthly budget and are compelled to go out and buy that gorgeous whatever that we simply must have, or when we can't help but hit our brakes in response to that tailgater, or cut someone off who has been frustrating us with their driving.

Returning to Freud's idea that the id cannot discriminate between an actual object and its internal image of the object, it is easy to see that simply conjuring up the image of something yummy to eat is not enough to assuage our hunger. So the soul learns to discriminate between the internal image and outer reality, and attempts to find the real object that conforms to its image. In this process, the second part of the tripartite structure— the ego—is born. The ego, then, evolves as the part of our structure that interfaces with the outside, while drawing its energy from the id.

Freud called it the "I" to indicate that it is the part of our psyche that we identify with as ourselves. Its job is one of accommodation, controlling the raw drive energy of the id and finding outlets for that energy, as well as finding ways of satisfying its imperatives that are personally useful, appropriate, and socially acceptable. The ego is the seat of this reality principle, in which we take both external and internal reality into consideration, modulating the often unrealistic, inappropriate, and immature urges of the id. So it is the reasonable and rational part of ourselves. In the following analogy, Freud describes the relationship of the ego to the id as being

> *like a man on horseback, who has to hold in check the superior strength of the horse; with this difference, that the rider tries to do so with his own strength while the ego uses borrowed forces. The analogy may be carried a little further. Often a rider, if he is not to be parted from his horse, is obliged to guide it where it wants to go; so in the same way the ego is in the habit of transforming the id's will into action as if it were its own.*[8]

The ego, then, attempts to control the id's impulses and is also fueled by its energy. The ego and the superego, which oversees it, have no energy of their own. They differentiate out of the id, and it remains the source of energy for the whole psychic system. Toward the end of his life, Freud summed up the function of psychoanalysis as bringing the id to consciousness, as expressed in his famous phrase, "Where *it* was, there should become *I*,"[9] or in mistranslated Freudian jargon, Where the id was, there the ego should be. Despite Freud's sense of its centrality in the work of psychoanalysis, the concept of the id had, by the 1960s, fallen into—interestingly enough—a chaos of different interpretations, and by the 1980s was in relative disuse amongst that community.

Moving the model closer to psychic reality was left to the next generation of psychoanalysts. In the early 1940s, the Scottish psychoanalyst William R. D. Fairbairn began publishing articles challenging some of Freud's basic assumptions—amongst them, his tripartite structural model. His work marked a shift from a drive-based model of psychic structure to a relational one, and so he was one of the pioneers of the object relations movement in psychological thought. Without going into great detail about his theory, and oversimplifying a bit for the purposes of our discussion, Fairbairn saw the ego as central, although his use of the term *ego* bears little relationship to how Freud used the term, and has more in common with the contemporary use of the term *self* in psychoanalytic circles. He saw one part of what he called the ego representing our conscious sense of self—the central ego discussed in Chapter 1—and two split-off or repressed parts representing unacceptable aspects of ourselves. Each of these three egos is bound up with objects, rather than existing in isolation. One of these, which he called the libidinal ego, replaces the id.

The libidinal ego is composed of unfulfilled infantile longings and dependencies, and so exists in a perpetual state of deprivation and voracious hunger for satisfaction. It is primitive and primal, but more structured than the id, and is object seeking rather than simply aimless drive energy. Sometimes its longings are sexual, but this is often defensive, layered over its real longings for contact and nurturance. As Fairbairn writes of the libidinal ego,

> The 'libidinal ego' corresponds, of course, to Freud's 'id'; but, whereas according to Freud's view the 'ego' is derivative of the 'id', according to my view the 'libidinal ego' (which corresponds to the 'id') is a derivative of the 'central ego' (which corresponds to the 'ego'). The 'libidinal ego' also differs

*from the 'id' in that it is conceived, not as a mere reservoir of instinctive im-
pulses, but as a dynamic structure comparable to the 'central ego', although
differing from the latter in various respects, e.g. in its more infantile character, in a lesser degree of organization, in a smaller measure of adaptation
to reality and in a greater devotion to internalized objects.*[10]

The libidinal ego, then, is a more structured and object-seeking version of the id. It is not fully sealed off from external reality as is the id, and
it has more shape in our psyche. This evolution of the id model is the basis of Almaas's model of the animal soul mentioned early on in this chapter. We see, then, a development of the model of this primitive part of our
structure, and it might be most accurate to conceive of these notions of
that structure as part of a continuum, with the deepest layers of the id
hidden far below the radar screen of awareness at one pole, and the most
conscious aspects of the animal soul at the other pole.

Extending Fairbairn's focus, in Almaas's animal soul the strivings are
not simply for relationship. Although the desire for affection and a sense
of social belonging are certainly part of what the animal soul is preoccupied with, self-preservation is the most fundamental driving force. Concern about the well-being of one's body, such as having enough to eat and
adequate shelter, are rooted here. This is the part of our structure where
our primitive and often irrational survival anxieties live. It is the animal
soul informing our consciousness when we never feel that we have enough
money, even though we might have a very hefty portfolio; when another
person's anger toward us feels life threatening; or when we are certain that
we have cancer based on some ephemeral physical symptom.

While Fairbairn let go of Freud's concept of the id as the seat of internal energy, it is retained in Almaas's model of the animal soul, and this
brings us to the central importance of working with this internal structure. We have seen that Freud believed that the energy fueling our various psychic structures resides in the id. It is our drive energy. These
structures, then, are the forms or molds that give a particular shape to this
energy of our soul. If we discriminate between the structure and the energy, we see that the energy itself is what animates our organism. It is our

life force, or as the Hindus call it, our *prana* or *shakti.* As the Jungian psychologist James Hillman says in his commentary on Gopi Krishna's autobiographical description of the awakening of his kundalini,

> Prana *is both a super-intelligent cosmic life-energy and the subtle biological conductor in the body, that is, it is both a universal life-force and a physiological actuality. It is both immaterial and material, both independent of here-and-now yet inextricably interwoven with the life of the body.*[11]

Our life energy, then, is what fuels our body. It is *not* the body, nor, as Hillman implies, is it *of* the body—rather, it is the body's source of energy. This is a crucial discrimination to make. Prana or shakti infuses physical matter, but it is its own dimension of reality—in other words, it has its own existence separate from matter.

This life energy becomes channeled into our various drives—our drive for self-preservation, our aggression, our sexual energy, and so on—and from a Freudian perspective, resides in the id, as we have seen. As we develop, our ego takes shape as the interface between our id impulses and external reality. We learn to accommodate to the outer environment, learn to behave ourselves, and become more or less what we consider "normal" as we mature. Our superego oversees this development, evaluating our behavior, thoughts, and feelings against its model of how we ought to be, and by the time we reach adulthood, much of our id energy is securely "bound," or repressed and contained. The more that our ego and superego suppress our drive energy, the more dampened down we feel. Although the extent of this binding varies from individual to individual, it is safe to say that the more successfully we have become civilized, the more cut off we are from our life force. Most of us end up feeling some degree of a lack of vitality and vibrancy, and our life might feel more or less drab and boring, gray and dull.

We have seen that the id can be regarded as the deepest level of the more structured animal soul. The more buried, confined, and rejected from consciousness the structure of the animal soul is, the more distorted it becomes. It is easy to understand why this is, if we remember that what we are dealing with is a primitive structure made up of life energy. Whenever life energy is confined and kept in the darkness of unconsciousness, it becomes twisted and negative. There is often a direct proportion to the degree of inner repression of our animal soul and the primitive, raw, and sometimes perverse quality of its desires and aggression. We often see this in the most proper or spiritually correct of people who have a hidden dark side that leaks out in some incongruous way. And this is an important thing to understand about our drive energy: just because it is suppressed doesn't mean that it goes away. It comes out somehow in the economy of our psyche, whether through implosion of our energy in depression and self-destructive behaviors or in spontaneous and inadvertent forms of acting out.

The animal soul is central to Ennea-type Eights, as we have seen, with the drive energy expressed through veils of personality structure. Typically, Eights are full of gusto, intense, impulsive, larger than life, and often more spontaneous and less inhibited than the other types. An Eight seems to revel in his lusty ways, but as Naranjo notes, "even though the lusty type is passionately in favor of his lust and of lust in general as a way of life, the very passionateness with which he embraces this outlook betrays a defensiveness—as if he needed to prove to himself and the rest of the world that what everyone else calls bad is not such."[12] The passion of lust comes out not as pure life energy, clean and direct, but rather through the distortion of prohibition. Central is an Eight's assumption that he is not entitled to gratify his desires, that others are out to stop or deprive him—that his libidinal and aggressive energy are bad and not acceptable. His drive energy finds release, but it takes on a pushiness, grabbiness, insatiability, and belligerent edge. As Naranjo says,

> We must consider that lust is more than hedonism. There is in lust not only pleasure, but pleasure in asserting the satisfaction of impulses, pleasure in the forbidden and, particularly, pleasure in fighting for pleasure. In addition to pleasure proper there is here an admixture of some pain that has been transformed into pleasure: either the pain of others who are "preyed upon" for one's satisfaction or the pain entailed by the effort to conquer the obstacles in the way to satisfaction. It is this that makes lust a passion for

intensity and not for pleasure alone. The extra intensity, the extra excitement, the "spice," comes not from instinctual satisfaction, but from a struggle and an implicit triumph.[13]

At the root of an Eight's guilt-enveloped lust may well be the inner knowing in the soul that the identification with the body central to lust is a lie. The truth is that our ultimate nature is not the body, is not physical form or matter, so to be oriented around satisfying the body's sensory and sensual desires is not in alignment with how things really are.

Although in contrast to the other types, Eights seem more alive and exuberant, full of "lust for life," inwardly they are often just as cut off from their vitality. Probably in direct proportion to their bravado, Eights have a thick layer of callousness and deadness separating them from contact with their vitality. It is as though their soul has become hardened, toughened, and desensitized. What is needed, then, for Eights as for all of us, is for the life energy contained in the inner structure of the animal soul to be liberated, so that its vitality can inform the soul in positive and wholesome ways.

This brings us to the virtue of Point Eight: *innocence*. Innocence has multiple meanings, a number of which can help us understand the orientation indicated by this virtue. It is defined as freedom from guilt or sin, especially through being unacquainted with evil—purity of heart, freedom from guile or cunning, harmlessness in intention, a lack of experience of the world, naïveté, and sexual inexperience. And we have Ichazo's definition of the virtue of innocence:

> *The innocent being responds freshly to each moment, without memory, judgment, or expectation. In innocence one experiences reality and one's connection to its flow.*

Experiencing reality in its freshness and immediacy means experiencing it without the veil of the past distorting our experience of it. It means experiencing it without the structures rooted in the past obscuring our soul, our mind, and our perception. The deepest of these structures, as we have seen, is that of the animal soul, so to live in such a state requires bringing it and as much as possible of its deepest layer, the id, to consciousness. Doing so frees up the life energy contained in these structures, so that we can indeed experience ourselves in the flow of reality. It ameliorates the guilt, and the "guile and cunning" implicit in the purely physical orientation of the animal soul, and allows us to become truly human.

This is not a task to be undertaken lightly or without adequate preparation and external structures, since it really is a dismantling of all the strictures that have made us into more or less civilized human beings. Attempting to control or suppress the animal soul, as many spiritual practices have tried to do over the centuries, is certainly understandable given the power contained in this structure. But this only results in feeling very dry and flat, lacking juice for our spiritual journey.

Working with and freeing the animal soul does not mean simply letting it out of its cage so that we can run wild, gratifying all of our desires with no regard for the consequences to ourselves or anyone else. This approach has been tried by many psychologists and spiritual teachers, hoping that in so doing, the animal soul would wear itself out. Letting the animal soul act out does have a place, especially for those in whom those drives have been profoundly bound up and rendered inaccessible. But such discharging is not the same thing as working through this structure. Without inquiry into it and experientially understanding its nature, the structure of the animal soul remains fixed no matter how much leeway we give it.

Nor is uninhibitedly acting on its impulses the same as freedom. Freedom—as opposed to license—in terms of the animal soul is liberating the life energy contained in that structure, such that the structure becomes progressively more transparent and our life energy flows freely through our soul. This is only possible when we directly experience how our life energy has become trapped and fixed in our felt belief of ourselves as primarily physical. When we know this directly, our identification with the body as our ultimate nature, our final ground, gets seen through and begins to unwind.

What is required first of all, is acknowledging that we have such an animalistic side to ourselves and letting ourselves get in touch with it. To do this entails challenging our prejudices and assumptions about it—engaging it with the attitude of the virtue of innocence. Approaching this structure with an attitude of innocence means experiencing it directly, beyond the veils of our preconceptions—especially our judgment of it as something bad or wrong. This involves seeing the taboos and prohibitions we have about this side of ourselves—societal ones as well as our own personal ones—and understanding that while these have served an important function in our development into civilized human beings, this suppression is no longer serving us, except to separate us from our life energy. So the pull of the personality to accommodate, to be and behave like everyone else, which is so crucial to the process of becoming socialized, must be faced.

As we increasingly are able to experience this raw and uncivilized part of ourselves fully in the moment, we progressively feel its shape becoming less solid. We see that structure, even this most rudimentary formation of the soul, is a fixedness; and that our inherent innocence is the absence of any shape whatsoever informing our soul. As the structure of the animal soul relaxes, the primeval quality of the pure life force that is inseparable from our soul is revealed. We see that this energy only animates the body but is not *of* the body—that the nature of our soul does not emanate from our physical form. As we experience this, we see that this life energy is, as the yogis say, cosmic—the life energy of all that is.

We also see that while the animal soul structure houses a part of our soul that is untouched by civilization and our conditioning, still existing in its primal state, that very encapsulation has maintained its innocence. A sense of the pristineness inherent to our soul is revealed as the identification with the body loosens. We contact the basic fluidity of our soul, its transparent and formless nature, prior to any structuring of it into an ongoing sense of self. Prior to its atmosphere becoming tinged with any predominant emotional attitude or leaning—prior to becoming colored by our passion. Prior to the shaping of our soul becoming set as we experience one thing or another—different emotions, environmental impacts, and impressions—through repetition. In the absence of these fixed patterns in our soul, we experience its nature as it is, before its molding into our personality structure.

Here we have no memory overlaying and prejudicing our experience, and so we see things freshly and purely. We see that our personality is really the molding of this viscosity that is our soul into fixedness, and that this shaping is the result of remembering repeating patterns moving through our soul till they no longer change. This retention of impressions—memory—lies at the root of the process of forming the personality. Without these memories acting as a filter for our ongoing experience, everything is new. We experience things as we did before the formation of memory, and so free of our conditioned way of experiencing ourselves and the world, since conditioning is learned and learning relies on memory. Without impressions from the past, which memory stores, we encounter things innocently, as they are.

We experience our very soul as a plasmatic flow, the pure substance of consciousness, and the more refined our perception becomes, the more we see that this fluidity is part of the movement of all that exists. We are indeed, as Ichazo says, in touch with reality and its flow. We are in touch with ourselves prior to the time when we began to identify with the body at the exclusion of True Nature. We see things in their full dimensionality, since the inculcated focus only on the physical is gone. We see that there is no such thing as matter devoid of its depth dimension, which is spirit. Nor does spirit exist independent of matter—they are one thing. The nature of ourselves and of our world is the Divine—True Nature and the universe are inseparable.

When we see with such freshness, we have regained the innocence we had when we were very small—we have indeed become like little children. And rather than being able to enter the kingdom of heaven at that point, we see that we are, and have always been, already there.

P O I N T   O N E —
A N G E R *and*
S E R E N I T Y

———— *◦/◦/◦* ————

The Great Way is not difficult
for those not attached to preferences.
When neither love nor hate arises,
all is clear and undisguised.
Separate by the smallest amount, however,
and you are as far from it as heaven is from earth.

If you wish to know the truth,
then hold to no opinions for or against anything.
To set up what you like against what you dislike
is a disease of the mind.

When the fundamental nature of things is not recognized
the mind's essential peace is disturbed to no avail.

—CHIEN-CHIH SENG-TS'AN,
THIRD ZEN PATRICARCH[1]

The passion of this point of the enneagram is encompassed by the word *anger,* but what that term signifies is something much more broad than simply feeling peeved, resentful, or outright enraged, although these are certainly frequent emotional experiences for Ennea-type Ones. As is true of all the passions, what is meant is a general attitude, in this case one that Ichazo characterized as "standing against reality," or as Naranjo elaborates, "a rejection of what is in terms of what is felt and believed should be."[2] This is an attitude, then, of reacting against what reality presents us with.

This mind-set of standing against reality is not the only form of reactivity in the personality—all of the passions are from this vantage point different forms of reaction against the truth of reality in all of its dimensionality. Looking at the passions we have discussed so far, we can see that one response to reality, inner or outer, is to tune it out and to go to sleep in the face of it—to become lazy, in other words, the passion of Point Nine. Another reaction, that represented at Point Eight, is to meet reality with a devouring attitude, responding to what is as food to fill our inner hunger, as rations for survival. While all of the passions are different styles of reactivity, what we are addressing in this chapter is the most blatant reactive pattern implicit in the personality, one that we encounter early on as we begin paying attention to what goes on inside of us.

Those familiar with the enneagram know that the personality style of Ones is oriented around a conviction that things are not right as they are, and that they should conform to a One's idea of how they ought to be. The attitude or feeling tone arising out of this belief, then, is an oppositional hostility toward what is. In Ones, this aggressively rejecting attitude is seldom as out front as the designation of this passion—anger—suggests. These are people in service of the good, the ethical, the virtuous, and what they deem to be the correct and proper, who take the moral high ground in whatever sphere of life they are involved in. They tend to be politically and spiritually correct, suppressing what does not accord, and so end up chafing under their excessive self-control. Because of this, their angry attitude manifests typically as an intolerant, critical, and resentful atmosphere rather than an overtly hostile one. In this sense, *resentment* best describes their characteristic reactive atmosphere.

As Almaas notes, "In resentment, there is aversion, which is made up of anger and rejection toward your experience."[3] This belligerent attitude is not simply a rejection of how things are but also a forceful attempt to make things conform to a One's inner picture of how they ought to be. This manifests in a One's tendency to point out and attempt to correct the perceived faults of themselves and of others, and may extend to trying to make the world itself conform to his or her idea of how things ought to be, often with the sense that if everything were perfect, then he or she could finally relax.

Obviously, this whole inner atmosphere is fraught with a tense watchfulness. It is a determined and righteous overseeing, checking for what might not be right, an attempt to supervise and regulate emanating from an inner position of certainty about what is correct. No discrimination between internal and external experience is being made here, since to the extent that such an attitude is prevalent internally toward one's own experience, it is likewise directed outwardly. Experience is experience, whether within the bounds of one's own body or beyond it.

Lest those of us who are not Ones feel prematurely relieved that what I am describing is mercifully not personally relevant, an inner glance might suggest otherwise. When we begin paying attention to our inner experience, one of the first things that we notice is an inner voice attempting to orchestrate what we are feeling, thinking, and even experiencing. The content varies, but the internal dialogue always has an evaluative and judgmental tone to it. Although we each have our own unique versions of this voice, the sound track generally sounds something like, *Boy,* that *was really stupid—what's the matter with you that you always feel/think/do that?* or *No wonder you're such a loser. Look at what you are feeling/thinking/doing!* or *That was a* terrible *thing you said to so-and-so—how can you be such an idiot—so insensitive and stupid!* Sometimes, conversely, this voice praises us, saying something to the effect of, *Wow, you did a really great job—you are such a good person!* or *You are so much better than so-and-so—just look at how idiotic she is!*

If we are involved in spiritual work, we might inwardly hear something like, *What a spiritual disaster you are—you're so attached/identified/unconscious/uncompassionate!* Or, if the evaluation is positive, *You are such a good meditator—look at how still you can sit in contrast to that poor slob over there who keeps moving all the time.* The common thread, regardless of what this voice is addressing, is evaluation—whether positive or negative—and frequent use of the words "should" and "ought." This inner structure judges how things are, and has very definite ideas about how they ought to be. Most of us do not question its pronouncements. We may internally argue with them or try to appease this voice, but its very power lies in the fact that we believe that its judgments are accurate.

This is our inner critic, whose function as part of our personality structure is to oversee and evaluate what is going on within us, as well as to assess our actions, and to criticize, reproach, punish, or praise what it observes. Freud was the first to conceptualize this structure, and as we have seen, his name for it in German is the *Über-Ich,* literally meaning the "over-I." Unfortunately, the denotation of this structure's job as overseer of our sense of self is lost in the English rendition of "superego," but for the sake of clarity, we will use that now-familiar term for this structure as we explore it.

As overseer of the ego, the superego's job is to inspect and appraise the self, making sure that it strives toward and conforms to the values, principles, and qualities that we consider to be ideal. So it is the repository and enforcer of our personal values and standards. Its dicta are rooted in our internal picture of perfection, and reality, whether internal or external, is measured against this mental image. Its judgments, then, are based on a comparison of reality with an inner representation of how things could and should optimally be. Implicit is the conviction that things should match this internal representation, and if things do not, they are wrong and unacceptable.

This image is what Freud called our ego ideal, or *Ich-Ideal* in German, meaning literally "the ideal me," and he used this term interchangeably with his later concept of the superego.* Since his time, the ego ideal has come to be seen as a subset of the superego, one set of its functions, rather than being synonymous with it. Our ego ideal includes our concepts of what the ideal self, the ideal partner, the ideal child, and the ideal relationship should look and be like. It also includes internal representations of actions that ought to be taken or should be avoided to safeguard our ideal sense of relationship, both intimate and global. In other words, part of our ego ideal is an internal image of actions that we should and shouldn't take, based on preserving and supporting our intimate relationships, our friendships, and our participation in our community, nation,

*Freud introduced the term *ego ideal* in 1914, and the term *superego* in 1923.

and as a member of humanity. Cheating on our husband or wife, betraying a friend's confidence, or stealing from others are just a few examples of commonly held prohibited actions, while being kind to others, honest, and accountable are examples of ideal actions.

These ideals form the basis of our egoic sense of conscience—our sense of what is right and what is wrong. As we can see, what the term *ego ideal* refers to is multidimensional. When trying to grasp experientially what it means, it is most useful to envision its internal images as holographic ones that encompass and include a multitude of beliefs and concepts, not simply visual images like internal snapshots. These images form the basis of the evaluations and judgments of our superego—or to look at it from the other side, behind our assessments and pronouncements lies this collection of internal representations of what is optimal.

Freud viewed the superego as largely unconscious, in the sense that most people are as unaware of this internal voice of imperatives and prohibitions as they are of their id impulses. What most people can't miss, however, are the feeling states resulting from attacks and ovations from it. When we violate our superego's standards based on our ego ideals, we tend—if our ego is healthy—to experience shame or guilt. We usually feel shame when we do not live up to the ways we would like to see ourselves—when we fall short of our ideal concept of self, in other words. If we are experiencing a sense of failure, lack, or weakness, our superego typically jumps on us, disparaging and belittling us, making us feel humiliated and mortified. When we transgress our personal code regarding others, we typically feel a sense of guilt and reproach ourselves more or less severely.

Shame protects the integrity of our sense of self, while guilt protects the integrity of the other. The fact that we feel shame when we violate an inner dictum, in other words, preserves the intactness of our sense of who we are; just as feeling guilty attests to the integrity of the other, against whom we should not have transgressed. On the other hand, when our superego praises us, we feel a sense of pride and our self-esteem is elevated.

It is important to recognize that not all negative or positive feelings about ourselves are rooted in superego evaluations. We may feel empty or lacking, for instance, and if no judgment is involved, neither is our superego. We are then simply experiencing what is called an ego state, a sense of deficiency implicit in identification with our personality. Likewise, if we are feeling good about ourselves and have a sense of well-being, this is not necessarily the result of accolades from our superego. It could be a by-product of contact with the deeper dimension of ourselves. So it is important to discriminate whether or not our affective state is the result of internal assessment rather than assuming that all negative or positive states are the result of inner dynamics involving our superego. This is a mistake many make as their awareness of their superego becomes heightened.

What *is* true is that until we have some degree of freedom from our superego, our ego states of deficiency are usually compounded by judgments and pronouncements about what a miserable human being we are for feeling this way, how if we had only been better we would not feel this way, and so on. Insult, indeed, is added to injury. If we are interested in inner unfoldment, such exacerbation of already difficult states is one of the biggest reasons and incentives to work with the superego till we have some disidentification from it, as we will discuss more fully later on.

The biggest thing that our superego is on the lookout for and does everything it can to prevent is unacceptable drives arising out of that "seething cauldron" of the id, as Freud described it. So the animal soul, which we explored at length in the last chapter, with all of its primitive drives, is the superego's biggest target. From a Freudian perspective, the superego attempts to control and repress our sexual and aggressive impulses that, if enacted, would endanger our social standing. This means impulses to do things that are considered taboo, unacceptable, are illegal, or are morally condemned by our culture. It punishes us if such barbaric and erotic thoughts and wishes even enter our consciousness, not to mention if we act upon them. The superego, then, is the civilizing force of the personality. In Calvin Hall's words,

> If the id is regarded as the product of evolution and the psychological representative of one's biological endowment, and the ego is the resultant of one's interaction with objective reality and the province of the higher mental processes, then the superego may be said to be the product of socialization and the vehicle of cultural tradition.[4]

Freud considered that culture and its values are passed on via our parents, and we internalize them through the agency of our superego. From this angle, the superego is the protector of civilization, as we see in Freud's answer to "what means does civilization employ in order to inhibit the aggressiveness which opposes it," referring to the aggressive drive of each individual:

> *His aggressiveness is introjected, internalized; it is, in point of fact, sent back to where it came from—that is, it is directed towards his own ego. There it is taken over by a portion of the ego, which sets itself over against the rest of the ego as super-ego, and which now, in the form of "conscience," is ready to put into action against the ego the same harsh aggressiveness that the ego would have liked to satisfy upon other, extraneous individuals. The tension between the harsh super-ego and the ego that is subjected to it, is called by us the sense of guilt; it expresses itself as a need for punishment. Civilization, therefore, obtains mastery over the individual's dangerous desire for aggression by weakening and disarming it and by setting up an agency within him to watch over it, like a garrison in a conquered city.[5]*

Conflicts between superego dictates and id impulses were, he believed, the source of neurotic suffering. From his perspective, the individual's quest for happiness, which means to him satisfaction of his drives, is forever at variance with what will be socially accepted. As he says,

> *... the two urges, the one towards personal happiness and the other towards union with other human beings must struggle with each other in every individual; and so, also, the two processes of individual and of cultural development must stand in hostile opposition to each other and mutually dispute the ground. But his struggle between the individual and society is not a derivative of the contradiction—probably an irreconcilable one— between the primal instincts of Eros and death. It is a dispute within the economics of the libido, comparable to the contest concerning the distribution of libido between ego and objects; and it does admit of an eventual accommodation in the individual, as, it may be hoped, it will also do in the fu-*

ture of civilization, however much that civilization may oppress the life of the individual to-day.[6]

While Freud believed that the structure of the superego arises somewhere around age five to six, at the end of the oedipal phase, and becomes a stable inner construct by around age nine to ten, current psychological thought sees its precursors appearing much earlier. By the end of the first year, a child is well aware of his or her mother's prohibitions and demands. But it is not until the end of the oedipal phase that these constraints become the child's own, and not until some years later that they are a stable and ongoing presence in the child's psyche. Prior to that time, when mother is out of sight, so are her injunctions.

Freud believed that the superego coalesces as an internal structure as a way of resolving oedipal conflicts—the phase-appropriate amorous feelings for the parent of the opposite sex. His theory was that the superego develops as a way of putting a lid on this taboo incestuous id longing and the accompanying desire to displace or do away with our same-sex parent, through identifying with that same-sex parent's moral code. By taking on the ego ideals of that parent, our own unacceptable sexual desire for the opposite-sex parent is given up.

By adopting his or her ego ideals and superego, we are in effect stating our alignment with that parent, rather than seeing him or her as an adversary in our quest for the affection of the parent we are having oedipal feelings for. Freud went so far as to theorize that we actually want to kill the same sex parent, and through adopting his or her superego, we resolve this forbidden wish. We are removing ourselves from such a competitive and challenging position vis-à-vis that parent, if only in our own minds, since our attempts to woo our oedipal love object are almost always—and fortunately—doomed to failure. By fully identifying with the superego of the same-sex parent and internalizing it as our own, our own superego becomes a stable and continuous part of our inner landscape. No longer are we most afraid of losing our parents' love—now our most constant fear is of displeasing our internalized parental figure, our superego.

While I disagree with Freud's theory that our passionate love for a parent during the oedipal phase is basically sexual in nature—I think such

infatuation only becomes sexualized if the parent interprets it that way—
it may well be that the superego arises as a way of coping with what is
clearly passionate love for one parent and the wish to take the other parent's place during this period. I also think that the notion of a murderous
desire toward our same-sex parent may be present when there is abnor-
mality, but I think it is a little extreme to assume that such an urge is
present in all of us.

Presenting an alternative picture, some psychologists say that our
superego is an internalized identification with the parent we most idealized, who might or might not be the same-sex parent. We create this internal structure as a way of having this beloved parent with us all the time
and as a way of becoming like him or her. Others say that our superego is
an amalgamation of both parents and other strong authority figures of
childhood. In either case, all agree that it is not how these people *actually*
were or behaved that becomes codified as our own superego—what we
identify with is their superegos, regardless of their actual actions.

Through the agency of the superego, as mentioned earlier, Freud saw
culture being passed down. Our parents' values and standards are perpetuated in this way, since what we adopt at an early age is our parents'
superegos, established when they were quite young. To him, this accounts
for the conservative tendency of society, resistant to change and disruptions of the status quo. Likewise, as we shall discuss, our own superego
functions to maintain our internal status quo.

Since our superego formed when we were an oedipal-aged child as an
internalization of parental figures, our sense of self in relationship to it remains that of a child relating to an adult. This is an important thing to
understand and to experientially see—that we are almost always a child in
relation to our superego. So an adult part of our structure—our superego—
relates to the part of our structure most of us identify with as ourselves as
though we were about three feet tall—or less. Our internal relationship,
then, with our superego reinforces our identification with ourselves as immature, dependent, and most importantly, small.

Freud observed that the superego is usually experienced as an inner
voice—the voice of our conscience—and this is because it is the internalization of many auditory commands or pronouncements of our parents and

other early authority figures. For this reason, we often experience our superego as someone other than ourselves. Some of us, however, take ourselves to be our superego, and so there is little or no distance between it and our ongoing sense of self. This is frequently the case for Ennea-type Ones.

Part of Freud's theory about the superego is that the aggression fueling it—and most of us have very attacking and hurtful superegos—is derived from the id itself as we saw earlier. So the aggressive drive residing in the id fuels the structure set up to inhibit it, and our aggression gets turned inward, on ourselves, rather than being acted out externally. He believed that the degree of aggression in our superego does not reflect the degree of severity with which our parents reprimanded us but rather that it reflects the degree of our *own* hostility toward our parents during the oedipal phase. The energy of the murderous impulses we had, according to Freud, toward the same-sex parent gets channeled into our superego's suppression of those impulses. As he says,

> A *considerable amount of aggressiveness must be developed in the child against the authority which prevents him from having his first, but none the less his most important, satisfactions, whatever the kind of instinctual deprivation that is demanded of him may be; but he is obliged to renounce the satisfaction of this revengeful aggressiveness. He finds his way out of this economically difficult situation with the help of familiar mechanisms. By means of identification he takes the unattackable authority into himself. The authority now turns into his super-ego and enters into possession of all the aggressiveness which a child would have liked to exercise against it.*[7]

Another thing about the superego's method of punishment is that it is very primitive. It is of the biblical sort: an eye for an eye, and so on. Adequate punishment is to experience the same degree of injury that one has caused. This is the idea of justice prevalent in primitive societies and also prevalent in a child's mind. As adults, then, we punish ourselves internally, causing ourselves to feel the same degree of hurt that we believe we have caused or that we might have caused, had we acted on our impulse.

In this primitive inner system of justice, there is no discrimination between the deed and the thought of it. Our superego punishes us as severely for a forbidden thought as it does for acting upon it. This is in line with the childlike magical thinking in which impetus and action internally feel the same. Interestingly, this corresponds to the Buddhist notion of karma, in which there is no discrimination made between volition and action. This reflects the inner law that our actions mirror inner processes.

—⁓— So why have we spent so much time looking at this psychological structure, and what does it have to do with spiritual development? First of all, while it is a developmental achievement for our psyches to form a superego, it also causes us great inner suffering. Without it, the framework of our ego structure is not complete since the superego is the capstone, the final layer of our psychological scaffolding. However, the more "well-adjusted" we are—the better a person we try to be—the more we suffer from it, as we see in the following observation of Freud's:

> *For the more virtuous a man is, the more distrustful is its {his super-ego's} behaviour, so that ultimately it is precisely those people who have carried saintliness furthest who reproach themselves with the worst sinfulness. This means that virtue forfeits some part of its promised reward; the docile and continent ego does not enjoy the trust of its mentor, and strives in vain, it would seem, to acquire it. The objection will at once be made that these difficulties are artificial ones, and it will be said that a stricter and more vigilant conscience is precisely the hallmark of a moral man.*[8]

The better we try to be according to our superego's standards, in other words, the more we suffer. Attempting to appease our superego is a vicious cycle, never yielding the hoped-for sense of inner peace and satisfaction. So if we wish to attain some degree of inner stillness and fulfillment, we need to see that it will not come from attempting to match our ego ideal, no matter how lofty or spiritual. The very attempt is doomed to failure.

Second, by virtue of the fact that when we are engaged with our superego, we are engaged in an inner dialogue in which one part of us—the one most of us identify with—is a child responding to another part of us that is the voice of adult authority. We are relating to ourselves, regardless of which side of the object relation we identify with, as though one part is a child and another is an adult, and this very fact supports an unreal view of reality. The truth is that most likely anyone reading this book is an adult, and to experience ourselves as a child is simply not how things really are. So to stay engaged with our superego only perpetuates our egoic identity, just as the superego preserves and sustains the status quo of civilization, as we have seen. Our familiar sense of self, built around a core self-representation of ourselves as a small child, is maintained and affirmed to the extent that we stay engaged in this internal relationship.

We have seen that the superego draws its energy from the id, and in turn uses that force to suppress the id's drives. As long as our superego usurps the energy of aggression from the id and turns it against ourselves, we do not have that energy available to us in a life-affirming way. Our energy instead goes into suppressing ourselves, especially the primitive and uncivilized aspects of ourselves structured as identity in the animal soul. The aggression animating our superego, then, is at its core the vibrant and effulgent energy of the id. It is the energy of our aliveness and vitality, filtered through this psychological structure. Rather than having this energy accessible to us, when it is turned against us in this way we become inhibited, tense, anxious, and depressed. This is the fuel we need to power our spiritual journey. This is the energy that propels the dynamism of our soul, allowing us to expand beyond our familiar sense of reality. It is the energy of love and desire for union with the Divine, articulated so beautifully in the poetry of the fourteenth-century Sufi mystic, Jelaluddin Rumi.

We can liken our psychological structure to a Russian babushka doll, with the superego forming the outer layer, our ego or sense of self forming the next layer, our soul child the next, with the animal soul contained within that, and the id nested still deeper. Inside of the id, we find emptiness, and when we experientially reach it, we are moving beyond all psychological structure and into the realm of Being. From an energetic point of view, it is the energy of Being that is the source of the id's energy. This is the dynamic side of Being, which we see expressed in movement and change, internal and external.

Rather than aligning ourselves with this dynamism at the heart of life itself, when we stay in relationship with our superego, and thus reinforce its structure, we stand against that movement. The extent to which we are identified with our superego, which is to say the extent to which we believe that this inner voice is real and necessary, rather than a kind of inner holographic illusion, is the extent to which our unfoldment is blocked. It's as simple as that.

If we wish to test this out, we have only to notice that following moments of great insight into ourselves or of openings and expansion of our consciousness in which we feel that we are in touch with dimensions of experience beyond our norm, a superego injunction typically quickly follows. Something to the effect of, *Aren't you getting a little too big for your britches?* or *You shouldn't feel so fulfilled when so many are suffering,* or *You ought to face reality—you made the whole thing up.* In this we see the conservative tendency of the superego discussed earlier from another angle, attempting to constrict our consciousness again, making us feel small once more, as a way of reconstructing our familiar sense of who we are and what reality is. Obviously, if we want to grow and develop, which means moving beyond our familiar experiential constraints, we must contend with our superego's function as the dragon at the temple gates, roaring at us to keep us from entering.

One might argue that a new and improved superego laden with spiritual ideals goading us on to be more virtuous, loving, giving, wise, etc. can only help us become better people and support our inner journey. This is a case of the means determining the ends in the sense that if we are rejecting our internal reality as it actually is and pushing ourselves to be other than we are, the result will not be virtue or realization. It will be at best a facade of virtue and realization, with a seething caldron of id excitation waiting in the wings to burst through its very spiritual inner constraints. Realization means realizing who and what we truly are—not realizing an ego ideal—and requires profound inner access and exploration. This journey requires the freedom to enter into and explore our direct experience, whatever it happens to be.

One might also argue that without our superego prodding us to do our spiritual practices, we would never meditate or do the various things that our particular path teaches as methods to help us awaken. In the early stages of our inner journey, there is some truth to this—it is often our superego that pushes us to practice. Its energy is needed to counteract and overcome the inertial undertow of the personality initially, but once our journey has its own momentum, this is no longer needed.

How, then, do we get out from under the tyrannical hold of our superego? Clearly, intellectual understanding will not resolve it, as those who have been aware of their inner critic for years can attest, whether through analysis or otherwise. One method taught in the Diamond Approach and described at length in a book written by my colleague Byron Brown* is that of learning to disengage from it. This way of working with it relies on reclaiming the aggressive energy directed toward ourselves through aiming it back at the superego. We have seen that the superego usurps the dynamism of our nature, blocking the natural unfoldment of our soul, and by mobilizing our vital energy through refusing to belittle or undermine ourselves, this method attempts to liberate that life force.

While this approach can be a good first step and useful for many, real freedom from buying into the superego's pronouncements and barbs ultimately lies in experientially understanding—feeling in our gut, so to speak—what exactly we are doing when we attack ourselves and why we do it. One of the main reasons we attack ourselves is that, as noted earlier, there is almost always a grain of truth in our superego's attacks. However, we need to ask ourselves whether we really must be battered internally in order to perceive the bit of truth being expressed. We need to separate that bit from the aggression involved in the attack, and see whether it is possible to open to that truth without making ourselves bad or wrong. If not, we need to investigate why not.

Another of the main things we are doing when we attack ourselves is staying in relationship to one or both parents internally. We are staying loyal and engaged with our history, our culture, and our family of origin. We are someone small at the mercy of our big superego, or if our character is such that we tend to identify with the big one, we are that in relation to a small other. Regardless of which side of the object relation we identify with, we are maintaining internally the basic object relation, that of self and other, and so are supporting the fundamental structure of our personality.

*See *Soul without Shame: A Guide to Liberating Yourself from the Judge Within* (Boston and London: Shambhala Publications, Inc., 1999).

The important thing is that we are staying in relationship to *something,* rather than separating and experiencing ourselves as autonomous and inwardly alone. The superego, then, protects us from feeling isolated and out of relationship, a situation intolerable and potentially life threatening to the small child we once were. Proximity to our early caretakers was crucial at that time, and our psychological maturation depended upon internalizing them and in effect carrying them with us.

Because we are dealing with an object relation involving two parts of ourselves at odds with each other when we attack ourselves, I have found that the best way of dealing with the superego initially is through dialogue between these two parts, whether verbally or in written form. Gestalt therapy, Voice Dialogue, and Internal Family Systems work all are methodologies that can promote understanding and reconciliation between these two parts of ourselves, alleviating the necessity to carry on our internal combat. Such methods can lead not only to a truce being proclaimed but in time to a thinning of these structures themselves.

When the inner dialogue stops, we experience quiet and stillness rather than the turbulence of inner noise. At first, this does feel as if we were alone, and fears may arise of being externally out of relationship, unable to be related to, or that we are losing our loved ones. As this transition is made, in time we see that our perceived aloneness is simply the lack of inner representations, and that all we are aware of is part of a vast and edgeless oneness. This sense of aloneness is only the remnant of a self-representation, an image of ourselves in our mind.

This inner quietude brings us to the virtue of Point One, *serenity.* Serenity literally means the state of being peaceful, calm, and clear. Originally this term was used in reference to the weather, signifying a cloudless and bright atmosphere, free of dramatic changes, turbulence, and storms. In relation to people, it means the same thing—an absence of perturbation and agitation. Like all of the virtues, realizing serenity requires primarily understanding and working with the passion associated with it—in this case, anger.

Arriving at serenity, then, requires a close look at the basis of our inner disharmony with reality—our standing against it. What we see is that our difficulties begin with the innate tendency of the mind to discriminate one thing from another. This is a natural development as we learn to conceptualize, forming concepts and thoughts when very young. We learn to compare one thing to another, the bigness of one thing as opposed to the smallness of another, for instance, or our experience in one moment versus our experience in another. We know one thing from another based on contrasts between the two. Comparative judgment forms the basis of knowing, and is an inherent property of our mental functioning as adults.

Comparative judgment in and of itself is neutral, and it remains so when we add preference to it: "This is different from that, and I prefer the former." "This feels good and that feels bad, and I don't want the one that feels bad." So far so good. Still somewhat neutral. We can have preferences toward one thing and away from another without a negative attitude toward what we are moving away from. For example, if we prefer chocolate ice cream to vanilla, we don't usually harbor negative feelings toward the latter. Or we might be drawn toward one style of art or clothing or literature, and that inclination toward the one and away from another is an uncontentious movement.

But add to this a value judgment: "This one is prettier/nicer/more interesting than that one, and so the first one is better," and you are off and running with inner turbulence. The stage is set for rejecting what is judged as inferior, and with the addition of rejection, comparative judgment becomes oppositional. We want to rid our experience of the inferior or bad state/emotion/thought/impulse based on this weighted judgment, and our inner landscape becomes a battleground. This is the basis of our superego. When we make the judgment that one thing is good and another is bad, if we notice carefully we will see that there is an internal charge, or an aggression involved. This charge is encapsulated by the word for the passion of this point, *anger.* It is a movement against, a hostile attitude toward, and an attempt to get rid of what we have decided is bad.

This attitude is a destructive and pernicious one, which finds expression in the various forms of violence that fill our nightly news. It manifests in all sorts of culturally accepted ways, such as nationalism in which one's own nation is held to be better than another, rooting for one sports team as the good one and the opposing team as the bad one, and all the other ways in which the good guys versus the bad guys finds expression.

One of the characteristics of this attitude, called splitting in psychological terminology, is that things become all good and all bad, black and white with no shades of gray. Like most other things, this attitude begins in our relationship to our inner experience. Some things we judge as acceptable and others as unacceptable, and we attempt to get rid of the latter.

Splitting is an early adaptive mechanism in which positive experiences with mother are separated in our infant and toddler psyche from negative experiences with her. We do this to protect the good from being overwhelmed by the bad, and this defense mechanism is especially strong when the mothering person is abusive or traumatizing. This helps the young child hold on to the good by experiencing the good mother and the bad one as two different people, in effect. It is not until we are around three years of age that we can see that these two sets of experience are of the same person. The typical childhood fears of the boogey man and of the dark are expressions of splitting off the bad and projecting it outside of ourselves. By adulthood, we are more or less able to perceive and tolerate what we consider the good and the bad parts of someone as attributes of the same person. But our proclivity toward splitting often arises even in the psychologically healthiest of us when under duress of some sort or when we feel threatened, as well as in the socially accepted forms mentioned above.

The key to working through our tendency to stand against reality is to feel directly the painfulness of rejecting aspects of ourselves and our experience in this way. This is the ultimate necessity to achieve the cherished hope of peace on earth someday—which is another way of describing serenity. It begins within each of us, and we only can begin moving toward it when we experientially connect with the hurt we are inflicting upon ourselves continuously in splitting our experience and rejecting one side of it. All of us have memories of childhood in which aspects of us or all of us was put down, criticized, and rejected; of something that was precious to us being judged and devalued; and of something we had done or created being trashed. Simply remembering these incidents brings up a deep sense of hurt, but what we fail to realize more often than not is that we continue to relate to ourselves in the same hurtful way.

When we look closely at our inner experience, what we often see is not a pretty picture. We are constantly evaluating our experience—what we are feeling, thinking, and doing—and judging it against our idea of how it should be, and rejecting what does not accord. Not only does this block the natural tendency of our soul to open up, unfold, and grow, but when we feel it directly, such a relationship to ourselves is continuously wounding. In the presence of rejection, we do not blossom—on the contrary, we wither. It's only when we really understand in a felt way how we are injuring ourselves that our attitude of standing against ourselves begins to relax. Until that time, we believe this is the appropriate way to relate to ourselves, that it is for our own good. And it is not enough to intellectually understand that relating to ourselves in this way is harmful. We have to feel it in our heart. Nor can we reject the self-rejection, since this is just a spiritual twist on the same old pattern.

When we understand experientially that we are harming ourselves, we lose the drive behind the pattern. We then naturally begin to relate to what is arising in our experience with an open, receptive, accepting, and welcoming frame of mind—with serenity, in a word. Instead of there being certain things that we can and cannot open to both inwardly and outwardly, we become serene, unruffled by whatever arises. Serenity means having no conditions that must be satisfied in order to allow, and is complete openness to whatever presents itself. This is only possible when our internal standards have been worked through, and we are able to meet reality exactly as it is. Rather than feeling split inside and divided into opposing inner camps, a sense of wholeness organically arises.

At this stage, Ichazo's definition of serenity becomes relevant:

> *It is emotional calm, expressed by a body at ease with itself and receptive to the energy of the Kath. Serenity is not a mental attitude but the natural expression of wholeness in a human being secure in his capacities and totally self-contained.*

The Kath is the name for the belly center in the tradition out of which the enneagram came, as transmitted by Ichazo. It is called the hara in Zen Buddhism and the tantien in Taoism. It encompasses the three bottom chakras, and the energies involved have to do with the id and the animal soul. We have seen that it is precisely the energies contained within them that our superego has the most difficulty with and often form the root of what we judge as bad, so Ichazo is pointing to the fact that true serenity is only possible when these energies are allowed, rather than split off. When our drives, no matter how animalistic they feel, are fully allowed and explored experientially, these energies open up and transform naturally. It is this integration that permits us to experience our ultimate just-rightness, our wholeness, our perfection.

Our soul can at long last begin to relax, letting go of the tension of vigilance in anticipation of the bad. A tranquil inner atmosphere, free of reactive oppositionality, pervades the soul, and in such an environment, we feel free to be ourselves and can unwind. We naturally settle into ourselves in the presence of inner calm, and our experience spontaneously deepens. We are able to be as we are, and the depths within infuse our consciousness. As this happens, we see that standing against anything blocks us from being ourselves—our deepest selves—our True Nature.

—⁓— Having now explored the passions and virtues at the top corner of the enneagram, we can look at them as a group. When we do so, what we see is that the issues represented and the specific pushes and pulls of our inner economy described correspond to Freud's tripartite map of the ego structure. At Point Eight we find the id, the repository of our instinctual drives and primitive unconscious motivations. At Point Nine we find the ego, our conscious sense of self, shaped as it is by accommodation with our early environment. And at Point One we find the superego, overseer of our sense of self, whose job it is to see that only what is acceptable be felt and acted upon. I'm quite sure that Freud knew nothing about the enneagram, and the fact of this correlation between these maps of the psyche points to the fact that they describe a fundamental truth about how the ego is structured.

These points, then, describe the cornerstones of our ego structure, which forms a many-layered veil separating us from the realm of Being. These parts of our ego structure altogether are pivotal in keeping us in a state of sleep, of unconsciousness about what lies beyond the perimeter of our ego, and so Points Eight and One are differentiations of this principle represented at Point Nine. Taken together, these points form the outer-directed corner, since what is represented by the passions here is fundamental to keeping our consciousness oriented outwardly, toward the surface of ourselves—our personality. The virtues of these points, likewise, are crucial in shifting that orientation to one of awakening to who we really are—our True Nature.

We turn now from the outer-directed corner of the enneagram to the image corner, which speaks directly about this superficial orientation.

THE
IMAGE
CORNER

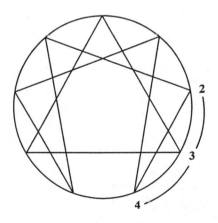

DIAGRAM 11

P O I N T   T H R E E —
D E C E I T *and*
V E R A C I T Y

—⟨⟩—

This world is nothing but the glory of Tao
    expressed through different names and forms
One who sees the things of this world
    as being real and self-existent
    has lost sight of the truth
To him, every word becomes a trap
    every thing becomes a prison

One who knows the truth
    that underlies all things
    lives in this world without danger
To him, every word reflects the universe
    every moment brings enlightenment

—LAO TZU[1]

Things are not as they appear. This is one of the oldest of spiritual teachings, many of which describe the world as illusion, and speak of it as a realm of appearances and lies. What does this mean? When we look around us, everything seems real enough and when we sense into ourselves, what we find seems also to be what truly is going on. As we turn to the passion and virtue of Point Three and those of its neighbors, Points Two and Four, this conundrum comes into focus. This corner of the enneagram deals with image, appearance, and presentation, and for this reason these three ennea-types make up what are referred to as the image types.

All three of these types are deeply concerned with how they come across and are perceived by others, and so are organized around the form and the front of things. With an ideal inner image of how they think they should be as a guide, these types attempt to morph or shape-shift into that form, molding the fluid medium of their souls into the rigid form shaped by their minds. They monitor their presentation very carefully, and so keep their attention focused on the surface of themselves rather than on what is going on deeper down. The packaging becomes more important than the substance.

Threes are far more successful at this shape-shifting than Twos or Fours, both of whom struggle, in the first case to shore up their image and in the second with, as Naranjo says, a denigrated self-image leading to depression. Twos and Fours are a little to the side of the central focus of their desired image, while Threes are spot-on, only befitting for this most central of image types. The difference is that Threes fully believe that they are the facade they are peddling to others. As Naranjo puts it, "the essence of their psychological aberration is the confusion of the self-image that they sell (and others buy) with what they are."[2]

In our last chapter we discussed how each of us has an ego ideal, an ideal picture that we carry around inside of us and measure ourselves and our actions against. While all the types attempt to live up to their ego ideal, the image types take this one step further, and try to present themselves *as* this ideal. And while there are general outlines to the ideal self specific to each of these types, there is also a certain fluidity to the image they present, since image types adapt to the person or group they are trying to be accepted by, portraying the ego ideal of the other. Here is where the passion of Point Three, *deceit,* begins. As mentioned earlier, at each corner of the enneagram, the passions of two wings of the point on the inner triangle can be viewed as refractions of that central passion. So all three image types share and are oriented around deception—or to put it more directly, lying about their reality. One aspect of this deceit is presenting themselves as though they were their ego ideal, and another is adjusting this image to fit a given situation.

Before moving more deeply into the subject of deception, we should look at whether it is appropriate to consider it the passion of this point, a question raised because of Naranjo's revision of Ichazo's teaching on this. As we have seen, the passion of each point is an inner attitude or affective atmosphere. The fixation of each point, on the other hand, is its core delusion. It is a fixed and distorted belief about reality since it is a view of reality devoid of its spiritual dimension, and it colors and slants one's perception and experience. It arises in the absence of the enlightened view of reality—the Holy Idea—associated with that point. The passion is primarily affective, while the fixation is primarily cognitive. Because of Threes' excessive focus on their self-image, Naranjo thinks it is more accurate for vanity to be considered the passion of Point Three, rather than deceit, as given by Ichazo. Deceit, he believes, better describes the distorted mind set—the fixation—of this type than does Ichazo's use of the term *vanity.* Vanity means an excessive pride especially in one's appearance, or alternatively the state of being futile, worthless, and empty of significance, while deceit means the act of misleading and tricking someone. A case could be made for either vanity or deceit as the passion, but it seems to me that the vanity of believing that one creates and sustains one's own world is the central delusion of Point Three, corresponding to the loss of the Holy Idea of Holy Law, and that deception is the way one convinces oneself and others that this is so. Also, veracity, the virtue of this point, is the opposite of deceit and not of vanity.

There are a number of levels to the deception necessary to maintain a Three's world. There is the deceiving of others in terms of shape-shifting to present themselves in such a way that others will approve of, admire, and love them. As mentioned above, while they might not know they are doing it, Threes have the uncanny ability to tune in to the ego ideal of the other and to present themselves as a pretty good facsimile of it, and are much better at this than Twos or Fours. Having sussed out the ideal carried by those in their early childhood environment, they not only sought to live up to it but ended up convincing others as well as themselves that they *were* it. Those familiar with the ennea-types know that Threes tend to present themselves as the cultural ideal of whatever milieu they grew up within, and adjust that image as their environment shifts in adulthood. For this reason, they are considered the chameleons of the enneagram, taking on the coloring of their surroundings.

This duplicity is not only a deceiving of others but more importantly a self-deception. The facade and presentation is so important to Threes that whatever else is going on within them gets left behind, especially those things that don't fit in with the ideal image they are attempting not simply to present but to actually become. This focus on image is a matter of *doing* rather than of simply *being* oneself. By this I mean that it takes a lot of internal, albeit unconscious, work to figure out what is ideal and to portray oneself as that, and also that presenting themselves not as they are is an effortful inner activity.

This is one side of the fact that Threes are the great doers of the enneagram. The other side is that just as deeply as a Three believes that she is what she appears to be, she also believes that her value lies in what she can achieve. Or, to put it differently, she fervently believes that she is what she does. Her accomplishments, then, are all-important so a Three stays on the go, producing and striving after success. Threes typically believe that it is up to them to generate sustenance and support in their lives, and so are very busy doing everything it takes to hold up their world.

Investing their image and achievements with ultimate value is another nuance, then, of their passion of deception. This is a lie shared by everyone, to one degree or another. The fact that deception is a passion of the ancient system of the enneagram, which maps not only characteristics of the individual types but also universal tendencies, points to its centrality in the life and functioning of the personality. The deception focused upon at this point is also becoming more of an issue for us all at this stage in history, since humanity is becoming progressively more individualistic and cultures throughout the world are emulating that of America, one of whose chief cultural characteristics is a Threeish orientation.

There are all sorts of lies that we tell, which are accepted aspects of the conventional world. There are the "little white lies" that are so much a part of the fabric of social life. The ones we tell to save face, spare another's feelings, or get ourselves out of a difficult jam, such as, "I'm so sorry for not returning your call—my message machine must not have picked it up," or "It would be lovely to spend more time with you—it's such a shame I'm so busy all the time," or "Don't you look marvelous!" In the world of business, lies are told to close a deal, to convince you that one product with the same ingredients as another is the better one, or that you simply must have it—whatever it is—to feel complete.

We have a whole new vocation—being a "spin doctor"—whose job it is to sell bad news as good news. This is a postmodern variation of public relations, the packaging of someone or something and marketing it to the world at large. So we pay people to twist reality and make it palatable, and in some instances desirable. Facts are distorted to achieve the desired affect, while in other cases the facts are fabricated altogether. Politics are full of spin. An example of this is the debate about what evidence actually existed to justify the American invasion of Iraq, and how much of what was told to the governments involved and the public was based on prevarication.

In a similar vein, the advertising industry works to sell things based on their packaging—physical as well as conceptual. To a greater extent than most of us realize, in our postmodern world the packaging has become more important than what's contained within it. Clothing labels are now proudly displayed, so that the wearer of a garment can partake of the glamour associated with the designer's name. Status is conferred by the approximation of one's presentation to one's cultural ideal, by the make of car one drives, or the neighborhood one lives in. The common lie is that the appearance something or someone has is itself the substance—a lie that we are taking more and more as reality.

We are most often aware that we are distorting the truth or giving it a particular patina when we lie to others, but are not usually aware of it when we lie to ourselves. We deceive ourselves in all kinds of ways—about what we think, what we feel, and what our relationship to our body is. We are convinced that we feel positively toward someone who, when we scratch the surface of our consciousness, we find we don't like at all; or we contort ourselves into believing that a work situation we really want or need is tolerable when deeper down we can't stand it; or when we think that we are doing our best to succeed at something when inevitably we do something to undermine our attainment. When we push ourselves beyond our physical or emotional limits without noticing because the job needs to get done, we are deceiving ourselves about what has ultimate value and what is really going on with us. One of our most universal lies is living as though and believing that we will never die, even though cognitively we know otherwise.

While each ennea-type specializes in one or more of our psychological defense mechanisms, all are based on protecting ourselves from the direct truth of our experience. For instance, we repress an idea or a feeling, such as anger or hatred toward someone we care about, not allowing it to surface into our consciousness. We use the defense of reaction formation by replacing a difficult thought or feeling with its opposite in our conscious awareness, for instance becoming very solicitous of someone toward whom we harbor hatred. We project unacceptable emotions and desires onto another, for example, fearing that another is out to harm us when unconsciously it is we who would like to hurt the other. We isolate an emotion from an action, such as screaming at someone without being aware of our anger. Or we undo a thought, feeling, or action through some form of expiation, as when we do something we consider bad and then punish ourselves in some way to remove the offense. While none of these defenses are outright ways of lying to ourselves, they are ways of keeping away deeper levels of our internal reality, which we experience as threatening. Threatening to what? we might ask. To our sense of who we are. Through it, then, we maintain our internal self-image.

While not typically classified as a defense mechanism, identification is the process ascribed by Naranjo as the defense mechanism of Point Three. Identification is the inner process by which we take on attitudes, values, and functions of another, and incorporate them into our own sense of self. Identification is defensive in the sense that we defend against the truth of who we are in this way. Threes in particular identify with familial and cultural ideals, incorporating them into their sense of who they are. This is the typical morphing or shape-shifting discussed earlier, in which a Three's inner reality becomes what is identified with. He shapes himself into an external ideal and so his internal sense of reality becomes indistinguishable from what is outside of him. In the process, he lives increasingly on the surface of himself. We will return to this idea later, as it is part of the key for understanding the passion and virtue of this point.

As we have seen, lying is for all of us intimately connected with maintaining and perpetuating a particular facade, both to others and to ourselves. We lie to ourselves and to others when our image, our self-presentation, becomes more important than who we really are. We also lie to ourselves when we believe that our value lies in our accomplishments. Behind these attitudes and orientations is the lie that the surface of things is what has value and importance. We lie to ourselves when we believe that the form is the substance, and as we're seeing, you don't have to be an image type to do this. And here is where the focus shifts in regard to this passion from a psychological issue to a spiritual one.

One of the hallmarks of our present age is this excessive emphasis on the world of form. There is some history to this modern and postmodern materialistic perspective. Beginning in the Renaissance of the fifteenth century and culminating in the so-called Age of Enlightenment in the eighteenth century, our Western worldview became increasingly denuded of its depth dimension—the realm of the spiritual—leaving only what could be perceived and measured by our physical senses as what could be considered to exist. So one of our deepest lies is that the material world is the ultimate truth, and hence that we are our bodies. While our identification with the body is nothing new—it seems to be implicit in having a personality structure—during this period this worldview became solidified and sanctioned as ultimate truth.

This is a lie most of us believe, that our physical form defines who we are. The scientific perspective that human beings are fundamentally creatures whose functioning, emotional states, and thought patterns are biological in origin is the modern version of this age-old untruth about ourselves. All of our religious and spiritual traditions throughout the centuries have been trying to convince us otherwise. We have discussed this deepest belief of the personality primarily when discussing the fall into the sleep of the ego at Point Nine, and here we see its underpinning—identification with our body.

Not only are we identified with our bodies but as a Threeish image consciousness subsumes mass consciousness, this focus on the surface results in an overemphasis on the outward physical form. So a major way that we lie to ourselves is in believing that our physical appearance is of crucial importance. In addition to the personality's identification with the body here, then, is its investment in how it looks. This endowment of the outer surface of our physical form with so much importance is stronger in the image types, but the number of magazines and television shows devoted to style, fashion, dieting, body building, makeup, hairstyles, and so on, as well as the value given to supermodels and the surfeit of beauty pageants, not to mention the rise in popularity of plastic surgery to make our bodies conform to the image we have of what they should look like, attest to this preoccupation in the culture at large.

This is not to say that our appearance is unimportant. Our body is what our soul inhabits in this life, and how it looks reflects much about the state of our soul. Neglect of one's appearance or body points to an imbalance, just as does the overinvestment of importance in it. As it is our vehicle for interaction with the rest of the world, its condition reflects the inner state of our soul and also tells us a lot about our relational orientation. If one is severely overweight or underweight without some physical cause, for instance, something is clearly out of synch in that person's psyche as well as in their relationship to others. Obesity tells us something about the psychological need for padding or insulation from contact with others, as well as exhibiting an inner hunger that food is turned to as a means of satisfying. Eating disorders based on starvation—anorexia and bulimia—point to disturbances in relationship with mother as well as a vicious perfectionism channeled into one's appearance.

During adolescence, we tend to be preoccupied with our appearance. As our bodies change and our sexuality emerges, we typically become absorbed in concern about our attractiveness to others, and so how we look becomes a major focus. Unquestioningly we measure our bodies against the standard of our current cultural physical ego ideal, and attempt to approximate it. Our identification with our form is usually of utmost importance during this period, and how we feel about our bodies at this stage brings to the surface, literally, earlier psychological conundrums that often affect the rest of our lives. While this engrossment in our physical appearance is phase-appropriate, it also reflects the centrality of its importance in the life of the personality, and many of us do not grow out of it. Our relationship with our body then becomes one in which we are deceiving ourselves about its ultimate significance.

We end up believing that our appearance is the cause of our joy or suffering, and that if we looked differently, we would feel differently. This is a misplacing of priorities, a lie about the source of satisfaction or its lack. It's the same as saying that if we change the shape of the container, what's in it would change also. Changes in our appearance brought about by that great outfit or darling pair of shoes, or at the other extreme, liposuction or tummy tucks, seldom change the character of our souls or bring us more than momentary happiness. The great irony is that the deeper our identification with our body, the less accurately we actually perceive and experience it.

Growing out of this physical identification is our delusion that we are ultimately separate entities, and out of this grows the ego structure, as we have seen. Deeper still, then, is the central illusion or untruth that the outer shell of who we are, our personality structure, is who we are and all that we are. This is analogous to believing that a wave on the surface of the ocean has its own ultimate reality, even though like everything that exists, it arises and fades away. This belief is part and parcel of egoic life, and when we are identified with our personality, we have a blind spot to anything beyond it. Until we begin to work on ourselves and have experiences of who we are beyond our personality, we don't even realize that the personality is an outer surface, not the entirety of who we are. We live our lives based on this self-deception, and our actions follow from it. What we do is largely geared toward supporting this facade, even though we are not usually consciously aware of this. This is the life of the personality— perpetuating and supporting itself.

Part and parcel of this identification with the personality, with its physical basis, is the belief that we are separate doers in life, or as Almaas puts it, that we are centers of action. On the face of it, this seems accurate enough: we experience ourselves in action all the time when not asleep, whether we are physically moving or thinking about something or feeling one thing or another. Our ongoing experience is one of activity, of constant change, with different sensations coming and going in our awareness. Without this dynamism, there would be no perception at all, since perception itself is based on one experience in contrast to another one. But rather than seeing that this is all happening *through* us, we come to believe that we are making our world happen. While most of us don't believe that we create the world we inhabit, we do cling to the belief that we are the major actor in the drama of our lives and that we are responsible for what happens, rather than life happening through us. As Almaas puts it, "If you did not believe that you are an independent doer, it wouldn't make sense to believe that you are inadequate or a failure."[3] Returning to our analogy, it is as though each separate wave were to believe that its movements were generated by itself.

The central question posed at Point Three, then, has to do with who we are and what we do. Are we the facade we present to others? And are we the image we hold of ourselves inside of our minds? Our ego structure is an amalgam of various mental representations of ourselves, our self-images. Are they in fact what define us? Or are we something that cannot be turned into a mental representation? One of the major developmental milestones in our psychological growth is the development of a stable and ongoing sense of self—the sense that we are such-and-such a person, with certain attributes, skills, and talents; that we come from a particular family with a particular ethnic and cultural history; that we are of a particular gender; that our bodies look a certain way; and that there are certain types of experiences that are part of our sense of self and others that are not.

But do these things really describe who and what we are? If we are wedded to our personality, we fervently believe that they do. If we are interested in exploring more of our potentiality as a human being—pushing our envelope, so to speak—what we find blocking that expansion is our concepts about these very things. Our inner pictures of who we are and the beliefs that are fundamental to those images act as walls that separate us from the rest of reality. Although invisible to us until we have moved beyond them, they contain and limit our experience by filtering it through veils made out of concepts. And to the extent that our soul is shaped by our personality structure, our sense of reality is filtered through our conceptual pictures. These pictures are rooted in our personal past, the images and mental representations that are the building blocks of the personality structure. Even our experience of our body is filtered through these inner representations of it, and so, as we saw earlier, we don't experience it as it truly is.

One of the effects this filtering of reality has is to create the illusion that we are something static. This is because these inner pictures themselves are relatively unchanging, creating the impression that we are something fixed and solid, moving through time and space. If we really understand things as they are, we see that who and what we are is not something unvarying as these representations. We see that the whole universe, including ourselves, is a continuous up-swelling, being generated anew in each instant. We are, in this sense, the expression of the dynamism of Being. This is the understanding of the Holy Idea of this point, Holy Law. As Almaas says,

> The perspective of Holy Law, then, illuminates the fact that the unity of Being is not a static existence, but rather, a dynamic presence that is continuously changing and transforming as a unified field. Here, we see the aliveness of Being and the universe, its energy and flow and vigorous transformation. This Holy idea confronts some of our very basic convictions about reality, but if we don't understand it, we cannot really understand what unfoldment means. This is because the unfoldment of the soul is Holy Law operating in one location, so when we perceive it, we are seeing in microcosm what is happening everywhere all the time. Holy Law is not an easy thing to swallow, since in the process of perceiving it, you—as you have known yourself—get swallowed up.[4]

Understanding this helps us to understand the relationship of image and of functioning, both central issues of Point Three. In one breath, we typically describe Threes as focused on their presentation and on their achievements, without questioning what the relationship is between the two and why both are so central to this type. It is only when we see things from the perspective of Holy Law that we understand how concern about these areas arises in the wake of its loss. While Naranjo has emphasized the centrality of image for those of this type, and Almaas points to functioning as most fundamental, it seems clear to me that both areas are what this point focuses upon. The connecting link is the self in relation to others and to the world around us. So the focus here is not primarily on what our nature is as human beings—this is the question of identity—but on what it means to be a person living a life on the planet—what it means to be an entity.

When our sense of self is experienced through the veil of self-images that make up the personality structure, we lose the perception of ourselves as a locus of dynamism inseparable from the continuously moving and changing fabric of the whole of reality. Not only do we then see ourselves as separate and static entities but we also experience ourselves as the source of action in our lives. We become to ourselves someone who moves through time, making this or that happen in our lives. We experience ourselves like our wave, cut off from the rest of the ocean, believing that our undulations are generated by ourselves. We no longer see our reality as it is, and this is the deepest lie: not living and perceiving the depth of reality, both inner and outer, as it is.

In the early days working with Naranjo, he referred to this corner of the enneagram as that concerned with living. We are perhaps beginning to understand why: when our illusions and self-deceptions start to fade, usually as a result of pursuing some form of spiritual work, we begin to understand who and what is living our lives. We see that we have come to believe that we are the outer shell of ourselves, the personality, and that this is what acts and interacts in our life. The more we experience the truth of things, the more that we see that our personal actions are simply the actions of Being occurring through our soul, and that living a life of truth includes an awareness of this reality. We progressively see that we are each a particular manifestation or arising of Being, acting and interacting in this world, each form of which is also an arising of Being. As human beings, we have the unique opportunity to know our deepest nature and to live it consciously, to fully experience ourselves as an embodiment of the Divine and for our actions and interactions to express that knowingness.

This is what it is to live a life of truth, and this brings us to the virtue of this point, *veracity*. Veracity means the truth of something as well as the truthfulness of a person. Ichazo's definition is as follows:

> *A healthy body can only express its own being; it cannot lie because it cannot be anything other than what it is.*

If we substitute the word "soul" for "body," this definition takes on a depth of meaning in line with what we have been discussing. Living a life informed by veracity, then, is a life in which we express the truth of who and what we are. This means a life informed by our deepest nature rather than one informed by the personality.

Obviously, this radically changes our priorities. Rather than being concerned with our image—our appearance and how we are perceived by others—and with the reception of our actions by the world implicit in the quest for success and achievement, instead we are grounded in the depth of who we are. Our interactions and our activities are then the expression of this depth rather than being oriented toward recognition by others. The irony is that without Being informing our consciousness, we experience ourselves as the generators of our lives, but our life is lived always in reference to the outside—how we are seen and what kind of recognition we get. When our life is informed progressively more fully by Being, our sense of ourselves is less and less dependent on the outside and more completely autonomous. We then have a vertical connection with our depth, and therefore are not so oriented toward the horizontal—the outer surface of reality.

For veracity to inform our consciousness, we need to see the truth of the extent to which we lie to ourselves. Movement toward veracity, then, means questioning and exploring all of the ways in which we deceive ourselves rather than believing our self-deceptions. This entails questioning and exploring how deeply we are enmeshed in the illusions of conventional reality, the consensus reality of the personality. We have discussed many levels of the deception implicit in the personality structure, and veracity is making them conscious. If what we have explored is experienced directly rather than simply intellectually, we will begin to feel more real. When we believe our personality and take its perspective to be the truth, we inevitably feel disconnected from reality, and so feel superficial and false. This is because we are identifying with something that does not have ultimate reality—it is simply a collection of mental representations of self and other. When we identify with it, we are staying firmly engaged in our inner holographic reality, our inner movie, which while it feels real enough when we are fully engaged in it, just as a movie does when we are completely engrossed in it, leaves us with a stale and empty feeling. This is because we are living on the surface of ourselves.

Understanding this in a way that transforms our soul is not a matter of doing anything. This is a pervasive misconception about working on ourselves, a Threeish orientation. There is nothing to do but be present and see the truth of what is happening within ourselves, and understand its nature. For a time it may feel that learning to be present in our bodies, our hearts, and the full dimensionality of our souls requires effort and feels very much like a doing. This is because we are resisting the inertial pull of the personality wanting to take us out of the immediacy of our direct experience. Being fully present means ceasing the constant ego activity of generating our inner reality. Learning to abide more fully in the now necessitates overcoming the undertow of that habitual inner activity. Becoming conscious of this pull and understanding what drives it is the beginning of the cessation of the doing inherent in the personality.

Behind this pull is identifying. Once we are able to be present to our direct experience, we inevitably begin to see the duplicities and prevarications that are part of our ongoing experience. When this happens, we are no longer fully identified with the contents we are experiencing. This is becoming veracious—getting real about what is going on inside of us. We have seen the many ways that we consciously distort and fabricate in our communications to others, and we have seen how we also do this unconsciously within ourselves, keeping ourselves from seeing the truth of our feelings and thoughts in their entirety. Without these self-deceptions, we cannot maintain our egoic sense of self, because without these veils, we would be in direct contact with the whole of ourselves, the full dimensionality of our reality. It is the personality's tendency to identify with whatever level of things it believes to be true, which keeps these veils in place, appearing real in our inner virtual reality.

From the perspective of Point Three, then, the Path is a matter of becoming increasingly honest about what is going on inside of ourselves and this requires skillfully working with our tendency to identify with our experience. When we are identified with what is going on inside of us, we do not see the contents clearly but rather are acting from them. Turning and facing the contents of our soul—the thoughts, the feelings, the sensations—means that we are already separating from them, and not treating them as our ground. So being honest about what is happening within implies disidentifying with it to some extent.

How do we go about doing this? Many spiritual schools teach practices designed to help one disidentify from the contents of their consciousness, often involving trying to let go of it or turning one's attention elsewhere, like on a fixed point or a mantra. While such practices can help us let go of the contents of our consciousness, actively moving away from them in this way can only result in transcending them rather than fully working through them. Transcending our psychological material might work temporarily, but it seldom, if ever, permanently resolves that content. The content does not go away, and so we must continue to sidestep it. These unresolved issues have the nasty habit of leaking out in all sorts of troublesome behaviors, like passive aggression, procrastination, and other more damaging actions that can wreak havoc in our lives and the lives of others. And, for many, trying to disidentify simply doesn't work.

There are some good reasons for this. First of all, the thoughts and feelings that we experience arise out of a sense of self in which they are consistent. The contents of our consciousness, then, are always in synch with our self-image—they are the thoughts and feelings of who we take ourselves to be. The person we take ourselves to be is attempting to let go of the inner experience of that person. We can then only be rejecting what is going on inside of us, rather than really letting go of it. Attempting to disidentify, even if it works momentarily, will not necessarily result in transformation of our soul because disidentifying is not an action. It is not something we can do or try to do. Disidentification *happens*. It occurs when we no longer believe the truth of what it is we are letting go of. The one who tries to let go of something is the very one generating the experience.

As Almaas says,

> *To be able to disidentify, to turn away from a certain experience, a certain self-image, your identity needs to be at a deeper level than the self-image at that moment. You cannot disidentify from something if you are identified with something that is more superficial than what you're intending to disidentify from. So if you are identified with a certain self-image*

and then some feeling arises and you find yourself unable to turn away from it, it might be because it is at a deeper level than you are operating at the moment. If it is deeper than you are, then you cannot disidentify. . . .

It is not possible to turn away from something if you are unconsciously identified with it. It's not possible, because you believe you are it, in a way that is deeper than your awareness at that moment. It is your ground. You cannot disidentify from your ground. First you have to become aware of it, understand it, then your awareness will be deeper than it.[5]

When we have an experience outside of the realm of those belonging to this sense of identity, like when we have a spiritual experience that takes us beyond the bounds of our personality, unless we know ourselves to be this spiritual dimension, the experience will not stick. We then have the all-too-familiar experience of our consciousness contracting back from its expanded state and returning to our familiar sense of reality and of who we are—returning to our ground. So we cannot disidentify with a feeling or a thought if the sense of self out of which it arises is who we believe we are—if we are identified with it, in other words.

What are we to do, then? Paradoxically, the path to true disidentification lies in completely plunging into our experience and experientially understanding what it is all about. This is not the same thing as our usual egoic inundation in reactivity in which we are completely aligned with our identification and operating from it. Here, we are fully allowing the contents of our consciousness while being fully present to it, with an open mind that takes no position about it. When we engage our experience in this way, insight and understanding naturally arise, and in time the whole worldview out of which the contents are arising comes into focus. Making experiential contact with it has the effect of opening it up, taking us deeper into ourselves. As we deepen, we let go of what is more superficial in our experience. As Almaas describes it,

What's needed then is an immersion experience—allowing whatever that experience is and becoming involved in it as completely as possible, in order to understand it. Notice in your experience of understanding yourself, part of the process is this immersion, is an involvement with the experience,

whether it is a belief, an emotion, a contraction in the body, a sense of frus-
tration, a sense of attachment to something—whatever is there is experienced
completely, without trying to get rid of it. When there is a complete involve-
ment with what is there in you, then after a while an understanding arises.
Without involvement, the understanding will not arise.[6]

As our consciousness opens to ever deeper levels of experience, we are
moving through distortions, illusions, and lies about who we are and
what reality is. Our ground progressively becomes deeper as we approach
a truer and more real experience of ourselves. Rather than our soul being
informed and shaped by our history and our self images that have arisen
out of it, our consciousness becomes more completely its True Nature. We
see that it is a lie that we occasionally experience Being—we see instead
that we *are* Being. We begin to feel like a real and genuine human being
rather than a shell trying to approximate a life. We are becoming veracity—
something real. Instead of expressing conventional reality, the proverbial
realm of appearances and lies, our actions become genuine expressions of
who we truly are. We increasingly live a life of truth, and the world
around us no longer seems like an empty husk but takes on its full dimensionality and profundity.

POINT TWO—
PRIDE *and*
HUMILITY

═══⟨∘∕∘⟩═══

The Sufi becomes more humble every hour, for every hour is drawing him nearer
to God. The Sufis see without knowledge, without sight, without information
received, and without observation, without description, without veiling, and
without veil. They are not themselves, but insofar as they exist at all, they
exist in God. Their movements are caused by God, and their words are the
words of God uttered by their tongues, and their sight is the sight of God,
which has entered into their eyes. So God Most High has said, "When I
love a servant, I, the Lord, am his ear so that he hears by Me; I am his
eye so that he sees by Me; and I am his tongue so that he speaks by Me;
and I am his hands so that he takes by Me."

—Ibn 'Arabi[1]

Few of us have an entirely realistic sense of ourselves. It is
rare for someone to have an objective perception of their
physical, emotional, and mental abilities and limits.
Most of us tend to overestimate or undervalue our en-
dowments and what we are capable of, vacillating between these two extremes of self-assessment.

Behind this difficulty often lies the passion of pride.
Our pride rests upon valuing and investing energy into
how we would like to *see* ourselves—our idealized self-
image—rather than perceiving ourselves directly, as we
really are. Those qualities and characteristics that don't
match how we would like to be form part of a deficient
self-image, which, as we shall see, is simply the other end
of the pride continuum.

What we take pride in varies greatly from person to person. Some of us pride ourselves in the belief that we don't have physical limits, that our energy is endless and that we have the stamina to do anything. Especially as we age, it may be quite challenging to acknowledge increasing limitations of our physical prowess, such as feelings of stiffness or lack of vitality. Not being able to do the things that we once could, like staying up late and then turning in a full day at work the next day, may be hard to accept. This is particularly true for those of us who have an investment in the vigor and strength of our bodies, such as those whose central self-image and identification in life has been as an athlete. On the other hand, others of us shelter ourselves from physical exertion, convinced that we don't have what it takes, and so don't reality-test what our physical edges truly are. Unless there is some actual handicap, this is often rooted in a self-image of being wimpy, fragile, delicate, and easily overwhelmed physically, which we are deeply identified with, and as a consequence, invested in, since it forms part of our sense of self.

Many of us either overestimate or underestimate our mental capacity. Some of us set great store in our intelligence, and our mental proficiency forms a major part of our self-image. Things that we don't understand might feel threatening, and we might avoid delving into a whole field of understanding, preferring to stay within the confines of what we know. The presence of someone whose mental acumen is superior to ours might feel challenging; or someone who seems to know more about the particular area in which we take pride in our understanding will feel like an adversary, potentially jeopardizing our self-esteem. Others of us are convinced that we are not smart, simply because the nature of our intelligence doesn't fit into what was expected of us or valued in our family or culture. This can create a lifelong sense of inferiority, and an ignoring of and lack of interest or value in the kind of intelligence that we actually have.

Emotionally, many of us are unrealistic about what we can and cannot handle. For example, some people put themselves in situations that typically illicit fear or pain, without expecting themselves to experience such emotions. Others purposefully place themselves in precisely those situations to prove to themselves that they are above such human frailties. Some people are invested in a self-image of being emotionally untouchable, while others pride themselves on being available, empathic, and sensitive. For those familiar with the enneagram, this setting store by one's emotional receptivity applies particularly, although not exclusively, to Enneatype Twos.

Likewise, the atmosphere of pride is central to Twos, although again it is not their exclusive domain. Recalling that this point is one of those in the image corner of the enneagram, the emphasis here is on imbuing our idealized image with weight, importance, and value. This image is superimposed over ourselves as we are, and forms a filter through which we experience and evaluate ourselves. As is true for all three of the points in this corner, our internal image of how we would like to be and think we should be is confused with who we actually are and what we are like. This image also becomes something we demand ourselves to conform to. Our energy, then, goes into supporting our idealized self rather than our real self. As Naranjo puts it, "We may envision pride as a passion for self-inflation; or, in other words, a passion for the aggrandizement of the self-image."[2] As he continues,

> In all three character ennea-types at this corner—II, III and IV—we may say that there operates a mistaken sense of "being" in what others see and value, so that it is the self-image rather than the true self upon which the psyche gravitates, out of which action flows, and on which is supported a person's sense of value.[3]

Self-inflation is not always obvious in some Twos, whose image involves being self-effacing and, as Naranjo used to say, falsely humble. However, pride is taken in these very qualities for this type of Two. In other Twos, haughtiness, inflated self-esteem, and the sense of being superior—special—are obvious in their demeanor. Whether it shows or not—whether the pride is more internalized or more externalized—every Two, to quote Naranjo, "flatters those who through nearness gratify his pride, disdains most of the rest in haughty superiority."[4] With the idealized image of being a lovable human being, a Two's investment in how he is received by important others—with love or with rejection—is paramount. His pride rises and falls depending upon how these special others feel about and relate to him. The generosity Twos take such pride in is largely a tactic in their quest to be loved. As Naranjo notes, "Fundamental to it [the pride-centered character] is the strategy of giving in the service of both seduction and self-elevation."[5]

The roots of a Two's pride are compensatory. As Naranjo explains below, pride is a repression of neediness in relation to the heart point's— Point Four's—passion of envy:

> *let me remark that to speak of a repression of neediness is practically equivalent to speaking of a repression of the psychological atmosphere of envy—and just as in the case of ennea-type I we understood anger as a reaction-formation to gluttony, we may in this case understand pride as a transformation of envy through the joint action of repression and histrionic emotionalism. Just as for the perfectionist it is self-indulgence that is most avoided, in the proud and histrionic character nothing is more avoided than the love thirst and the sense of unlovability that are characteristics of envy. Thus we may say that through a combination of repression and histrionic emotionalism envy is transformed into pride and . . . succorance into nurturance.[6]*

To explain this a bit further, we need to understand that neediness is one of the most difficult feelings for a Two to tolerate. As Naranjo explicates, acknowledging that she is needy of love is, for a Two, tantamount to saying that she is unworthy of it, since if she were worthy of love, she would already have received it. To feel or express neediness challenges the idealized image she holds of being lovable, and to challenge that would be unbearable because her self-esteem depends upon approximating this image. So a Two's repression of need both supports her pride and in turn, makes acknowledging need devastating.

Pride being not only one of the seven deadly sins but considered the most fundamental one, it is universal to all ego structures. So while it is a more central issue for Twos, it is nonetheless relevant for all of us. Often, the difference between our reality and how we would like it to be is intolerable, and so we escape into prideful grandiosity about ourselves. This is because we have ceased to value who we really are, and instead turned our attention to a mental construct of how we would like ourselves to be.

This is an extremely important thing to understand about our pride: it rests upon qualities and characteristics that may have some basis in reality, although not always, but nonetheless exist as part of a picture in our mind—that of our idealized self-image.

Before delving further into the question of pride, it is important to differentiate between this investment in a mental construct, and genuine satisfaction in ourselves and our accomplishments. When we have done a good job at something or have been promoted at work based on our performance, when we have delivered a successful lecture that was well received or painted a picture that has a certain magic to it, we naturally feel a sense of accomplishment, pleasure, and satisfaction in ourselves. This is a far cry from investing our imaginary picture of ourselves with pride. Realistic satisfaction in ourselves is also not the same thing as using such tangible accomplishments to inflate ourselves and feel superior to others. Linguistically, we do not differentiate between these two usages of the word *pride.* Dreamed-up superiority and realistic personal satisfaction in something achieved or in qualities possessed are both definitions of pride found in the dictionary, but obviously, one exists mostly or even exclusively in the imagination and the other in reality. It is the difference between inordinate self-esteem and a pragmatic and felt sense of one's true worth.

Psychoanalyst Karen Horney, founder of one of the neo-Freudian schools of the 1930s and '40s, was probably the first to psychologically elaborate the question of pride in detail. In order to resolve this lack of differentiation, she refers to the first sort of pride as "neurotic pride," and to the second as "healthy pride." As we shall see, the first is the passion of this point, and the second has to do with the virtue. For our purposes, when we use the term *pride,* we are referring to an overinvestment in the self, which is indistinguishable from our self-image.

The other, and closely related, crucial difference between these two definitions of pride is that neurotic pride makes us extremely vulnerable and easily hurt because it rests on the flimsy ground of a mental construction. Experiences in life challenge and buffet our idealized self-image, making it precarious and assailable in direct proportion to our investment in it. The degree of discrepancy between our reality and our grandiose picture of ourselves reflects how painful that reality is to us, and the less reality based our pride is, the more brittle it is.

What Horney calls healthy pride, on the other hand, is rooted in actuality rather than in the subjectivity of our own inner world. Rather than reality challenging it, reality affirms it. As Horney says of pride,

> *Neurotic pride furthermore rests on the attributes which a person arrogates to himself in his imagination, on all those belonging to his particular idealized image. Here the peculiar nature of neurotic pride comes into clear relief. The neurotic is not proud of the human being he actually is. Knowing his wrong perspective on himself, we are not surprised that his pride blots out difficulties and limitations. But it goes farther than this. Mostly he is not even proud of his existing assets. He may be but hazily aware of them; he may actually deny them. But even if he is cognizant of them they carry no weight for him.*[7]

Pride, then, is pride in our self-image rather than in who we actually are. It rests upon an estrangement from self, forming a gap between ourselves as we are and the internal image that we have of ourselves. As Horney continues,

> *The idealized image is a product of his imagination. But this is not something which is created overnight. Incessant work of intellect and imagination, most of it unconscious, goes into maintaining the private fictitious world through rationalizations, justifications, externalizations, reconciling irreconcilables—in short, through finding ways to make things appear different from what they are. The more a person is alienated from himself, the more his mind becomes supreme reality.*[8]

This is solid psychological understanding, but the implications reach beyond the realm of psychology. From this perspective, we can see that working through our pride is a matter of becoming more and more realistic about ourselves, and instead of shoring up a picture of ourselves in our minds, learning to perceive and to value ourselves as we are. As we have seen, often we take pride in qualities or capacities that we actually have, but when they remain part of our self-image rather than part of our felt sense of ourselves, we are likewise estranged from them. The logical implication of this takes us well beyond psychological understanding: as long as there is any kind of mental construct acting as a subjective filter through which we experience ourselves, the roots of pride remain intact.

And to speak of a chasm between our subjective sense of self and ourselves as we are is another way of describing the personality itself, which as we have seen, is composed of mental representations that we take to be reality yet which have no ultimate existence. This is because they are constructions in the mind, rather than direct experience in the here and now.

Pride, then, is the personality's investment in itself. It is the value it gives to itself in order to buttress itself. It is the fuel that gives energy to our mental constructs. Without it, our investment in the images we carry of ourselves collapses. Almaas has described pride as the assertion of the ego, in which it supports its own greatness. Ultimately, pride is a spiritual issue, and one that can only be resolved by moving beyond identification with our personality structure. We will return to this theme a bit further along.

Our pride is compensatory, as we have seen—this is also standard psychology. To the extent that we feel unloved and unworthy, we tend to inflate ourselves in our own minds, taking the sting out of these painful feelings. As Horney says in describing the neurotic, which for our purposes we can translate as anyone identified with their personality structure,

> His self-idealization is an attempt to remedy the damage done {by early unfavorable constellations} by lifting himself in his mind above the crude reality of himself and others. And, as in the stories of the devil's pact, he gets all the glory in imagination and sometimes in reality. But instead of solid self-confidence he gets a glittering gift of most questionable value: neurotic pride.[9]

We have explored pride so far as self-inflation, but as we delve into its compensatory nature, it becomes clear that it is part of a process that has two opposite extremes of self-assessment, as alluded to at the beginning. The inevitable other side of puffing ourselves up is self-diminishment.

This is not usually thought of as pride, but if we understand how pride works, this self-disparagement is an inevitable part of the whole gestalt. Likewise, to the extent that our self-importance depends upon the diminishment of that of others, the one needs the other. Implicit in pride, then, are two sides, one of which is superior and significant, and the other of which is inferior and insignificant. These two poles form the two sides of an object relation—an image of self and of other—and as in any object relation, we can identify with either side at any given time.

Many of us, especially Twos, vacillate between feeling that we are vastly superior to others, invested with special gifts and abilities, and are just plain better, more lovable human beings and conversely feeling that we are profoundly inferior to others, devoid of anything special, and utterly unlovable. The latter pole is seldom seen for the prideful position that it is, but this becomes obvious when we focus on the assertion of being the *most* inferior, the *most* lacking in anything remarkable, and so on. It is an overinflation of deficiency. The mechanism of pride, then, is ultimately a polarization of value, with one side compensating for the other.

Since our pride is not rooted in our direct experience of ourselves but rather in an image of ourselves invested with value, it is easily wounded. As Horney says,

> *It can be hurt as easily from within as from without. The two typical reactions to hurt pride are shame and humiliation. We will feel ashamed if we do, think, or feel something that violates our pride. And we will feel humiliated if others do something that hurts our pride, or fail to do what our pride requires of them. In any reaction of shame or humiliation that seems out of place or out of proportion we must answer these two questions: What in the particular situation has aroused this response? And what special underlying pride has been hurt by it? They are closely interrelated, and neither can be given a quick answer.*[10]

As she notes, sometimes we do not feel the shame and humiliation directly, but instead feel secondary emotions of rage and fear. We are angry, then, at someone who has injured our pride, or afraid of someone who might assault it. Our attempts to deflect or avoid injury to our pride are essentially efforts to avoid being catapulted to the other extreme position—attempts to avoid our own self-diminishment and consequent self-hatred.

When reality confronts and challenges our prideful self-estimation, threatening to throw us into self-diminishment, we often attempt to restore our wounded pride in a variety of ways. We may deny that the humiliating situation happened or claim that we were misunderstood. We might justify our behavior that did not live up to our idealized image, claiming that the other pushed us into acting that way or that he or she had it coming. We might try to get revenge upon the other who so humiliated us, settling the score. Or we might lose interest in those who have humiliated us by not including us, for instance, convincing ourselves that it didn't matter to us anyway.

Just as pride is psychologically compensatory for a deficient self-image, as we have seen, it is also a counterbalancing mechanism from a spiritual perspective. Putting it plainly, our pride is an attempt to offset awareness of the ultimate emptiness of our personality structure. We have seen that the personality or ego is really only a mental representation and so has no ultimate existence. This is why it is frequently referred to in spiritual literature as an empty illusion. It is inherently insubstantial and because of that when we are identified with it, deep down we feel devoid of substance and therefore lacking and vulnerable.

Our core experience is one of emptiness—this is inevitable when we are identified with our personality—and this emptiness is not the rich and profound emptiness the Buddhists refer to as *shunyata*. Rather, it is a painful sense of being flimsy and meager, which most of us experience indirectly as a gnawing sense of insignificance, inconsequentiality, and negligibility. This is often excruciating to experience directly, and so to make life bearable, our pride steps in saying in effect, "No, you are not nothing! You really *are* someone, and someone very special indeed." In this way, our pride supports the supposed reality of our personality structure and infuses it with importance and value. Or, at the other end of the same polarity, our pride may say, "Yes, you really *are* deficient—let me count the ways," supporting our identification with our shell. To really take ourselves in as we are threatens the whole structure.

So our pride stands in the way of seeing things as they really are. It stands in the way of recognizing our assets and our limitations, and on a deeper level, it stands in the way of recognizing the ultimate unreality of our personality, our constructed sense of self. From this perspective, we can see that for us to believe that we are our personality is an expression of pride. We are asserting that this fabricated sense of self is what we are, and in the same breath denying that our ultimate nature is what we are. It is as though we were standing in the face of the Divine, and saying, "I exist in my own right—I have my own beingness apart from you!" Obviously, then, pride is implicit whenever we are identified with our personality—whenever we experience ourselves separate from Being.

Just as our pride obscures both our limitations and our assets, and blurs the ultimate unreality of the personality, it also blinds us to our true function as human beings. When we are identified with it, we believe ourselves to have a self-importance and significance that is not objective, but this belief is a reflection, however distorted, of a truth. From the perspective of the personality, we are either special or we are negligible. Neither is an accurate assessment of our true place. Each of us is unique and special, just as each cell in our bodies is unique and special. Each of us is important and has our own job to do—not at the expense of others but alongside others. Likewise, each of us has a particular place in the body of humanity; and from a larger perspective, humanity has a particular place within the body of the whole universe.

Because pride is implicit when we are identified with our personality, it is a pernicious obstacle to spiritual work. It begins the moment we start congratulating ourselves for our ability to meditate so well, to have such powerful insights, to be so compassionate to the other person, and so on. The other side of pride's coin arises when we condemn ourselves for not being able to sit as still as the meditator next to us, for having absolutely no self-awareness, or for being so materialistic, hardhearted, selfish, and so on. Not only are we evaluating ourselves but we are also elevating and lowering our self-esteem. We are conferring or withholding value from ourselves based on our approximation to our internal image of what a spiritual person should be like.

Likewise, when we have a deep experience or insight, an instance of movement beyond the veil of our personality structure, our pride tends to reassert itself in our self-congratulation: "Wow, what a high state I'm in! Obviously, this is proof of my progress and specialness!" When we do this, we are distancing ourselves from the direct experience by turning it into an inner image, and we are also using our experience to infuse ourselves with value. We are treating our experiences as acquisitions, commodities we are accumulating and adding to ourselves. We are pinning medals or gold stars onto ourselves, at least in our imagination. Spiritual work is really the opposite. It is a matter of losing more and more of ourselves.

This is what the late Tibetan Buddhist teacher Chögyam Trungpa Rinpoche described as spiritual materialism:

> The problem is that ego can convert anything to its own use, even spirituality. Ego is constantly attempting to acquire and apply the teachings of spirituality for its own benefit. The teachings are treated as an external thing, external to "me," a philosophy which we try to imitate. We do not actually want to identify with or become the teachings. So if our teacher speaks of renunciation of ego, we attempt to mimic renunciation of ego. We go through the motions, make appropriate gestures, but we really do not want to sacrifice any part of our way of life. We become skillful actors, and while playing deaf and dumb to the real meaning of the teachings, we find some comfort in pretending to follow the path.[11]

We may collect and catalogue our experiences or our spiritual knowledge, using them to convince ourselves of our development. We may take pride in how perfectly we perform our prostrations, meditations, and spiritual study. We may pride ourselves in how beautifully we fold our robes or hold our malah, or even how compassionately we behave or how devoted to our practice we are. When we do this, we are simply collecting evidence, albeit very spiritual proof, to convince ourselves of our substantiality. As Trungpa continues,

> Our vast collections of knowledge and experience are just part of ego's display, part of the grandiose quality of ego. We display them to the world

and, in so doing, reassure ourselves that we exist, safe and secure, as "spiritual" people.[12]

From a slightly different angle, the eminent psychologist Carl Jung describes how we inflate ourselves as a way of offsetting our doubts about our spiritual understanding. Undoubtedly drawing from his own experience, this is typical of the use of pride by the fear types:

If we now consider the fact that, as a result of psychic compensation, great humility stands very close to pride, and that "pride goeth before a fall," we can easily discover behind the haughtiness certain traits of an anxious sense of inferiority. In fact we shall see clearly how this uncertainty forces the enthusiast to puff up his truths, of which he feels none too sure, and to win proselytes to his side in order that his followers may prove to himself the value and trustworthiness of his own convictions. Nor is he altogether so happy in his fund of knowledge as to be able to hold out alone; at bottom he feels isolated by it, and the secret fear of being left alone with it induces him to trot out his opinions and interpretations in and out of season, because only when convincing someone else does he feel safe from gnawing doubts.[13]

When pride gets attached to our spiritual openings, they lose their transformative effect upon us. As the Buddhist meditation teacher and prolific author Jack Kornfield says,

{Experiences} do not in themselves produce wisdom. Some people have had many of these experiences, yet learned very little. Even great openings of heart, kundalini processes, and visions can turn into spiritual pride or become old memories. As with a near-death experience or a car accident, some people will change a great deal and others will return to old constricted habits shortly thereafter. Spiritual experiences in themselves do not count for much.[14]

Our peak experiences can simply inflate our personality, puffing it up to cosmic proportions. This keeps us stuck in our familiar sense of self, but with new spiritual trappings that blind us to what is really going on. When we do this, we are defending against the truth of our situation— that we are firmly entrenched in our identification with our personality— and we are infusing it with a sense of value and importance that is out of synch with the fact that it has no ultimate reality. It exists only in our minds.

Stories abound of spiritual teachers whose self-inflation has blinded them to a realistic sense of themselves and their limitations, leading to catastrophes for their students. As Mariana Caplan describes in her book about premature claims to enlightenment, *Halfway Up the Mountain,*

> *Among individuals who have prematurely presumed their own enlightenment, there is most often significant ego inflation. Such individuals have a subjective and grandiose belief about their own spiritual stature and attainment. Inflation can be so commanding and so convincing that it consumes everything in its wake, including conscience, discrimination, and, at times, basic sanity.*
>
> *. . . Inflation wears many different masks: a sense of superiority, vanity, self-satisfaction, a feeling of being special, an over-estimation of one's spiritual development and capacities, pride in one's spiritual accomplishments and stature, aloofness, the feeling that no one is able to understand one's experience. Each of these is a mask of ego inflation, worn in delusion, with each wearer believing that his or her mask represents the true face.*[15]

As she quotes Jung explaining, such inflation is the result of the personality appropriating to itself spiritual states that belong, in fact, to no one since they have their own existence. When the personality seizes upon such states and uses them to puff itself up, this is the beginning of trouble and sometimes danger for someone professing to be a teacher. Their grandiosity causes them to lose sight of where their contact with True Nature begins and where the personality ends. The two get mixed together—contact with one's depths becomes abrogated by the personality—leading to messianic pretensions in some cases and to claims of infallibility in others.

When a teacher closes the door to scrutiny, either internal or external, when he stops looking objectively at his process or when he becomes defensive and turns the tables on a student by making her questioning of his motives or behavior her own issue, it's a good sign that pride is operating. When a teacher acts out his animal soul either sexually or in the accumulation of riches, and justifies such behavior as appropriate to his stature or as beneficial to his students, it is another indication that grandiosity is obscuring that teacher's vision. When a teacher claims that she has a corner on spiritual understanding and invalidates other teachers, pride is inflating her sense of self. Such behavior is the source of cults, and it is dangerous not only for students but for the teacher himself or herself, as their continual unfoldment—implicit in spiritual development—turns into a cul-de-sac.

The more developed a person becomes, the more they have a realistic sense of what their capacities and limitations actually are. Development means moving beyond the veils of our personality structure. As we work on ourselves, these veils progressively thin and we experience the deepest nature of ourselves and of reality. We are moving beyond our self-enclosed, subjective world into experiencing things as they are beyond that holographic sense of things. We are, in this sense, becoming more objective. We become more objective about the nature of reality, and that includes ourselves. This objectivity or realism is the virtue of this point, humility. Like all of the virtues, it is one of the major hallmarks of true spiritual development.

Humility is a much-misunderstood word and state. We often conceive of it as self-deprecation, replete with images of groveling and refusing to accept anything positive being given to or said about ourselves. The dictionary defines humility as being humble, which in turn it defines as having a low opinion of oneself and of one's importance or merit, feeling a lack of worth, having an abject attitude and demeanor, as well as the absence of vanity and pride.[16] The first part of this definition sounds pretty much like the opposite pole of pride discussed earlier, reflecting the perspective of the personality in which pride and self-disparagement are the only options.

From a spiritual perspective—that is, from outside the realm of the personality—humility is something quite different. When we understand what humility is from this objective perspective, we see that the personality imitates it in the distorted form of diminishing oneself. Ichazo's definition of humility gives us a good clue to its meaning in the sense of being a true virtue:

> *It is acceptance of the limits of the body, its capacities. The intellect holds unreal beliefs about its own powers. The body knows precisely what it can and cannot do. Humility in its largest sense is the knowledge of the true human position in the cosmic scale.*

To paraphrase this in language more applicable to our discussion, humility is the recognition and acknowledgment of both our limitations and our capacities. When we are identified with our personality structure, we experience ourselves through beliefs about ourselves, both inflated and deflated ones, as we have discussed at length. When we are objective about ourselves, we know not only the limits of our body but of our soul. And finally, humility is an inner knowing of not only our personal place but of the place of humanity within the cosmos.

Humility, then, is seeing ourselves and our abilities clearly. It is realism that distinguishes the passion and the virtue of this point. It is a realistic self-assessment grounded in how we actually are, not as we might wish ourselves to be. It involves the absence of the superimposition of our idealized image over our sense of ourselves.

This means, for one thing, recognizing our physical edges—knowing how much energy we have in general and for a specific thing. It means, particulary for Twos, not taking on more than we actually have the stamina for, and it also means not underestimating what we are capable of. In terms of how we live, it means realism about time. It means knowing what we have time for and when we are committing ourselves to things that are beyond what we can objectively do in that time frame. It means not overextending or making promises to fulfill things for others that are not possible for us or that we don't actually want to do.

Humility means having a realistic sense of the limits of our intelligence, as well as a recognition of the kind of intelligence we have. Not measuring ourselves against an inner or outer yardstick, we are able to honor the particular sensitivity of understanding that each of us possesses, and humility also means the absence of a sense of superiority regarding our particular form of intelligence. It simply means seeing it as it is.

Humility involves profound acceptance of ourselves and of our experience, regardless of what it is, and this points us toward seeing how this virtue provides an orientation toward inner development. The more developed we are, the more we are in touch with our direct experience. Without filtering our experience through a concept of what is acceptable and unacceptable based on an image we hold in our minds, we are simply in touch with what is. So being in touch with ourselves as we really are, regardless of what it is that we find when we make such contact with ourselves, is approaching our process with the attitude of humility.

This means allowing the full range of our emotions, rather than only letting ourselves experience the ones that fit in to our ideal image. This includes our anger, hatred, greed, selfishness, and all of the other negative emotions that don't fit into most people's pictures of what a developed person feels. If we do not allow ourselves our full emotional breadth, how can we possibly understand and work through our reactivity? We can only suppress states that don't correspond to our image, and all this does is distance us further from ourselves. We might develop a very realized image, but it will only be appearance rather than bona fide unfoldment. This orientation doesn't mean license to act out our darkest and most negative states but rather the freedom to explore them all, and in so doing, move through them.

Obviously, it is not a simple thing to drop our concepts of how we ideally should be. But the more that we make contact with our reality as it is and begin to question our expectations of ourselves, the more the discrepancy between what is and our ideal image becomes apparent, and this is the beginning. This is frequently painful at first, and it is so in proportion to the store we have set by needing to live up to our ideal. However, contacting the truth about ourselves, even if it is difficult to tolerate, inevitably brings its own particular kind of satisfaction. In the depths of our hearts, we know the truth when we experience it, and when we do, we know that we are on safe ground, rather than on the artificial and therefore tenuous foundations of our beliefs and illusions about how things are.

Contacting the truth about ourselves has a particular sweetness—a sense of genuineness, authenticity, and true worth. Rather than getting a sense of value from approximating our ideal image, we progressively find true value in reality.

Realizing humility is not easy. In one of the most famous accounts of attempting to cultivate the virtues, one of America's Founding Fathers, Benjamin Franklin, found this out during his project to attain "moral perfection," launched when he was in his early twenties. Franklin's project has struck some, such as the author D. H. Lawrence, as a naive attempt at self-improvement, while others, including the philosopher Jacob Needleman perceive in it "the sort of program of self-struggle that has always formed the basis of the search for inner freedom and moral power."[17] Franklin's initial list of virtues that he sought to cultivate omitted humility, and he added it when a Quaker friend helpfully noted frequent instances in which he displayed pride, being "overbearing and rather insolent." His instructions for developing humility (Franklin most likely being a Seven) said simply, "Imitate Jesus and Socrates."[18] This was one of the virtues Franklin never mastered, as we see in this excerpt from his recent biography by Walter Isaacson:

> "I cannot boast of much success in acquiring the reality of this virtue, but I had a good deal with regard to the appearance of it," he wrote. . . . "There is perhaps no one of our natural passions so hard to subdue as pride; to disguise it, struggle with it, beat it down, stifle it, mortify it as much as one pleases, it is still alive and will every now and then peep out and show itself." This battle against pride would challenge—and amuse—him for the rest of his life. "You will see it perhaps often in this history. For even if I could conceive that I had completely overcome it, I would probably be proud of my humility."[19]

Indeed, Franklin is not alone in only approximating true humility through presenting an image of it. This is the personality's only option. Authentic humility is not possible if we are identified with our personality structure. Humility is the result of moving beyond our egoic sense of self, which needs pride to survive as a virtual reality in our consciousness. We can only do this if we are engaged in genuine inner work that gradually chips away at and in time dissolves our very need for being seen and held in high esteem by others. Since humility is realism about ourselves, it is not dependent upon how we are regarded by others or how we measure up to anyone or anything. It is something we know in our own hearts.

This is indeed freedom and true autonomy. We become liberated from the prison of our inner imperatives and therefore of our inner constraints, becoming free to be ourselves—not in the libertine way so characteristic of Twos, who chafe under any kind of limitation, but in the true sense of being able to be and to live the truth of ourselves.

Humility is needed to see the truth, whether about ourselves or about the nature of reality. Without it, we are attempting to see things through the occluded lens of structure, the structured sense of self of the ego. It is a great paradox to the mind that only when we acknowledge and accept our actual limitations as well as our capacities, when we have an objective sense of our own personal edges, that we are able to get in touch with the boundlessness and limitlessness of our deepest nature. This is because when we see ourselves as we really are, we see also what our nature is. Without the need to live up to a self-image, the sense of self gradually becomes more diffuse and in time dissolves completely, leaving our soul open to its nature.

As humility informs our soul, the rigid structure of our personality melts, and our infinite potential becomes accessible. Our capacity develops not only to flow with our own process without attempting to manipulate it but also to participate in the dynamic unfoldment of all of the universe. From a spiritual perspective, our place as human beings is that of having the potential to make conscious all of the dimensions of existence, to be windows experiencing and expressing True Nature in our individual lives. Recognizing and fulfilling this function is not a matter of pride, but one of realism.

As we progressively see the truth, we begin to understand what we human beings are: we see and we know that the Divine is acting through us. This is the initial sense of things. We might experience ourselves as Its servant—that what we are all about is being of service to our deepest nature. As our dualism thins—as there is less of a sense of us on the one hand

and the Divine on the other, or to put it differently, as our sense of our-selves in relation to the Divine as an other diminishes—we recognize that we *are* the Divine. There are not two—me and True Nature—but rather there is just the one thing that is everything, including ourselves. This is the realization that I am True Nature, or as the great Vedantic teacher, Sri Nisargadatta Maharaj, titled one of his books, *I Am That.*

From some religious perspectives, believing that we are the Divine is the ultimate pride. We find this in belief systems in which the Divine is conceived of as an other, and in which we attempt to emulate Its qualities and receive Its grace, but It remains something separate. This dualistic approach to the Divine reflects the dualism of the personality, in which units of object relations, different variations of the sense of self and of other, coalesce into the egoic sense of self. As we move beyond these basic conceptual frames of our ego structure, this dualism dissolves, as we see in mystics of even the most dualistic of religions in which merging with the Divine overtakes them.

The ultimate humility is knowing and experiencing ourselves as the mouthpiece of God, the instrument of Being and Its expression. When we really *get* that everything that we are and everything that we do is the be-ingness and the action of True Nature, our humility is complete. We are then utterly realistic, living fully in the real world, knowing as Ichazo says, "the true human position on the cosmic scale."

P O I N T   F O U R —
E N V Y *a n d*
E Q U A N I M I T Y

———⊸⦿⦿⊸———

*Looking into life we notice how it continually moves between contrasts: rise
and fall, success and failure, loss and gain, honor and blame. We feel how
our heart responds to all this with happiness and sorrow, delight and despair,
disappointment and satisfaction, hope and fear. These waves of emotion carry
us up and fling us down; and no sooner do we find rest, then we are in the
power of a new wave again. How can we expect to get a footing on the crest
of the waves? How can we erect the building of our lives in the midst of
this ever-restless ocean of existence, if not on the Island Equanimity.*
—NYANAPONIKA THERA[1]

Most of us are not content with ourselves as we are, nor
are most content with what we have. As the saying goes,
"The grass is always greener on the other side of the
fence." Almost invariably, how others are or what they
possess seems inherently better. We cast an envious eye
toward them, scanning and comparing to see who has it
better than we do. We seem to have a kind of perceptual
illusion, perceiving others as possessing abilities, qualities, and characteristics that appear far more desirable
than the ones we have, and coveting what we see.

From another angle, we have only to consider how often we are wholeheartedly happy for the good fortune of
another without wishing that we, too, were also its recip-

ient, or were receiving it instead of the other, to get in touch with our envy. How often do we simply rejoice for another person when they have come by a windfall or a promotion, especially when it was one that we also wanted? How often do we appreciate how much better a job another did at something than we did? How often do we admire another's beauty, which we consider greater than ours? How often, if we are ourselves single, do we feel joy because a friend has become engaged? Even though we might be loath to admit it, we often find ourselves taking some satisfaction when another experiences misfortune. How often are we wholeheartedly sorry for another—especially another who has it better than us—when they lose of a chunk of income in a stock market dip, are beaten by a competitor at something, or go through an unwanted separation or divorce?

The good or bad fortune of another is something that we personalize—do we have it or not? How does what I have compare to what they have? And most of the time, it looks better over there. Curiously, while we may experience ourselves as lacking and deficient, we seldom perceive others that way, even though most people typically experience themselves, whether consciously or not, as equally empty. We tend to project fullness, completeness, satisfaction, happiness, and all other positive states onto others, and from our vantage point, they seem to have what it is we do not.

In America, we tend to envy the rich and famous, while in other cultures it might be royalty or the upper classes who arouse covetousness. We need look no further than the numerous magazines and television shows devoted to tracking these cultural icons to see how we are mesmerized by those who seem to have it all, and we rarely notice that all that they possess often brings them far less happiness than we have. When we do this, we are simply projecting our ideals onto these people, and then envying them for approximating them. Ultimately, we are perceiving and projecting our own goodness, the beneficence of our nature, outside of ourselves and then envying those we have endowed with it.

The more sinister side of envy shows its face when our tracking of our icons involves looking for the dirt about them. When we take secret delight in the losses and suffering of those we envy whether from a distance or up close, it is our covetousness showing its dark side. Envy is the breeding ground of gossip, slander, and backbiting. When we engage in it, we are attempting to harm or to spoil those we envy. We see the positive, the good, the ultimate outside of ourselves, and we can't stand it. We want to hurt it or at least bring it down a notch.

Envy has dogged spiritual seekers throughout the centuries. As St. John of the Cross, the sixteenth-century Spanish mystic, writes in speaking of religious beginners,

> *For, with respect to envy, many of them are wont to experience movements of displeasure at the spiritual good of others, which cause them a certain sensible grief at being outstripped upon this road, so that they would prefer not to hear others praised; for they become displeased at others' virtues and sometimes they cannot refrain from contradicting what is said in praise of them, depreciating it as far as they can; and their annoyance thereat grows because the same is not said of them, for they would fain be preferred in everything. All this is clean contrary to charity, which as Saint Paul says, rejoices in goodness. And, if charity has any envy, it is a holy envy, comprising grief at not having the virtues of others, yet also joy because others have them, and delight when others outstrip us in the service of God, wherein we ourselves are so remiss.*[2]

It is not only those new to inner work who experience envy of their fellow travelers. Even those who have worked on themselves for decades often have difficulty acknowledging and celebrating the development of their colleagues. Envy is at the root of this, since in direct proportion to our investment in being seen as evolved, admitting another's fuller embodiment of Being threatens our self-esteem. What is being warded off is the painful sense of not living up to our spiritual self-image. This creates great difficulty in some spiritual communities when members have difficulty recognizing and appreciating another's development that might be different or has surpassed their own, or in begrudging the achievements, celebrity, or respect that a fellow voyager receives. Spiritual envy is the source of the tendency rampant in spiritual communities to point out the flaws in another, to focus on where they are not developed rather than where they are, and to undermine the esteem another is held in. Jesus Christ encapsulated this phenomenon in his statement, "No prophet is recognized in his own country."

Our envy comes out most dramatically in connection with the life arena our consciousness is the most centered around—in enneagrammatic terms, which instinct is the most dominant in our personality—self-preservation, social, or sexual. This is of course true with all of the passions. All of the passions, especially that of our ennea-type, will come out the most strongly in relation to the arena of life that we have the most difficulty and insecurity about—that of our instinctual subtype. And getting in touch with what life arena arouses our passion the most strongly is a good way to identify our subtype.

If the self-preservation instinct is the most highlighted, we tend to envy the physical security another possesses. Perceiving that another has it monetarily better than us will arouse our covetousness—we might envy another's income or their stock portfolio or their inherited wealth. We might cast a longing and begrudging eye toward the splendor of another's home—its largeness, elegance, or location—or toward the furnishings and artwork we find there. We might envy the health, stamina, or physical prowess of another; or their capacity to take care of themselves. The perceived superiority of another in relation to those things that have to do with survival and physical well-being would be the source of our envy.

Related to both the preservation and sexual instinct, it is rare that people are fully content with their bodies, and this is especially true during adolescence, but some of us never outgrow this dissatisfaction. Comparing the shape and appearance of our physical form to what our culture considers ideal is a preoccupation for many, and the source of great income for those who profit from defining and helping others achieve some ideal form. Beauty and fashion magazines show us how we should look and who amongst us we should try to look more like. Those who fit the image are fascinating to many of us, and we invest them with perfection and then envy them for it.

If the life arena we are most sensitive about is social, having to do with our capacity to be regarded as a friend, where we are in the social pecking order of our particular culture or group, or our standing in the world at large, our envy will also come out here. We might simply envy another's social ease—their capacity to entertain, make small talk, or to feel comfortable in a group of people. On the other hand, we might covet another's prestige, power, social respect, or accolades. We might cast a green eye toward their social standing, their popularity, or their fame. Or we might envy those who know and have access to the famous and notable.

If the sexual instinct is the most dominant one in our life, the area of intimate relationship is where our envy is be aroused. We might be envious of another's allure, their capacity to attract another or to hold another's interest. We might be covetous of those in a relationship if we are not, and yearn to also have a partner. Or, if we are in a relationship, we might cast a longing eye outside of our relationship, believing that another's partner is better or more attractive than ours, or that being alone is preferable. We might be highly aware of the pecking order in terms of sexual attractiveness—who is the most enticing. We might envy another's number of sexual conquests or their sexual proficiency, perceived or imagined. The area of sensuality in general will arouse our covetousness— envying those who seem to have the most pleasure in their lives. We might also believe, because of our insecurity in this area, that others are more attractive, and begrudge them for it. We might be jealous of them, afraid that they might jeopardize our relationship, luring or stealing our partner away—projecting our envy.

Relationally, some of us suffer from only being interested in those who are not drawn to us, and end up in serial relationships characterized by longing for another who is never quite available. For many, this kind of relationship is the only one that is exciting enough to keep them engaged. Others are only interested in those who are married or otherwise committed to another, and attempt to seduce them away. In both cases, envy is at work and suffering is at hand.

Our envy, then, is not random. Research has shown that it is elicited in the life domains that are the most important to us, areas of life that our sense of self is deeply connected with. Quoting the contemporary psychologist Peter Salovey, who edited a compilation of research on jealousy and envy,

> *Envy is most likely to be experienced when comparisons with another person (a rival) are negative for the self, and these comparisons are in a domain that is especially important and relevant to self-definition.*

Jealousy, although closely related, is not the same thing as envy. As Salovey says about jealousy,

> *Jealousy is most likely to be experienced when the termination of an important, interdependent relationship with another person is threatened by a rival whose characteristics in especially important domains—that is, domains relevant to self-definition—appear to be better than our own.*[3]

Jealousy is an intolerance or suspicion of rivalry or unfaithfulness, hostility toward a rival one believes holds the advantage, and a vigilant guarding of one's possessions. On the other hand, envy is "a painful or resentful awareness of an advantage enjoyed by another joined with the desire to possess the same advantage."[4] Malice is an obsolete definition of envy, but while linguistically antiquated, it is definitely part of the whole dynamic of envy.

There are degrees of envy, beginning with admiring how another person is or some quality that they possess, like eloquence, gregariousness, great physical beauty, or a particular talent, and wishing that we had it, as well. Appreciation and enjoyment of how the other person is or what they possess is still present. As envy progresses along its continuum, we are unhappy to see that another is a particular way or has something that we wish we had, and instead we feel hostility toward them. We begrudge what they have. This is because seeing that they have something desirable that we lack threatens to trigger our inner sense of deficiency, making us feel bad about ourselves. To defend against that, we feel enmity toward them.

In its full flowering, the envious state is one of deep inner turbulence and unrest. We feel a painful sense of discontent and frustration because we don't possess what it is that we envy. We might agonize about it, berating and shaming ourselves for not being as fortunate as the coveted one, and at the same time being filled with antagonism toward this source of our envy. Our envy then can reach the extreme of malice, our not-so-obsolete definition, and of hatred. Hatred is ultimately a drive to get rid of the object causing us such upset. It is the desire to annihilate, to destroy, to wipe out. If we completely allow the movement of hatred within our souls, we see that it is an attempt to obliterate the source of inner disturbance in an attempt to restore peace to our consciousness.

As Melanie Klein, one of the generation of psychoanalysts following Freud, who was the first psychologist to write extensively about the psychology of envy, describes,

> *Envy is the angry feeling that another person possesses and enjoys something desirable—the envious impulse being to take it away or to spoil it. Moreover, envy implies the subject's relation to one person only and goes back to the earliest exclusive relation to the mother. Jealousy is based on envy, but involves a relation to at least two people; it is mainly concerned with love that the subject feels is his due and has been taken away, or is in danger of being taken away from him by his rival. In the everyday conception of jealousy, a man or a woman feels deprived of the loved person by somebody else.* [5]

As Klein notes, in jealousy love is still present and the intent is to protect it, while in envy the drive is to spoil and damage what is considered good. Probably a Four, Klein considers envy the basest of the seven deadly sins: "I would even suggest that it is unconsciously felt to be the greatest sin of all, because it spoils and harms the good object which is the source of life." [6]

The reason that I think she was probably a Four is that her perceptions of infant behavior in regard to the breast seem to be filtered through a decidedly adult and very Fourish lens. As she says,

> *My work has taught me that the first object to be envied is the feeding breast, for the infant feels that it possesses everything he desires and that it has an unlimited flow of milk, and love which the breast keeps for its own gratification. This feeling adds to his sense of grievance and hate, and the result is a disturbed relation to the mother.*
>
> *. . . The infant's feelings seem to be that when the breast deprives him, it becomes bad because it keeps the milk, love, and care associated with the good breast all to itself. He hates and envies what he feels to be the mean and grudging breast.*
>
> *It is perhaps more understandable that the satisfactory breast is also envied. The very ease with which the milk comes—though the infant feels gratified by it—also gives rise to envy because this gift seems something so unattainable.* [7]

To those of us who are not Fours—and perhaps to many Fours as well—this seems a markedly far-fetched interpretation of infant behavior and emotions. It does, however, tell us a great deal about how a Four tends to perceive things.

Envy is the reactive tendency and inner affective atmosphere—the passion—that is the strongest one that Fours have to contend with. As one of the image types—those ennea-types on either side of and including Point Three—the existential dilemma for Fours is coping with continually falling short of their idealized image. As Naranjo puts it,

> *While an ennea-type III person identifies with that part of the self that coincides with the idealized image, the ennea-type IV individual identifies with that part of the psyche that* fails *to fit the idealized image, and is always striving to achieve the unattainable. Here is a person animated by a vanity that fails to reach its goal because of the admixture of the sense of scarcity and worthlessness (of point 5).*[8]

With the inner drive of all of the image types to fulfill their idealized image coming from their Three wing, while partaking of the sense of depleted emptiness of their other wing, Point Five, Fours are left with a sense of dearth. They interpret this as a sign of badness, whether they are conscious or not of this deep conviction about themselves, and turn their gaze outward for the good that they feel they don't have. Their inner orientation is, as Naranjo continues, "a forceful reaching out, an intense demand for that which is missed." As he notes, their inner atmosphere is one of turmoil and turbulence, in contrast to the quiet resignation of Fives, since envy is a vicious cycle:

> *The emotional state of envy involves a painful sense of lack and a craving toward that which is felt lacking; the situation involves a sense of goodness as something outside oneself which needs to be incorporated.*
>
> *Though an understandable reaction to early frustration and deprivation, envy constitutes a self-frustrating factor in the psyche, for the excessive craving for love that it entails never answers the chronic sense of inner*

scarcity and badness, but on the contrary, stimulates further frustration and pain.[9]

The basic assumption around which a Four's character is built, then, is the sense that who they are fails to measure up to how they ought to be. In this conviction we can feel the echoes of Four's heart point, Ennea-type One. Rather than attempting as Ones do to become better people, they are resigned to their fundamental bereftness and badness. Goodness seems to reside outside, something that others are and that others possess, something that it is hopeless for a Four to attempt to find within himself or herself. Turning their attention outside of themselves, they long to acquire, take in, incorporate whatever looks like goodness, in a perpetually melancholic—because hopeless—stance.

With a Four's conviction of inner badness and of lack, the good that she does take in from others never can satisfy her for very long. Inevitably, there doesn't seem to be enough of it to fill and satisfy her or it didn't turn out to be as advertised, and so a Four's yearning is perpetuated. So is her self-image of being someone whose hopes are never realized, whose desires are never fulfilled. Others seem to have the happiness that eludes her—the perfect partner, the satisfying life. The grass out there upon which she focuses remains eternally more verdant elsewhere.

Envy is intimately connected with a Four's central defense mechanism of introjection. As Naranjo says in this regard,

> *We may say that the bad self-image of type IV is the direct expression of an introjected self-rejecting parent and that an envious neediness results from the chronic self-hate entailed by such an introject—the need of external approval and love being in the nature of a need to compensate for the inability to love oneself.*[10]

As we have seen, the inner sense of scarcity coupled with badness propels a Four's envy. But this is clearly not their exclusive domain. It is something that we all contend with. Envy is based on the premise that another has something that we don't, and that that thing they possess, whether an actual object or a personal attribute or quality, is superior to what we have. Sometimes when we envy another, we are perceiving a real characteristic or possession of another, but sometimes we are simply projecting something of our own nature. In both cases, we see that thing out there as better than what we have.

Envy, then, is a response to disparity and discrepancy. Comparative judgment, inherited as it were from Four's heart point, One, is involved. One thing is better than another. What we consider as goodness exists in one place and not another. One of us has it, and the other doesn't, and when we are engaged in envy, that good thing exists outside of ourselves. Implicitly, there is a preference for what we have judged as better, and added to that is the judgment that what we have is inferior. Once this judgment is made, we turn away from, reject, and essentially hate who we are and what we have.

We hunger for that other, better thing that resides outside of ourselves, coming from the belief—real or imagined—that we don't have it, and at the same time, that we need it but cannot get it. Our envy, then, is driven by a voracious dearth, a yawning emptiness. What adds maliciousness to envy is both the sense of unfairness about not possessing it and the despair that we cannot learn, develop, or acquire that superior thing. We feel a sense of hopelessness about having it as our own. It will perpetually reside outside of ourselves. This is terribly frustrating, to long for something and feel at the same time complete despair about ever getting it. This leads us to feel hostility toward what we consider goodness. We start to hate the source of our envy, because it makes us feel so devastatingly lacking and helpless to do anything about it.

According to some of the psychologists who believe that envy is innate—including Klein, Otto Kernberg, and Carl Jung—the origin of envy lies in the simple fact that to an infant the source of sustenance and love resides outside of itself, in the mother's breast. As the Jungian-oriented Ann and Barry Ulanov write in their interesting book about envy, *Cinderella and Her Sisters: The Envied and the Envying,*

> *We do not just admire it {the good} and receive it gratefully; we look*
> *upon it with hostility because the source of our comfort, food, and love orig-*

inates outside of ourselves. Like the demonic archetype personified as Satan, we turn away from the source precisely because we are not it. Envy extinguishes gratitude.[11]

This extinguishing of gratitude is the spoiling of the good that Klein refers to, and which we will return to later.

Other psychologists such as Heinz Kohut, D. W. Winnicott, and Leslie Farber see the origin of envy in disruptions in the relationship with the mother. The infant's needs are not accurately attuned to, resulting in overfeeding, in deprivation, or in cycles of both. According to the Ulanovs,

> *The child's instinctual hunger and accompanying fantasies remain unsatisfied and split off from the psyche, thus forming those pockets of unconscious envy and rage that siphon off energy and inhibit growth. If a child gets stuck at this level of anger and frustration, then envy takes the form of a voracious hunger, needing to be concealed even from the child itself, severely repressed to keep its ego from being entirely overwhelmed. Such envy, suffered unconsciously rather than acknowledged, makes one feel an eternal victim, the left-out menial sitting in the ashes, overworked and underappreciated, with a paranoid conviction that others always get more than oneself.*[12]

Rather than acknowledge dependency on goodness outside of ourselves, we turn to envy of it. In this, we see envy's connection to pride. As the Ulanovs continue,

> *We can also see why pride stands alongside envy, occupying the highest place in the list of Seven Deadly Sins that dates back to medieval times. Pride means, "I am the Good. I don't need you to give it to me. I am altogether self-sufficient." The undoing of envious pride and phantom self-sufficiency follows up on our acknowledgment of the fact of dependence. Winnicott says, with his usual eloquent brevity: "Gratitude is dependence that is acknowledged."*[13]

In this movement, we turn away from the source of satisfaction and fulfillment because we are not it and because we despair of gaining it. The irony is that envy is driven by a voracious hunger and yet stands in the way of satisfying it, condemning us to continue coveting when we are under its sway, and at the same time making us refuse to take in what it is that we covet.

As the psychoanalyst and contemporary teacher of psychology at Harvard Medical School Harold Boris understands envy, it is not so much particular qualities or possessions that we covet but rather the *wherewithal* to acquire them. As he eloquently puts it,

> *Envy is what in some measure the have-nots feel toward the haves. It arises out of a state of mind in which we scrutinize what others have in order to compare to what we ourselves possess. Through that other unwinking green-eyed monster, jealousy, our perturbed gaze goes to the intimacy others enjoy with one another, from which we are excluded. But when the eye of envy is agape, it is* the wherewithal out of which they have fashioned and enjoy *that intimacy that we canvass with awe or fear. Jealousy contemplates people in relation to one another in respect to who chooses whom; envy remarks only one's self and others as to who has what.*

The very fact that we don't have what we consider good is an indictment against us.

> *Not only do we feel deficient and defective and filled with hate but in our aloneness, by our aloneness, we feel diminished, even humiliated. Others, by comparison, seem comfortably above the fray—and this burnished supposition adds insult to our injury and exacerbates our pain. It is not just that we are left wanting: it is as if we are judged and found wanting. We whisper to ourselves that it doesn't matter, that we have what it takes, that what the other has is worthless or worse, so that we are not consumed by the covet of it.*[14]

He goes on to describe envy as a relationship. In the language we have been using, it is the emotion, the affect in an object relation in which the other is withholding from the self. When we are caught in this object relation, we refuse to take in the good.

This refusal to take in the positive is what led Melanie Klein to begin her groundbreaking exploration of envy in the first place. She was attempting to understand why it was that some people refused to be healed in therapy. The Ulanovs describe the stance of such a patient as, "I want the analysis to work and I don't want it to work because you might get credit for it."[15] The therapist would be seen as good and the patient inevitably as bad. One of the keys to understanding envy, then, is the idealized good splitting away from the persecutory bad. The one who envies is the bad, deficient one and the envied is the perfect, good one. Rather than dealing with whole people, then, both the envied or the envying become abstracted, rendered all good or all bad.

We see this aspect of envy dramatically operating internationally in the curious phenomenon of hatred that those receiving aid feel toward the more affluent countries who help them—biting the hand that feeds, as the saying goes. Currently the West, and in particular the United States, the most prosperous of countries, are the objects of the wrath of the have-not societies. Those who rid Iraq of its despot in the early twenty-first century became themselves targets in what one might suppose would be a grateful nation. While the pros and cons of this "liberation" can undoubtedly be debated, it is also clear that envy plays a large part in the enmity currently being displayed in the Muslim and Third World.

No discussion of envy would be complete without discussing Freud's concept of penis envy, his premise that little girls are discontent with their own genitals and are angry that they don't have a phallus, and covet one. He saw this disappointment and sense of inferiority as the basis of femininity, and chronologically placed the emergence of penis envy during the oedipal phase, from two and a half to six years of age. Most psychologists have subsequently come to see that gender identification begins in the first year of life, and that while there may be a period between eighteen and twenty-four months of age in which toddlers become aware of gender differences and penis envy arises, for most females it is a passing phase. Disruptions in mother-child interactions may lead to a more generalized sense of a lack of self-worth and in turn, a devaluing of one's genitals. This can lead to envy of those of the opposite sex—not simply for little girls but for little boys as well. Breast envy is considered the equivalent to penis envy for little boys, along with envy of their father's larger penis.

This is the psychological theory. In practice, none of us escaped childhood without some degree of disruption in our relationships with our mothers, resulting in various sorts of psychological issues and various kinds of envy. That's what having a personality structure is all about. (This does not contradict the fact that some of us emerge into adulthood more disturbed than others, depending both on constitutional factors and actual childhood vicissitudes.) Like all of the passions, envy is rooted in an inner sense of lack or emptiness, which, as we have seen, is implicit in being identified with our personality structure. Our personality forms around the basic premise that we are a separate person, and as we have seen, this creates an inner sense of emptiness, which later we experience as the various deficiency states. The personality or ego is a mental construct, shaped out of our experiences and our history, defining us as such-and-such a person who has been through such-and-such experiences and so feels and behaves in these ways and not those ways. This construct that is our sense of self limits and encloses all of the vastness of our potentiality, limits our access to the rest of reality outside of our delimiting beliefs about who we are and what reality is like. It also generates the conviction that the source of gratification, goodness, satisfaction, and fulfillment resides outside of ourselves, just as our mothers did.

If we are identified with our personality structure, we are ipso facto disconnected from what we experience as goodness—our True Nature. Inevitably, when we are identified with this construct, there is an emptiness at the core of us, since the spaciousness and vastness of our nature has been fenced in. Like any creature kept in a cage, we feel confined and separated from our natural habitat and inevitably feel that something basic is lacking. We tell ourselves that we are fundamentally bad, and this is the reason we are so deprived. We acclimate to our limited circumstances, and often console ourselves with believing our confinement is the best we can hope for. Most of us tend to long for what is beyond our particular enclosure, believing that if we were in a different situation or had the trappings that another possesses, or that if we simply were more like that other one over there who seems to have the fullness that we lack, then we would be content.

Returning to our old friend Freud, we find he was onto something: our gender identity is intimately tied up with our sense of self, and as long as we are identified with our personality structure, our relationship to our own genitals and to the opposite sex will be disrupted. In varying degrees, the emptiness at the core of our personality structure will lead to character traits that are based on difficulty contacting and taking in the good, and in turn that translate into difficulty experiencing the fullness and completeness of our own gender identity. This leads to character traits rooted in envy of the opposite sex.

If we are female, we might avoid our emptiness by becoming promiscuous in an attempt to take in the good genitally, or we might be only attracted to those already in a relationship in an attempt to take the goodness away from another. We might develop a phallic character style, becoming pushy, bossy, and needing to dominate in an attempt to act out the goodness that we unconsciously believe is possessed by the opposite sex. Or we might blame men for our sense of deficiency, believing that they have taken it from us.

If we are male, we might need to put women down in various ways, unconsciously blaming them for the inner sense of lack that we experience. This is undoubtedly the psychology behind some men's need to relegate women to second-class status, a dynamic played out globally in centuries of patriarchy, which we are slowly moving out of in the West. Likewise, if we are male, our sense of being a have-not often leads us to translate that sense into the conscious or unconscious sizing up and envying of another's supposedly larger genitalia, regardless of what sex that person is.

We have seen that envying involves splitting others and ourselves in our minds into all good and all bad. When we envy another, we are in one movement idealizing the other and what they have, and rejecting ourselves and what we have. We and they cease to be whole people but become split up into parts. When we envy another, we do not see them in the context of being a whole individual with difficulties, gifts, existential dilemmas. They or parts of them simply become idealized as the good, and that is all we see. The Latin root of the word *envy* is *invidere,* which means "to look upon." The eyes of envy, then, look upon another—but covetously and with malice. We do not see another in their entirely, nor do we see ourselves as a whole being. We and they become depersonalized.

Instead of seeing another in their own right and in their own terms, we see them relative to ourselves, and when we envy, we always come up short. We are rejecting ourselves and refusing to inhabit our own experience. We want to substitute the experience of the other, over there, who matches our ideal image. As the Ulanovs describe it,

> *When we envy we are not willing to find and live with our own self, with all the hard and nasty work that that involves. Instead we want to seize another more glittering self. We may severely damage other persons with this violent thrust at their being, but more seriously, we refuse what is our own. We hunger and desire to be a person of substance, but we are unwilling to nurture the only substance we can ever possess—our own. Because ours is so dim to us, we seize on what others have that is clearly visible and try to grab it from those who did in fact welcome it and give it room to grow. In our unwillingness to accept what is really our own, we do not want the other person to have anything either. So a piece of music or a poem another has written becomes a mere product to be imitated, no longer an expression of a whole human life struggling to articulate a vision. A beauty of face becomes no more than a surface appearance, a fashion to ape, never a presentation of a particular self where face and clothes mirror soul. Talent becomes an acquisition, a means to power, ease, or fame, no longer rooted in a person's way of life or expressing multiple and subtle choices and sacrifices to develop particular gifts.*

And most importantly,

> *When we envy we almost always miss what is our own, for we are never at the place where we are but only where the other is.*[16]

Which brings us to what is needed to work through our envy—the virtue of this point, equanimity. Equanimity literally means "with equal mind," and has come to connote emotional balance, even when under stress. This balance is only possible when we bear all of ourselves with an equal mind and heart. Envy is the movement of abandoning ourselves when we do not fit an inner picture of how we think we are supposed to be, and grasping after those qualities in another. Equanimity is an openness to the whole of ourselves. This means forsaking the ideal images in our minds, instead of deserting and discarding ourselves.

The following is Ichazo's definition of this virtue:

> It is balance. A whole being lives in complete harmony with his environment. His moves are economical and always appropriate to his circumstances. He is not emotionally affected by external stimuli but responds to them exactly as much as is necessary.

This is only possible when we do not measure ourselves against others and don't take what we encounter in life personally, as a statement about us, but rather take it on its own terms.

Equanimity is considered in Buddhism one of the marks of enlightenment—in fact, the highest one. The word for it in Pali is *upekkha,* coming from the Sanskrit word *upeksha,* with *upa-* meaning "over" and *–iksh* meaning "to look." It means, then, to see from the broadest panorama, from the highest view, in contrast to the nearsightedness of envy. It means getting the big picture of things, and with this view, everything falls into perspective. As the contemporary Buddhist meditation teacher Sharon Salzberg writes of upekkha,

> The four boundless states that we call the brahma-viharas or divine abodes culminate with equanimity. In Pali equanimity is called upekkha, which means "balance," and its characteristic is to arrest the mind before it falls into extremes. Equanimity is a spacious stillness of mind, a radiant calm that allows us to be present fully with all the different changing experiences that constitute our world and our lives.[17]

In Buddhism, upekkha is sometimes translated as "serenity," but in the language of the enneagram, although closely related—since One is the heart point of Four—they are not the same thing. Serenity has to do with allowing reality and our experience to be as it is, without adding to it a value judgment of good or bad. Rather than standing against what we have decided is wrong and attempting to make it right, when our soul is informed by the virtue of serenity we are without aggression toward what we encounter inwardly or outwardly. Equanimity, on the other hand, literally means "with equal mind." The emphasis here is not so much on a lack of aggression toward reality, but on a lack of covetousness. When we are equanimous, we are in a state of emotional balance, which begins with a balanced view of ourselves and others. When our soul is informed by equanimity, there is no attempt to move away from our experience and ourselves, and to incorporate what looks better to us. Equanimity at its core is a heart quality. As the meditation teachers Joseph Goldstein and Jack Kornfield say in their book on insight meditation, "Equanimity is developed as we learn to keep our heart open through the changing circumstances of our life and practice."[18]

Only when we are able to open to our changing states, when we are able to take in the whole of ourselves, to see and be with it all just as it is, are we able to do the same with others. When we can perceive and appreciate the entirety of others, we are at peace with them and can live in harmony with them. Otherwise we are divided within ourselves, and our relationship to others can only be likewise divisive. Our inner atmosphere is then stormy, filled with emotional reactivity in which we are pulling away from one thing and yearning for another, and our envy of others is simply its externalization. When we envy, our hearts are closed both to ourselves and to the envied. We are filled with malice and hatred, and the very act of envying blocks us from taking in the goodness that we long for.

Without openness and appreciation toward whatever we consider goodness, we are caught in a vicious cycle of hungering for goodness while at the same time being unable to take it in. Klein saw the resolution of envy as gratitude, which she viewed as gratefulness for enjoyment and its source. Our capacity to appreciate and take in the goodness of another and of what life presents us with depends upon ceasing to see it as an object doled out to some and not to others. It requires seeing goodness as something implicit in our nature itself.

When we are able to rejoice and delight in the beauty, brilliance, abundance, or development of another, we are acknowledging it as part of the wholeness that we are. We lose our separateness, and what we consider goodness ceases to be a commodity that some have and others don't but rather is part of the fabric of the whole. As the Ulanovs put it,

> *Envying or being envied shows the good as a commodity to be possessed and ourselves as the happy potential owner of the prize or its potential would-be robber. When we correspond to goodness, and put the parts together, we see that goodness is not an object but an inner integrity, not a predictable thing guaranteed to make us happy, but a relationship with something alive and responsive to small specific events in our lives. Goodness is not a norm or set of rules which we fall short of achieving and then blame ourselves for failing, but a radiance making perceptible the essential being of all things, no matter how trivial.*[19]

Like all of the virtues, developing equanimity begins within our moment-to-moment experience. Our relationship to our own internal process—to the constantly changing kaleidoscope of thoughts, feelings, and sensations—is where equanimity starts. The very attitude of equanimity—not valuing one experience over another—allows us to be with the whole of our experience, and in so doing, to experience our wholeness. Ceasing to relate from within the object relation fundamental to envy—that of the haves and the have-nots—necessitates being open to whatever it is that we have. Only when we can be with what we have, which starts with being with whatever experience is presenting itself within and without, are we receptive to allowing anything in. Our very attitude of openness to whatever we have—our equanimity—aligns us with our deepest nature, since it is the totality of all things. Our receptivity of heart connects us with the beneficence of our nature, the source of all that exists, and as we touch it, our hunger is answered, our soul is transformed.

—∿— We have explored the passions and virtues of those points that relate directly to our self-image and to living on the surface of ourselves—the image corner. Each of the passions of these points is based upon our mistaken sense of identity, the belief that we *are* our personality. This belief, as we have seen, is the core self-deception (the passion of Point Three) that is primary to the issues raised at these three points. Hence, the passions of Points Two and Four are differentiations of that of Point Three. The virtues of all three points are likewise rooted in getting real about our true situation, and are—as are all the virtues—pivotal in our inner work.

As our exploration of these points concludes, we turn now to those of the fear corner of the enneagram.

THE
FEAR
CORNER

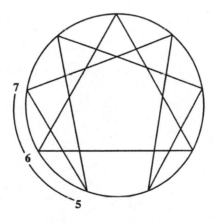

DIAGRAM 12

CHAPTER 8

POINT SIX—
FEAR *and*
COURAGE

*Be vigilant, and allow no one to mislead you
by saying:
"Here it is!" or
"There it is!"
For it is within you
that the Son of Man dwells.*

—FROM *THE GOSPEL OF
MARY MAGDALENE*[1]

Our lives today in the West are, by and large, far less centered around survival than in previous eras in which having enough to eat depended entirely on Mother Nature's
whims, and when lawlessness was more the rule than the
exception. While we moderns, for the most part, no
longer have as a central focus of our lives where we will
find food and shelter as our ancient ancestors did, this has
not diminished our fear. Instead of being worried about
acquiring the means for sustenance, we now worry about
not destroying ourselves. As we begin our exploration of
the passions and virtues of the fear corner of the enneagram, we turn our attention to this very human experience of fright in its many forms, which forms the central
thread of all three of these points.

Our technology has proliferated exponentially since the so-called Age of Enlightenment in the eighteenth century, leading to the industrialization of the nineteenth and globalization of the twentieth centuries. This double-edged sword has given us the power to not only radically improve our quality of life but has also at this point become a threat to our very existence. As we move into the twenty-first century, we stand on the edge of being able to live in space and colonize other planets, as well as to decimate the ecological balance and the environment on this one. We have the power, in the form of atomic and hydrogen bombs, weapons of mass destruction, and biological warfare to destroy ourselves many times over. Improvements in medicine and diet are allowing us to live far longer than our ancestors could dream of, and while this has made sixty the new thirty in some people's minds, overpopulation is one of the biggest threats to the survival of our species.

Hand in hand with this technological explosion has come the receding in our consciousness of the centrality of the numinous, of a transcendent reality many refer to as God or the Divine. In counterpoint to the ascent of scientific knowledge in the eighteenth century, religious authority declined as the arbiter of what is real. The Church and so God slowly lost their central place in our understanding of reality, and science's mechanistic understanding of life as well as of ourselves led to an increasing soullessness. Industrialization led to individuals becoming only specks in the masses of humanity, and modern and postmodern life, with all of its sophistication and physical comforts, has become increasingly bereft of a sense of profundity and significance.

Ample grounds, indeed, for a new, improved postmodern version of survival anxiety. The existential philosophers of the early twentieth century—Heidegger, Camus, and Sartre, to name a few—made the German word *Angst* part of our vocabulary, signifying the fear and dread that characterize the modern psyche. Civilization has allowed us an ease of life unknown in ancient times, yet are we any less afraid? All of our increased stability and security has not diminished to any significant degree the amount of anxiety experienced by most people. *Fear,* then, the passion of Point Six, far from being eradicated, has only had a face-lift.

While fear is the central emotional atmosphere of Ennea-type Sixes, as we are seeing, you don't have to be a Six to be afraid. Fear is one of the underpinnings of postmodern life, and as long as we are identified with our personality structure, we live in fear. We will further explore this point later. Many people who study the enneagram erroneously decide that they are Sixes because of the degree of fear, anxiety, worry, distrust, and doubt that they live with, but each of the nine types has its own kind of fear and all nine can be seen as different responses to survival anxiety. This is because whenever we are disconnected from our inner ground—the ground of Being—we are insecure.* This is a natural law. What determines our type, from the perspective highlighted at Point Six of the enneagram— that of fear—is the question of *what* we are afraid of.

If we are afraid of creating conflict by making ourselves or our needs too obvious, it is likely that we are a Nine. If we are afraid that there is something fundamentally wrong with us or that who we are is not enough or good enough, it is likely that we are a One. If we are afraid of rejection, being needy, and of not being loved, it is likely we are a Two. If we are afraid of failure, it is likely we are a Three. If we are afraid of being abandoned, of our sadness, and of feeling lost, it is likely we are a Four. If we are afraid of entanglements and of losing what we have, it is likely we are a Five. If we are afraid of boredom, of grunt work, and of being exposed as a charlatan, it is likely we are a Seven. If we are afraid of being weak and not being in charge or on top of things, it is likely we are an Eight. If, on the other hand, we are simply afraid of everything and everyone to one degree or another, if fear itself in a nameless, faceless way is the driving force of our psyche, then it is likely that we are a Six.

Likewise, the life arena around which our fear is based is that associated with our instinctual subtype. While the root of all fear is our instinct for self-preservation, the two other instincts used in the map of the enneagram refract out of that fundamental instinct in the same way that all of the ennea-types can be seen as refractions of the principle of sleep or

---

*Almaas's book *Facets of Unity* is based on the premise that all of the ennea-types arise in reaction to the loss of contact with Being in early childhood, particularly with the dimension of Being in which we experience unconditional love and holding, supporting a sense of trust and security in the soul. This dimension is referred to in the various traditions as that of cosmic or divine love, in which the universe is experienced as beneficent and loving. Each of the types, then, is based on a lack of basic trust in life, the world, and reality in general.

ignorance at Point Nine. This means that those of us in whom the social subtype predominates feel that we will not survive unless we are part of the group, while those of the sexual subtype believe deep down that our survival is assured only through intimate relationship.

If our fear primarily revolves around concerns about livelihood and sustenance, we are likely to be a self-preservation subtype. Worries and insecurity about our physical safety, income, our home environment, food, and the health of our body are forefront for those of this subtype. If our fear has to do with our social standing, our degree of prestige, our sense of belonging, and of having friends, we are most likely a social subtype. Feeling socially insecure, afraid of being left out, and needing status dominate for those of this subtype. If our fear has to do with whether or not we are loved by a special someone and whether or not we are sexually attractive to others, we are most likely a sexual subtype. Concerns about closeness, intimacy, pleasure, and sexuality itself dominate for those of this subtype.

While all of us experience some degree of fear about some area of our lives, the Six personality style is the quintessential fear type, as we see by its location at the center of the fear corner of the enneagram. The ennea-types of its wings, Seven and Five, are also fear types—they are oriented around different responses to existential fear, which is at the forefront for each of these types. For Sixes, fear itself is the central preoccupation, even if it is functioning unconsciously. It is the driving force of their personality, with the possibility of physical annihilation seeming to lurk just behind the next corner. This may sound rather extreme, but if we explore a Six's psyche closely, it is indeed how things feel to him or her—again, not necessarily consciously. The basic mind-set is that the world is a dangerous place and that one's survival is by no means assured. A Six feels ill equipped to deal with life's vicissitudes, and so is hypervigilant, on anxious lookout for where the presumed threat might come from. Sixes tend to have a wired, furtive, and insecure aspect about them, as though they are perpetually on guard. They are, as Almaas puts it, defensively suspicious, with "an alert, paranoid kind of suspiciousness, always being on the look-out for danger."[2]

As those familiar with the enneagram know, there are two types of Sixes: those identified with their fear—phobic types—and those identified with countering their fear and proving that they are not afraid—

counterphobic types. The latter may look strong and powerful, but the amount of energy they put into demonstrating how courageous and unafraid of risks and challenges they are belies their fear orientation. Phobic Sixes appear timid, uncertain, hesitant, fearful, and furtive; and frequently seek out strong authority figures or belief systems that they can devote themselves to as a way of assuaging their uncertainty. Likewise, counterphobic Sixes come across as decisive, firm, pugnacious, and argumentative, and often find themselves opposing those in authority and debunking prevailing trends of thought. They are frequently mistaken for Eights, but lack the Eight's self-assured indomitability, and instead appear aggressively suspicious, belligerent, and defensive in their attempt to prove that they are not afraid and don't feel vulnerable. As Naranjo says of the counterphobic Six in relation to the passion of fear,

> . . . we need to point out, as in the case of anger and other emotions, that this important emotional state need not be directly manifested in behavior. It may be, alternatively, manifest in the over-compensation of a conscious attitude of heroic striving. The counter-phobic denial of fear is no different in essence from the covering up of anger through excessive gentleness and control, the covering up of selfishness through excessive yielding, and other forms of compensation manifested throughout the range of characters, particularly in some of the sub-ennea-types.[3]

Naranjo, in recent years, has equated the phobic Six with the self-preservation subtype, the counterphobic with the sexual subtype, and has added a third type of Six, equated with the social subtype. This third type he describes as a "'Prussian character' in reference to the stereotype of dutiful and authoritarian German rigidity."[4] This type of Six is rule bound and humorless, legalistic and controlled, substituting adherence to external guidelines for an inner sense of guidance and confidence. While it is not clear to me that these three types of Sixes neatly correspond to the instinctual subtypes, Sixes do have one of these character styles as dominant in their personality.

Regardless of the subtype or dominant style of a Six, their personality structure revolves around fear. Convinced that the world is an unsafe and hostile environment and that others are driven by selfishness, Sixes—until they have done a great deal of inner work—are fixed in their cynical perspective that goodness and supportiveness not only are unobtainable but don't really exist. They tend to doubt the positive, not with an open attitude of finding out whether or not it exists and is reliable but with a prejudice that it does not. Not only do they doubt the positive outside of themselves but perhaps even more distressingly within themselves as well. They doubt their motivations, question their impulses, and are basically afraid of their inner reality, experiencing it as deceptive and untrustworthy. This is particularly true of that seat of preconceptual instinctual drives, the id; and so they typically have a fearful attitude toward what is arising spontaneously from within them, particularly if it is aggressive or sexual. It is their conviction of the unreliability of themselves, others, and the world that gives them a peculiar kind of certainty, but one that leaves them in an underlying state of fear and anxiety.

All of us, to the extent that we are identified with our personality, share the Six's cynicism about reality and its resulting passion of fear. This attitude or fixed perspective and its consequential affective atmosphere is simply another of the building blocks for the foundation of the personality, regardless of what ennea-type we are. So it is important for all of us to understand the nature of our fear.

The subject of anxiety was crucial in Freud's theories of neurosis, since he viewed neurotic symptoms as attempts to cope with it, or "bind" it. Anxiety, then, he saw as the central problem of neurosis. Because of its centrality in psychoanalytic thought, his perceptions are very helpful in our understanding of this passion. Freud evolved an understanding over time, believing at first that all anxiety could be traced to inadequately discharged libido, or sexual energy. In his second theory of anxiety, elucidated in 1926, he saw anxiety as a survival mechanism, warning us of impending danger, both internal and external, which allows us to take action to avoid it. While Freud's focus on repressed sexuality as the core of most psychological problems—which it might well have been in the culture he lived within—is no longer considered accurate by most psychologists, many of his deductions about how we function still have great validity.

Freud made a distinction between fear and anxiety. As he says,

Anxiety [Angst] *has an unmistakable relation to* expectation: *it is anxiety* about *something. It has a quality of* indefiniteness and lack of object. *In precise speech, we use the term "fear"* [Furcht] *rather than "anxiety"* [Angst] *if it has found an object.*[5]

In both cases, he saw that these affects are responses to what we consider danger, meaning something that we believe might harm us. Fear, then, refers to an unpleasant anticipation of a realistic external danger whose source we are consciously aware of. Confusing things a bit, he called this fear "realistic anxiety" since it is objective and reality based. Anxiety, on the other hand, is the sense of an internal danger whose source we are not conscious of, and he refers to this as "neurotic anxiety." As he continues,

Real danger is a danger that is known, and realistic anxiety is anxiety about a known danger of this sort. Neurotic anxiety is anxiety about an unknown danger. Neurotic anxiety is thus a danger that has still to be discovered.

We might be afraid as our car skids on an icy road, for instance, or while walking down a dark street in a bad neighborhood; while on the other hand, we might experience free-floating neurotic anxiety without knowing exactly why it is arising when walking into a room of strangers, for instance, or while contemplating not going to work. Freud believed that neurotic anxiety is an inner signal that something we consider dangerous is threatening to arise in our consciousness, primarily some forbidden aggressive or sexual—id—desire.

He saw that there are two reactions to real danger: experiencing anxiety and taking protective action to avoid the danger. If we are afraid of something, we do what we can to defend ourselves. Likewise, Freud postulated that in neurotic anxiety, we experience anxiety and try to master or bind it to protect ourselves. Also, as he says,

In some cases the characteristics of realistic anxiety and neurotic anxiety are mingled. The danger is known and real but the anxiety in regard to it is over-great, greater than seems proper to us. It is this surplus of anxiety that betrays the presence of a neurotic element.[6]

Anxiety, then, is a warning signal to the organism that danger is present, and he believed that this is its evolutionary function, supporting our capacity for self-preservation. Sometimes, however, our response to anxiety is paralysis rather than withdrawing from the danger. In this case, Freud saw the presence of neurosis, and attempted to understand why.

Pursuing the question of what we regard as dangerous situations, Freud came to the conclusion that we perceive danger when our own strength is outweighed by the threat. We feel helpless in the face of it, either physically if the danger is external or psychically if the danger is arising from the id, the seat of our instincts. He referred to such situations of helplessness as traumatic situations. Traumatic situations are experiences that overload our system with too much stimuli for us to master or to discharge, and they automatically trigger anxiety. Freud saw us being particularly susceptible to trauma in infancy and early childhood when we are so helpless physically and our ego is so unformed.

In our early years, realistic anxiety arises frequently, since we lack the physical means to perceive, anticipate, and get rid of an external danger. Also, until our ego structure develops, we are easily overwhelmed with stimuli that we cannot cope with or contain, which Freud saw as giving rise to anxiety. As an infant and young child, for instance, prolonged separation from our mother, or the absence of food or love are traumatic. Inner demands are not being met and we are helpless to do anything about them, and such situations fill us with anxiety. Such situations impact us deeply. From the perspective of the soul, before our psychic structure is fully developed, our consciousness is the most open and therefore vulnerable during our early years. This is why the events that occur during these years leave such strong impressions on our souls, and in response to which our ego structure develops.

The prototype of such experiences Freud saw as the *birth trauma*, in which we are suddenly overwhelmed by stimuli that we have been protected from within the womb. A number of psychologists, including Otto Rank, extended Freud's thinking about birth trauma, seeing it as the source of neurosis. Freud himself, while originally receptive to the idea, came to feel that it was inaccurate and in the course of thinking it through, entirely revised his understanding of anxiety. Following in Rank's footsteps, in the latter part of the twentieth century a number of New Age therapies emerged that aim at re-experiencing our birth and working through whatever trauma remains from it in the hope of resolving our neuroses. Like Freud, I think that our situation is much more complicated than this, and while such work may have benefits for some, it does not appear to be the ultimate panacea.

Situations in which we are overloaded with stimuli that we cannot cope with—traumas—occur in some form or other for most of us in our early years, but they are not confined to childhood. Trauma can occur throughout our lives, brought about by events like natural disasters; being in an automobile, train, or plane accident; losing a loved one; or being in combat. Any situation in our adult lives that triggers emotions that we can neither master nor discharge, and as such threatens to reduce us to an infantile state, triggers anxiety. We now speak of posttraumatic stress symptoms, and have developed therapies for working with them.

Freud believed that all of our adult fears that are not reality based harken back to our early experiences of helplessness in the face of danger. Neurotic anxiety, then, is the triggering of the memory of realistic anxiety: whenever a situation in life arises that is similar to one we experienced as traumatic, signal anxiety arises, warning us of the immanence of danger so that we can avoid it. When faced with such situations, we unconsciously experience ourselves as the helpless young one who first experienced a similar trauma. Too much trauma can be debilitating, but on the other hand, if we have been overprotected as a child, this identification with our helplessness is also exacerbated, as we see in Freud's observation:

> *The undesirable result of 'spoiling' a small child is to magnify the importance of the danger of losing the object (the object being a protection against every situation of helplessness) in comparison with every other danger. It therefore encourages the individual to remain in the state of childhood, the period of life which is characterized by motor and psychical helplessness.*[7]

We saw that Freud connected neurotic anxiety with instinctual demands that threaten to overwhelm the person's ego. Inner urges when expressed or acted upon early in a person's life that were responded to with punishment or a withdrawal of love came to be seen as dangerous ones. Neurotic anxiety manifests in free-floating apprehensiveness, in which a person seems afraid of everything, including themselves, and lives in fear of something dreadful happening. At the core, such anxiety is the fear that unacceptable instinctual drives—aggressive or sexual—will overcome the ego's defenses and that he or she will lose control and be helplessly driven by them. Although the danger usually seems to be out-side of themselves, what such people are really afraid of is their own id. This is clearly the case with phobic Sixes—they are afraid of and thus vic-timized by their disowned drives.

A second way that neurotic anxiety manifests is in phobias—intense, irrational fears that are way out of proportion to the actual danger they present. Some people have phobias about snakes, spiders, mice, open spaces, closed spaces, crowds, deep water, heights, flying or driving, to name just a few. Freud postulated that the thing one is afraid of is or rep-resents something that the person unconsciously wants but cannot allow, primarily either something having to do with sexual or aggressive in-stincts, including in the latter his postulated death instinct. Fear of heights, for instance, might represent a secret desire to jump. Fear of snakes is typically seen by Freudians as a forbidden fascination with and desire for the penis. Fear of knives is interpreted as a taboo desire to attack someone. Fear of being raped might indicate a secret wish for being sexu-ally dominated.

In such cases, the memory of punishment as a child for either the sex-ual or aggressive urge involved in the phobia maintains its forbidden and frightening quality. What we are phobic about, then, triggers in our un-conscious both the instinctual urge and the remembered repercussions when we went for it as a child. This naturally makes us afraid of that ob-ject, since it represents taboo temptation as well as recrimination. In this way, this form of neurotic anxiety is based on the memory of realistic anx-iety—acting on this urge historically put us in what we experienced at the time as a dangerous situation with our early caretakers.

While this seems accurate in many cases, in others, phobias do not ap-pear to be expressions of warded-off desire but rather seem to be based on early traumatic experiences with what one is afraid of. Getting stuck in an elevator as a child, for instance, can lead to a lifelong fear of them. Or having been attacked by dogs when young can lead to a deep apprehension of them. In such cases, the memory of traumatic reality anxiety leaves a deep imprint on the soul.

A third kind of neurotic anxiety is expressed in panic behavior, in which we act out some form of aberrant behavior with no apparent provocation. From time to time we hear about instances of wealthy people shoplifting or of someone going berserk and shooting others for no apparent reason. We might experience such behavior ourselves in a more innocuous form when we blurt something out that we had not meant to say to someone, usually something hostile or lascivious. In these cases, impulses are being acted out as a way of discharging the tension and anxiety involved in holding them back. While we might feel terrible for letting such behaviors slip out, when this happens we often feel a sense of relief, a sense that the pressure has been released internally.

Freud saw that what we are afraid of changes at different stages in our early life:

> *If we dwell on these situations of danger for a moment, we can say that in fact a particular determinant of anxiety (that is, a situation of danger) is allotted to every age of development as being appropriate to it. The danger of psychical helplessness fits the stage of the ego's early immaturity; the danger of loss of an object (or loss of love) fits the lack of self-sufficiency in the first years of childhood; the danger of being castrated fits the phallic phase; and finally fear of the super-ego, which assumes a special position, fits the period of latency.*

The fear of castration isn't one that everyone these days agrees actually arises in children. The sexualization of the oedipal period seems to many, including myself, to be an aberration rather than the norm, and the corresponding fear of loss of the genitals as retribution for attraction to the parent of the opposite sex likewise seems to be the exception rather than the rule. It may be that the more narcissistically oriented a person's personality structure is, the more this type of experience occurs.

While particular fears are phase-appropriate, Freud saw that we do not entirely outgrow them. We typically unconsciously continue to experience these dangers as adults, and the degree to which this is so determines our degree of neurosis. While not the Freudian view, the reason for this is obviously that our egoic sense of self is made up of many self-images that formed at these different phases. As Freud continues,

> *In the course of development the old determinants of anxiety should be dropped, since the situations of danger corresponding to them have lost their importance owing to the strengthening of the ego. But this only occurs incompletely. Many people are unable to surmount the fear of loss of love; they never become sufficiently independent of other people's love and in this respect carry on their behaviour as infants. Fear of the super-ego should normally never cease, since, in the form of moral anxiety, it is indispensable in social relations, and only in the rarest cases can an individual become independent of human society.*[8]

Fear of the superego is the third type of anxiety Freud identified, which he called moral or social anxiety. It is the fear of not living up to our ego ideal. If we believe that our ego structure is necessary, then a superego is also. If, on the other hand, we have a spiritual orientation, the superego, as part of our ego structure, is something to move beyond, as we discussed in Chapter 4.

In the first generation of psychoanalysts coming after Freud, a new tradition began to develop in which interpersonal relationship rather than inner drives was seen as the determining developmental factor. One of the most influential and radical of these new psychoanalysts was Harry Stack Sullivan, who practiced from the 1920s through the '40s. He is important for our understanding of fear and anxiety since he gives us a very different perspective on them.

Like Freud, he discriminated between fear and anxiety. While experienced by the infant as the same thing, he saw their source being quite different. Quoting psychoanalysts Jay Greenberg and Stephen Mitchell on Sullivan's perspective, in their overview of the major psychoanalysts and psychoanalytic movements,

Fear is caused either by violent disturbances in perceptions (such as loud noises or cold) or dangers posed to the existence or biological integrity of the organism (hunger or pain); anxiety, in the highly specific manner in which Sullivan uses the term, is "caught" from caretakers. He suggests that anxiety in those around the infant is picked up, even if the anxiety has nothing to do with the infant per se.[9]

Without picking up anxiety from its caregivers, Sullivan postulated that an infant's development would proceed without any hitches. The most cataclysmic early experiences, he says, are those of escalating anxiety in which the infant or child "catches" its caretaker's anxiety, and becomes anxious itself, which in turn increases the caretaker's anxiety, and so on. In fact, rather than pain and pleasure being the organizing principle for experience (as in Freudian psychology), Sullivan says that it is formed around the distinction between anxious and nonanxious states. Experiences of "good mother" are experiences of nonanxious mother; experiences of "bad mother" are those of anxious mother.

The child learns to anticipate behaviors that evoke tenderness, approval, and calmness in the mothering person, and as a result make the child less anxious. These form the basis of the child's sense of "good-me." On the other hand, behaviors that make mother anxious and thus the child, form the sense of "bad-me." Those areas of personality that arouse extremely high anxiety in mother are almost unbearable for the child, who forms an amnesia about the behaviors leading to this state, and they remain unintegrated in the child's personality, dissociated and forming the sense of "not-me." Avoiding anxiety and finding security becomes the driving force in the personality, and as Greenberg and Mitchell tell us,

Thus, within Sullivan's system anxiety about anxiety is at the core of all psychopathology and constitutes the basic organizational principle of the self. Original experience with anxiety, because it entails such intense helplessness and passivity, leaves behind a residue of terror and generates a phobic attitude toward experiences of even mild degrees of anxiety. The self operates solely on the need for security, based on the principle that anxiety is to be avoided at all costs and that power, status, and prestige in one's own eyes and in the eyes of others is the broadest and surest route to safety.[10]

With such a focus on anxiety as central to the personality structure, Sullivan's view articulates clearly the perspective of our psychology from the Six perspective. It seems likely that the formation of the personality as he describes it resonates for Sixes, and at the same time it highlights aspects of psychological organization common to all of us.

Obviously, the personality's quest for security via prestige, status, and power rarely if ever resolves anyone's anxiety, and if it does, it does so only momentarily. The more prestige, status, and power we have, the more we end up worrying that we will lose them, and so our anxiety goads us on to greater and greater striving after them, creating a vicious cycle. Whenever we look outside of ourselves for security, our search becomes endless. We can live in a gated community, we can install elaborate alarm systems, we can invest in any number of insurance policies, and we can take preemptive action, attacking countries we believe are a threat to ours, but as we have seen in the wars in Vietnam and Iraq, such moves only lead us into a quagmire. This is because of the way that we function psychologically: with an inner reservoir of undigested anxiety left over from our childhoods, it is impossible to feel secure unless we work through it. What has shaped our personality structure is our insecurity, and so clearly the only solution is to work through that structure by opening up the fear contained within it. Rather than seeking security, then, the way through the fear is exploring our lack of security.

For many of us, questing after prestige, power, and status are not the main ways that we try to allay our fear and anxiety. This is the social subtype solution—or rather, its attempt at one. For self-preservation subtypes, safety is sought through physical and financial security, while for sexual types refuge from fear is sought through intimate relationship. Each of the ennea-types looks for safety and security in its own characteristic way—Nines through creating harmony, Ones through becoming perfect, Twos through being loved, Threes through success, Fours through not being left out, Fives through withdrawal, Sevens through plans about the future, and Eights through control and dominance.

I have, you will note, left out Sixes. This is because their quest for security embodies most purely and is the most expressive of the universal
tendency to look outside of ourselves for it. Sixes look to what they perceive as an outer pillar of strength to allay their anxiety, whether that rock
is someone in authority, or a philosophy, a religion, or other belief system.
Even counterphobic Sixes, who appear irreverent and antagonistic toward
authority, are nonetheless constellated around it. They remain in relationship with some sort of authority, deriving and supporting their sense of
self from their oppositionality to it.

The common thread, then, in all of the personality's attempts to find
refuge from fear, uncertainty, anxiety, and doubt is always by looking outside of itself. The rub is that we can never have enough outer supports in
place to make ourselves feel entirely safe because our insecurity is an internal matter once our basic needs for food and shelter have been covered.
While survival anxiety—the fear that arises when our survival is actually
at risk—is something that can only be resolved through obtaining what
we need to sustain ourselves from the outer world, this is not the anxiety
that objectively bedevils most of those likely to be reading this book. In
fact, the more physical comforts we have, the more anxiety we often feel.
This tells us that our insecurity, in Freudian terms, is mostly neurotic
rather than realistic.

Its resolution, then, is to be found within ourselves. This brings us to
the virtue of this point, *courage.* Ichazo's definition is the following:

> *It is the recognition of the individual's responsibility for his own exis-*
> *tence. In the position of courage, the body moves naturally to preserve itself.*

This points to the fact that security is to be found within ourselves, and
that what interferes the most with our capacity to take care of ourselves is
our anxiety. What does it mean to find security within ourselves? This is
not a matter of finding security in our bodies, which can get injured, become sick, and always die; nor in our abilities or our skills, since these are
just the expression of who we are. Rather, it lies in finding out what our
nature really is, and discovering that in *that* lies our only true safety.

It takes great courage to do things in our lives that might trigger what we fear the most, which we discussed earlier in this chapter in terms of our ennea-type and subtype. If we are a One, for instance, taking an action or showing something about ourselves that we don't consider perfect or even good requires great courage. If we are a Two, doing or saying something to someone important to us that poses the risk of losing their love and acceptance requires courageousness. And so on around the enneagram.

Our anxiety is often out of proportion to our actual situation, and it can inhibit and sometimes paralyze us from fully living. We hold ourselves back from plunging into our lives, from taking risks and immersing ourselves in our experience. We doubt and question, uncertain whether it is safe or not to fully enter into what presents itself, fully enter into ourselves and our direct experience. We are afraid of things outside of ourselves, but when we really explore it, it is mostly ourselves that we are afraid of. We are afraid of our wants and desires, afraid of our impulses, afraid of what will happen if we are spontaneous. We are afraid to be ourselves, for fear that we will not live up to our ego ideal or that our sexuality or our aggression will run away with us, as Freud described. We are afraid of triggering anxiety in others, as Sullivan tells us, and in turn increasing our own. We turn outward because we are afraid that there is nothing trustworthy inside of ourselves, nothing we can depend upon, and this forsaking of ourselves becomes a self-fulfilling prophecy: without being grounded in ourselves, we stand no chance of getting in touch with what is immutable, unchanging, and utterly dependable—our deepest nature.

The most difficult thing that a person can do is open to and explore their inner reality. Universally, courage is at its deepest level of meaning the courage to face ourselves. *Action,* the virtue of Point Nine, which is the heart point of Point Six, is implicit here. Instead of being externally directed, true action, as we have seen, is dividing our attention, with at least half of it focused inwardly, and exploring what we find within ourselves. Courage has to do with what it takes to pay attention to our inner reality, above and beyond overcoming the inertial pull of unconsciousness. We might think that courage is fearlessness, but the truest form of courage is not the absence of fear but rather facing what we need to face even though we remain afraid.

What is the nature of the fear that we must not be deflected by if we are to explore and thus transform our inner reality? The first level of it is risking the moral anxiety described by Freud: to pay attention to what is going on inside of us necessitates facing our own judgments about what we find. So the first big challenge in inner work is having the courage to cease simply going along with our superego's demands about how we should and shouldn't be, what's okay to feel and to think and what isn't, and to question these assumptions. This is a step that few of us actually take—challenging our beliefs about how we ought and ought not be. To do so feels like going against all of our conditioning—it means ceasing to go along with societal and familial mores and standards. And this can be very scary. It can feel as if we were going to lose our parents or step out of our culture, but this is not really the case. It *does* mean that we do so in our own minds. We let go of the voice of our authority figures, and this means moving out of our inner relationship with them in which we feel small and they seem big.

The next level of fear that confronts us as we journey inward has to do with our neurotic anxiety, in Freud's terminology. To understand this, we need to back up a little bit. Much of our fear is projected. Projection, as those familiar with the enneagram know, is the defense mechanism of Sixes. When we encounter a situation that realistically contains some danger to us of bodily harm or of a threat to our security and aspirations, the degree of fear that we experience is very often far greater than the actual situation warrants, as we saw earlier. When this occurs, we are overlaying the memory of situations in early childhood in which we felt helpless in relationship to some threat. This happens far more often than most of us care to recognize, and when it does, we unconsciously relate to the situation as though we were a frightened young child. Recognizing this, making it conscious, and working with the sense of self and other—the object relation—that the situation is triggering is where courage is needed here.

Another aspect of our projection has to do with projecting our own aggression. We often believe that others are more threatening and malevolent than they actually are, and for some of us, much of the fear we live with is based on this belief. When we explore this, we find that we have invested these menacing others with our own disavowed belligerence. We encounter this kind of projection of aggression and hostility whenever we lump together an ethnicity or a nationality and perceive them en masse as the bad guys or the enemy. Individuals lose their separateness and are folded into our internal sense of a menacing and potentially harmful other. It is really our own aggression and hatred that we are seeing in them when we do this. This disowning of some of these less savory and "uncivilized" emotions and drives is typical of those of us who try especially hard to be good, upstanding people. Courage, then, is needed to open to the possibility that we have far more aggressive and destructive urges than most of us are conscious of, and allowing and digesting them is key to reclaiming our power and inner authority.

Owning our aggressive drives—our animosity, cruelty, hatred, and selfishness—leads us in a paradoxical way to two changes in perception. One is a shift in how we experience the world around us, and the other is in how we experience ourselves and our nature. The first has to do with confronting our deep-seated conviction that the world is an unsupportive and potentially dangerous place. To the extent that our aggression is projected, we are blind to the benevolence and loving presence that is the fabric of all that exists, including ourselves. Our projection forms a kind of blanket that darkens what we perceive, both around us but also within ourselves, blocking out the luminosity that is present and more fundamental to the nature of everything.

From Freud's point of view, anxiety is the fear of bodily or psychological harm, the latter being rooted in the former. From Sullivan's point of view, it is presumably the same. The ultimate root of our fear and anxiety, then, is our belief that we are these bodily creatures—that our bodies define who and what we are. We see in this assumption how identification with our physical form, which is highlighted at Point Nine—the heart point of Six—underlies our fear. We discussed in Chapter 2 how this identification is the foundation upon which our personality is built.

When we have the courage to question the very assumptions that we unconsciously hold about the nature of our physicality, we find that our sense of what it means to be a human being changes. Rather than perceiving the nature of both ourselves and others to be that of highly developed animals whose underlying imperative is survival of the fittest, we find that while this is part of our biological programming, our nature transcends that. When we courageously penetrate our inner experience, including that of our bodies, we find that our nature as well as the nature of all form is something incandescent and indestructible. When we know this directly, the ground upon which all of our fear and anxiety has been based disappears. We have the courage, then, to relax and let go of our vigilance, letting ourselves be held by the loving support of reality. In this way, we open to the objective level of Six's heart point, Point Nine.

While it is true that our bodies can be harmed, eventually we may come to know that we are, as everything is, this luminosity. Then we may understand that death, that experience we all fear in direct proportion to our identification with our bodies, is not what we have thought. In time, we may find that death is simply the transition from one form to another, and when we truly know this, this is the end of our fear.

P O I N T   S E V E N —

G L U T T O N Y *and*

S O B R I E T Y

All this talk and turmoil and noise and movement and desire is
outside the veil; inside the veil is silence and calm and peace.
— ABU YAZID AL-BISTAMI[1]

We are pleasure-loving creatures. Aversion to pain and attraction to pleasure is hard-wired into our physiology, and
is a survival mechanism that we share with all of the other
sensate organisms. Our attraction to pleasure moves us
toward what will enhance and sustain us, while our aversion to pain alerts us to and so allows us to move away from
any threat to our organism. This dislike for what is painful
keeps us from harming ourselves, and when we are still too
young to speak, gives our parents cues about what is and
isn't working for our developing organism via our expressions of pleasure and of pain. When we are very young,
we have almost no patience with what is painful to us, nor
are we tolerant when our needs are not immediately met.
Having little capacity to wait for gratification is part of
what it is to be a child. So far, so good. The rub is continuing to live our lives driven by our quest for pleasure
and our avoidance of pain, as most of us do to some degree, and this is the difficulty highlighted at Point Seven.

For better or worse, seeking pleasure and avoiding pain continues well into physical adulthood for most of us. It is behind many of the more blatant difficulties people struggle with in their lives—overeating and overindulgence in sweets and chocolate, alcoholism, drug abuse, sexual addictiveness, addiction to shopping and so getting into credit card debt, gambling, and so on. Our sense of reality goes out the window in our drivenness toward consumption in our pursuit of pleasure.

These are obvious areas in which our intemperateness throws our lives and our bodies out of balance, but built increasingly into the fabric of our postmodern lives are all sorts of other ways in which our addiction to pleasure shows up in the form of titillation and stimulation. New and improved types of entertainment and amusement keep appearing—better, bigger, and flatter televisions accessing more and more stations, a continual stream of new movies, personal music systems to carry around with us, personal computers with all sorts of engrossing programs, DVDs, and so on. The acquiring of endless amounts of information via the Internet and entertaining ourselves with computer games and message boards offers us limitless opportunities for escape.

There are the old-fashioned and time-honored ways we get away from anything painful, like avoiding seeing difficulties in our financial situation, our relationships, or in our work life, and instead of facing reality, losing ourselves in an unrealistically rosy picture of what is going on. Closely connected is the universal tendency to check out of the present through daydreaming and fantasizing. One of the most accepted ways that many of us attempt to evade our emotional pain is through intellectualizing—moving into our heads and living from the neck up. Whenever we escape into our own mental world, you can bet that we are trying to move away from some discomfort.

A characteristic of being an adult is facing things as they really are and doing what objectively needs to be done in our lives, regardless of the degree of comfort or discomfort we experience. Fulfillment, for an adult, is not necessarily a matter of always experiencing pleasure—or perhaps more accurately, it is a matter of discovering the enjoyment of meeting challenges, of taking responsibility, and of growing from our interactions in life, even if they are difficult. As adults, if we are driven by pleasure seeking and pain avoidance, we are simply children masquerading as grown-ups. But, realistically, as a spiritual teacher I know once said, there are very few true adults of the species.

We Americans are notorious for our conspicuous consumption, our drive to acquire more and more things, and we do it trying to find happiness. Wealth has come to be defined in quantitative terms rather than qualitative terms. How many things and how much money we have has become the yardstick of our affluence, while the quality of our lives gets lost in the scramble to acquire ever more. Do we truly enjoy and appreciate the numerous things that we have, or are we simply oriented toward gaining more? In this quest for more, we hope to fill ourselves and finally be fulfilled, seldom asking ourselves whether or not this strategy, which is national and becoming international, is working.

The passion we are dealing with here is *gluttony*. Gluttony does not simply mean the overindulgence in food or drink, although this is one of the most common ways we think of it. It also means "greedy or excessive indulgence in any desire or faculty."[2] In its larger meaning, as Naranjo notes, it is a "passion for pleasure,"[3] which underlies this overindulgence. It is an attitude of taking in, of consuming what is pleasurable, and has a very oral quality to it. It is not so much a drive for *immersion* in a pleasurable experience, which, as we have seen, is what lust, the passion of Point Eight, is all about. Gluttony, rather, is a desire to taste, to sample many and varied things, as opposed to deeply experiencing them. It is, in this sense, a shopping mentality. It is a drive toward pleasant stimulation, whether it is of the senses, of the emotions, or of the mind. Naranjo quotes Ichazo describing gluttony as "wanting more," reflecting the insatiability implicit in this passion. So there is a taking in, but not a filling up. Consuming rather than digesting is the focus, and inevitably this leads to dissatisfaction and a sense of insufficiency, masked by pursuit of more stimulation.

Our gluttony is not confined to what on the surface appears pleasurable, and this can make spotting it tricky. St. John of the Cross, for instance, speaks of those addicted to the sweetness and pleasure of spiritual practices, overindulging in asceticism:

Therefore, besides the imperfections into which the seeking for sweetness of this kind makes them fall, the gluttony which they now have makes them continually go to extremes, so that they pass beyond the limits of moderation within which the virtues are acquired and wherein they have their being. For some of these persons, attracted by the pleasure which they find therein, kill themselves with penances, and others weaken themselves with fast, by performing more than their frailty can bear, without the order or advice of any, but rather endeavouring to avoid those whom they should obey in such matters. . . .[4]

While on the surface this might not look like a drive toward pleasure, when we look more closely we see the particular pleasure that comes from intense feeling, even when it is overindulgence in what is painful.

Closely allied with this overzealousness in spiritual practices is emotional gluttony. Getting swept away by our emotional currents is one of the ways that many of us engage our gluttony, sometimes under the guise of working on our issues. Whatever reaction arises inside of us takes us over, and we feel helpless under its sway, tossed and turned by its powerful surges of feeling. For many of us, the intensity of feeling itself is as intoxicating as any drug, and so we unconsciously whip up difficult situations and crises in our lives to get our fix. It is important to see that when we engage in this kind of emotional gluttony, which is called hysteria in psychological nomenclature, we are not fully experiencing the emotions themselves. We are consumed by them, but are not completely entering into them, and are experiencing them with some resistance and at a certain remove, which sometimes takes a lot of introspection to realize.

For Ennea-type Sevens, gluttony is their suffering, even though at first glance it might not appear as such. Sevens, with their affable, enthusiastic, upbeat energy don't seem to suffer the way the other types do. They tend to focus on the bright side of things, perpetually optimistic and filled with plans for the future. They are inclined to be interested in all sorts of things, especially interesting ideas—broad global ones that synthesize knowledge from many different sources and disciplines are especially enticing. Amicable and perky, they can be quite charming and loquacious; holding forth, teaching, telling stories and entertaining others. It takes a little scratching below their sunny surface to understand how they are a fear type. Only when we begin to see how much energy they are investing in being "up," and how driven they are toward the positive, do we begin to suspect that they are afraid of and indeed running from pain. And in many Sevens, we see the result: we can sense an underlying depression, a kind of dry unhappiness, an unemotional dissatisfaction.

In their conscious or unconscious aversion to pain, they limit their direct experience of themselves and, consequentially, of life and this is the ultimate source of their suffering. They tend to experience things from the safe remove of their minds, testing life to see whether or not it might be safe to enter into it completely. When they want to fully dive into things, they find that they can't completely, since they are trapped in their personality's defenses against direct engagement. They can only exaggerate their experience without fully being able to be inside of it.

Their emotional life, as a rule, tends to be truncated and somewhat dried out, even if they are very vocal about it and can describe it eloquently. The juiciness of their inner world and the wetness of their pain seems to have evaporated off long ago from having their attention averted from it. This can be quite confusing to others, since Sevens can describe their suffering in great detail and in fact can often go on and on about it, but it is from a distance, seeing it clearly but from far away. Like the mappers and planners that they are, they experience it in a reified way, losing the actual territory in their concepts and depictions of it.

As with all defensive maneuvers in the psyche, what we are trying to protect becomes inaccessible to us as our defenses crystallize. For Sevens, attempting to protect themselves early on from pain, which for a child often feels frightening and overwhelming, ends up cutting them off from the vitality and vibrancy of themselves and of life. Out of their fear of being engulfed and subsumed by the unpleasant aspects of their emotional life, they retreated from it, moving into their minds. Attempting to understand their suffering seemed like the safest and best way of dealing with it. The movement away from their pain, however, ends up creating its own kind of anguish. It is the anguish of not being able to fully immerse themselves in their inner life, and instead participating from a secure distance.

Aversion to his pain, then, blocks a Seven's contact with himself. Without this immediacy of direct experience, he cannot contact and hence trust the natural process of his soul. He loses touch with the way things naturally shift and change, and ends up rationally knowing that things occur this way or that and tend to move in this direction or that direction, but has lost the feel for this natural movement, the direct contact with it. As a result, he may wind up knowing a great deal about how things work in his mind, but he does not experience his own internal movements and so cannot relax into his own process.*

When we see this, we can easily understand a story told by the late Sufi teacher Idries Shah, whose teaching was communicated primarily through such tales. In one of them, a man asks two groups of miserable-looking people how they came to be in such a state. The first group tells him that they ended up this way by being afraid of hell. The second group tells him that they are in their sad condition because they desired paradise. The third group of people he comes upon are radiant with joy and yet look as though they have endured a great deal. He asks them how they came to be as they are, and they tell him that the spirit of truth is responsible. They have seen reality and so all else has lost its allure. The moral of the story is that seeking truth, rather than fear of pain or the desire for happiness, is the correct orientation toward inner work, since seeking happiness makes you its prisoner just as surely as does pain.

What drives most people at the beginning to get involved with some form of inner work is their pain. They know that they are suffering, and they want to be happy. Often, people who are in emotional distress go into psychotherapy or some other form of growth work in the hope that they will get "fixed"—made better and happier. Early in their search, people often move toward forms of inner work that promise that they can get there quickly and easily. Some stay with these methods and keep trying, while for others it is only after exhausting a lot of these methods that they realize that real transformation is not sudden nor is it painless. While the de-

---

*With most of the passions, their origin in the loss of that point's Holy Idea is obvious. It is not so here. In what I am describing, perhaps we can see the connection: how gluttony not only is the outcome of the loss of perception of the natural unfoldment of one's soul—Holy Plan—but also supports and reinforces the estrangement from this Holy Idea.

sire to be free from suffering is an appropriate motivation initially, somewhere along the line our orientation has to change for real development to occur, as we will discuss more fully when we explore the virtue.

Some people get involved with a teacher who is able to transmit a high state of Being to them. Transmission is one of the time-honored methods of spiritual development. The hidden or perhaps not-so-hidden trap in such an approach in which the student is dependent upon the teacher for states is, first of all, this very dependency, and second, the lack of digestion of the student's own psychological obstacles to Being. "Catching" a state of consciousness in this way can be—though of course is not always—a way of bypassing the difficult inner work of confronting our resistances and psychological barriers. Unless we confront them, however, spiritual experiences can only be intermittent, like clouds that appear in the sky or don't, depending on the weather, rather than being readily accessible to us.

When we have not worked through our psychological material, it is possible to maintain a high state of consciousness in some cases, but to do so we must limit the challenges to our psyche. Living in isolation or in silence, out of reach of what might trigger our personality is one way of doing this. In many traditions, celibacy is another way of lessening the influences that might arouse our psychological material. There's nothing like intimate relationship and sexuality to bring up whatever is unresolved in our personality, so eliminating this stimulus is the traditional way of dealing with this problematic life arena.

Spiritual teachings throughout the centuries have sought to help us transcend our psychological material, the source of our suffering, through various practices and methods. Without the technology of psychological understanding afforded to us in the last century, this was the best option. Transcendence, getting up and out of our egoic reality, is the goal in many practices, and while much of the methodology to do this is very sophisticated in many traditions, few individuals are actually able to move beyond their personality structures in this way. Happily, things are changing, and learning how to effectively work with our psychology in such a way that it becomes more transparent to our depths is now possible. But it is not easy work. It requires *confronting* rather than *overcoming* our suffering.

Sevens are notorious for leaving psychological and spiritual work when the glitz wears off and the hard work in the trenches of the psyche begins. They have the reputation of being spiritual dilettantes, leaving a path when the going gets tough. This is, of course, a broad generalization and not the case for all Sevens, nor is this pattern by any means confined to them. But what is true is that if a Seven hangs in, he will, like all of us, pretty quickly be confronted with the depth of his suffering, and this is where things get difficult for him. The urge to leave, to move away from the pain and from the confrontation with their limitations is sometimes an irresistible one for Sevens, and they often are lured away by another teaching or teacher, who promises to be more of the "real thing," looking as though they will get them to enlightenment faster and more painlessly.

Obviously, you don't have to be a Seven to be a spiritual shopper, and again, I want to underline the fact that not all Sevens are. Many people move from one spiritual scene to another, attracted by one guru and then another, and spend the whole of their spiritual life trying out rather than really taking in and working with a teaching or a teacher. But we can skim the surface in this way even though we stay on a particular path or with a particular teacher. We can keep ourselves from fully engaging and being immersed in our inner life, remaining slightly outside of it and looking on, out of our fear of fully entering into ourselves. The spiritual shopping mentality of gluttony is old news in spiritual life. St. John of the Cross, writing in the sixteenth century, describes those who engage in it as follows:

> . . . when they have once failed to find pleasure in this or some other exercise, they have great disinclination and repugnance to return to it, and at times they abandon it. They are, in fact, as we have said, like children, who are not influenced by reason, and who act, not from rational motives but from inclination. Such persons expend all their effort in seeking spiritual pleasure and consolation; they never tire, therefore, of reading books; and they begin, now one meditation, now another, in their pursuit of this pleasure which they desire to experience in the things of God. But God, very justly, wisely and lovingly, denies it to them, for otherwise this spiritual gluttony and inordinate appetite would breed innumerable evils.[5]

As in the Sufi story recounted above, how deeply the work that we do transforms us has everything to do with our relationship to what Freud called the pleasure principle. Early in his explorations, Freud postulated that one of the basic principles regulating psychic functioning was our movement toward pleasure and our movement away from what, roughly translated from the German *Unlust,* is somewhat awkwardly rendered "unpleasure." Pleasure is a guiding principle especially during our early years as we learn to operate and maneuver through the world in our tiny bodies, and our tolerance for what is unpleasurable is minimal as children. We have to learn to tolerate delays in the gratification of our desires, and this involves developing the cognitive capacity to understand with our minds what is going on. As he said of what he initially called the pleasure-unpleasure (*Lust-Unlust* in German) principle,

> *These processes strive towards gaining pleasure; psychical activity draws back from any event which might arouse unpleasure. (Here we have repression.) Our dreams at night and our waking tendency to tear ourselves away from distressing impressions are remnants of the dominance of this principle and proofs of its power.*[6]

Initially Freud defined pleasure in biological terms: it was the lowering of stimulation impinging on our psyche. Because we are motivated by our desire for pleasure, our actions are necessarily directed toward the discharge of excessive internal pressure. From his perspective, then, and characteristic of his whole orientation toward human psychology, pleasure is something purely intrapsychic, having to do with the discharge of our internal forces, rather than something interpsychic, shaped by and stemming from environmental factors.

Later psychologists moved away from this view, understanding that our concepts of pleasure and unpleasure are influenced to a great extent by those around us in early childhood, and seeing that for many, stimulation is pleasurable. If our early caretakers consider quietude pleasurable, or alternatively, if they consider excitement pleasurable, this has a profound influence on what we consider pleasurable ourselves. Freud himself in his later years abandoned his view that pleasure consists of the diminishment of tension and stimulation, and postulated that it might have to do with the alternation of tension and relaxation, as we see below:

> *Pleasure and unpleasure . . . cannot be referred to an increase or decrease of a quantity (which we describe as "tension due to stimulus"), although they obviously have a great deal to do with that factor. It appears that they depend, not on this quantitative factor, but on some characteristic of it which we can only describe as a qualitative one. If we were able to say what this qualitative characteristic is, we should be much further advanced in psychology. Perhaps it is the rhythm, the temporal sequence of changes, rises and falls in the quantity of stimulus. We do not know.*[7]

Although Freud abandoned his efforts to define the nature of pleasure itself, what did remain clear to him is that it has to do with satisfying internal drives. Initially, when our state of "psychical rest," as he puts it, is disturbed by our internal needs,

> *. . . whatever was thought of (wished for) was simply presented in a hallucinatory manner, just as still happens to-day with our dream-thoughts every night. It was only the non-occurrence of the expected satisfaction, the disappointment experienced, that led to the abandonment of this attempt at satisfaction by means of hallucination. Instead of it, the psychical apparatus had to decide to form a conception of the real circumstances in the external world and to endeavour to make a real alteration in them. A new principle of mental functioning was thus introduced; what was presented in the mind was no longer what was agreeable but what was real, even if it happened to be disagreeable.*[8]

Thus what he called the reality principle was born. Instead of simply imagining what we wish for, which Freud believed we do at the beginning and is the source of our dreams and fantasy life, we begin to perceive what is really going on in the external world since just imagining doesn't fulfill the need. In this way we learn to perceive whether or not and how our needs can be gratified, and so learn to navigate external reality in search of satisfaction. This is the birth of the ego (in the psychological sense of this word), the interface between our internal drives and external reality.*

As the reality principle kicks in, there is an increasing ability to delay gratification of our desires and postpone the avoidance of what doesn't feel good to us. As we have discussed, as infants and young children we can't tolerate any postponement in gratification of our needs for comfort and in getting away from what feels bad to us. This is partially because our mental structure has not developed to the point at which we have a concept of time. Without that, everything is immediate, and our needs feel that way to us, as well.

For instance, when we are very young, we have no concept that eating a balanced meal is important for the development of our bodies and nervous system. We would just as soon replace ice cream or candy for dinner. In time we develop the understanding that if we eat a good meal, dessert will follow, and we can delay our wish for something sweet. Likewise, when we have a scrape as a young child, tolerating the pain of the treatment for it can be unbearable. When we are older, we understand that the pain will start going away if we let ourselves be treated, even though it hurts a lot more temporarily. We behave, in this sense, like little animals when very young in terms of pleasure and pain, and as we mature, we are able to conceptualize things in our minds, which allows us this capacity for postponing our being run automatically by the pleasure principle. As the reality principle supersedes being purely impelled by the pleasure principle, we can recognize what is realistic in terms of getting our inner desires met and how best to go about that. Learning to delay gratification is part of this increasing realism, which develops as we mature.

Freudian psychology basically boils down to viewing ourselves as being dominated and propelled by drives, which when thwarted lead to all sorts of neurotic manifestations. Life is a balancing act between our inner imperatives and the constraints upon them by outer reality. Later psychologists diverged from this view, many of whom, including the Scottish

---

* We might note here that the Seven's orientation toward imagining gratification and mapping and planning her way toward it is a leftover of what Freud perceived as our earliest strategy toward meeting our need for pleasure.

psychoanalyst W. R. D. Fairbairn, saw us as object oriented from the beginning. Pleasure and avoidance of unpleasure, Fairbairn suggests, is not the guiding principle behind our behavior. Rather, it is about searching for and maintaining contact with others. Our psychological disturbances, then, are not based on conflicts about our drive-based urges but rather on difficulties and vicissitudes in our relationships with others. In fact, Fairbairn saw purely pleasure-seeking behaviors as the result of breakdowns in the more fundamental drive toward positive relationship with an other. Drive theory was out the window. The aggressive instinct, like the libidinal drive for pleasure, he also saw as the result of the deterioration in object relations rather than as something innate.

Many psychologists contemporary with Fairbairn and those of succeeding generations also took issue with Freud's drive theory, and the whole understanding of object relations developed out of this diverging interpersonal perspective of the building blocks of the personality structure. This disagreement about what drives us humans has created two major trends in psychological thinking, which have often been strongly at odds with each other. The conflict comes down to the question of whether we are primarily social creatures or whether we are primarily individuals.

It reflects, as Greenberg and Mitchell note, two fundamentally different philosophical perspectives about the nature of human beings, which have been at the core of the Western philosophical and political debate for centuries. The drive/structural school reflects the perspective that "human satisfaction and goals are fundamentally personal and individual. Human beings pursue their own separate aims, argue Hobbes and Locke, and these atomistic, discordant pursuits are likely to interfere with each other."[9] It is out of this camp, they note, that the American political institutions were born. The relational/structure school of psychological theory arises out of the perspective shared by Rousseau, Hegel, and culminating in Marx, that human satisfaction and the realization of our goals is only possible within the community, since we are fundamentally social creatures and cannot have a meaningful existence apart from others. While some see these two points of view as irreconcilable and mutually exclusive, it seems to me that our search for happiness involves both our drive to fulfill ourselves as individuals *and* through our relationships.

Both schools of psychological thought apply to different aspects of who and what we are. Observing infants and young children, it does not make sense to entirely dismiss drive theory, since our inner needs so obviously function as motivation in many ways when we are very young. Our natural tendency to move toward what is pleasurable and to move away from what is not is clearly one of the driving forces of our behavior, but it alone cannot fully explain our behavior. This is obvious when we consider that many of us persist in behaviors that cause us suffering rather than pleasure. As Greenberg and Mitchell put it,

> People are notoriously inept at finding pleasure; they repeatedly engineer situations which make them unhappy. Only a fundamental need for human contact at any cost accounts for the perpetuation of unpleasure in the lives of so many people.[10]

Another thing that accounts for our persistence in patterns that are unsatisfying (and, parenthetically, supports the drive-theory view) is that they do bring us a certain kind of pleasure—that of familiarity. It is this inertia about maintaining the known, regardless of how unhappy it makes us, that is at the core of much of the perpetuation of our tendencies. In fact, only when we recognize the comfort that sustaining the familiar brings to us do we begin to unlock its hold upon us.

While the question of whether pleasure is drive based or relationally based is an important one in psychology since it determines how we approach our suffering therapeutically, our allegiance to moving toward pleasure and away from pain is *itself* the overarching issue from a spiritual perspective. There are a few reasons for this. As we have discussed earlier, if our orientation is toward pleasure, we will orient toward *enjoyable* experiences rather than toward the *truth* of our experience. When we do this, we are perpetuating the gluttony of the personality, rather than aligning ourselves with the attitude of the soul informed by Being. We are relating to spiritual experience as though it were something yummy to consume, and in so doing, preserve our sense of self as empty and in need of being filled. Breaking it down further, we are maintaining the attitude of being a hungry mouth needing to be fed. No matter how many high experiences we have, if our orientation toward inner work is striving after them, we remain identified with being a someone who is having spiritual experiences, and this someone can only be the personality. The glimpses of reality beyond our personality only end up sustaining and supporting the personality itself with its basic inner sense of emptiness and lack.

For our inner work to be truly transforming, we need to value truth above pleasure, as Shah's story tells us. Instead of going for the high and maintaining the attitude of being a seeker after those lofty states, we must directly engage the content of our soul, regardless of how it feels to us. When we attempt to fill ourselves, even when the content is spiritual, we are tacitly assuming that we are an inner black hole, a mouth needing to be fed, an emptiness; and when we are identified with our personality, we feel as if we were just that. But to find out who and what we really are, what our nature truly is, we must face into and engage that sense of emptiness rather than trying to fill it. When we do this, we are radically shifting our inner orientation, and this shift is all-important for the outcome of our endeavor. Rather than relating to ourselves as an emptiness needing to be filled, we begin to relate to ourselves as the journey *itself.* Rather than being focused on what will fill us or on what stimulates us to react, behave, or feel one way or another, then, our process itself becomes forefront. This is a dramatic shift of focus from the object of our experience to the subject, and without it, who we take ourselves to be does not change.

The attitude of gluttony, then, is the attitude of seeking, and as long as we are under its sway, it prevents us from finding. Part of this is being addicted to experience itself, especially experience that feels positive to us. This dependence upon the stimulation of experience skews our inner work, since some of the most important things that we find within ourselves have to do with stillness and cessation. And, the Absolute, the deepest dimension of reality, is characterized by the cessation of experience itself.

To become a finder rather than a seeker, then, we need to move beyond the pleasure principle. Characteristic of our allegiance to the pleasure principle is a flight from reality. This is what makes it problematic in our lives. A sign of mental illness is removal from reality, but few of us are living entirely in reality. The extent to which we do so is the extent of our awakeness to what is. It is the extent to which we are living in what Gurdjieff called the real world—the world experienced as it really is: informed by Being.

Obviously, we have been discussing the virtue of this point, which is called *sobriety*. We tend to associate this word with abstinence from drugs or alcohol, and that is certainly one of its definitions. It also is defined as restraint in appetite, and denotes one guided by sane and sound reason, showing no excessive or extreme qualities, and being serious and thoughtful.[11] As a virtue, it is this very quality we have been discussing: being firmly grounded in reality rather than being swept away by our inner drives and their resulting fantasies. "Thoughtful" here doesn't mean being lost in our minds but rather is used in the sense of the opposite of being impulsive. It has to do with being fully informed by the reality principle, but taken further than Freud took it—into the real world beyond that of the personality.

Ichazo defines the virtue of sobriety as follows:

> It gives the body its sense of proportion. A being in the state of sobriety is firmly grounded in the moment, taking in no more and no less than it needs, expending precisely as much energy as necessary.

Substituting the word *soul* for *body* brings us closer to an experiential sense of sobriety, although undoubtedly when we are sober in the sense meant here, our body becomes more balanced and less adrenaline driven. Our physical as well as emotional needs come into proportion, informed by what we really require as opposed to what we want. As Ichazo says, sobriety is about being in the here and now rather than lost in our thoughts, dreams, and fantasies, or spending our lives rehashing the past in our minds or anticipating the future as most of us do.

The sense of realism that is expressed by this virtue necessitates being with whatever arises in our moment-to-moment experience, again regardless of whether it is pleasurable or painful. To be fully in the present moment, in other words, means being open to our experience, no matter what it is. This is pivotal in inner work aimed at realization because of the fact that Being is a *presence,* and presence can only be experienced by fully inhabiting the present moment—moment after moment. Even the term *realization* that I have just used is based on the understanding that enlightenment means being fully real and therefore fully in reality.

To become sober, then, we need to work through our adherence to the pleasure principle. Or to recast things a little differently, we need to understand that true satisfaction and fulfillment lies in valuing the truth of our experience rather than in opting for what feels good and avoiding what doesn't. In a sense, then, we are taking the pleasure principle a step deeper, getting to the source of what really satisfies our soul.

For us to make this shift, we need to understand that what has happened is that a physiological given—the pleasure principle—has gotten translated into something psychological as we grew up. Our bodies naturally recoil from something painful, and this is necessary and useful for our physical survival. We learned as children to repress emotions, impulses, and thoughts that were too much for our developing psychological structure to tolerate, "disappearing" them from our consciousness. The memory of them did not go away, however, but simply became encapsulated and shut away in our souls, and it is these hidden-away memories that surface when we spend any period of time away from outer escape and stimulation, and also when we shift our attention inwardly. Working through our personality structure, which has developed in counterpoint to all of these pockets of undigested experiences, is a matter of becoming present to them, opening them up, and metabolizing them. As we do this bit by bit, we are transforming these lumps of experience and absorbing our personality structure. It becomes food for our growth, and in the process, our soul matures.

Rather than running from our suffering out of fear, we are engaging it in the only way that will ultimately resolve it. Instead of behaving like children, perpetuating an attitude toward ourselves of escapism, of following our emotional preferences, of basing our behavior on what we feel like or don't feel like doing, we act like true adults. Sobriety, then, is not being intoxicated and swept away by our emotions or our minds. It means not becoming drunk with our experience, no matter how lofty and transcendent it is. It also means not indulging and exaggerating our pain, but rather experiencing both extremes directly, fully, in a balanced way. It means not getting swept away by an emotional current, pulled out to sea by its undertow, and drowning in it. It means ceasing to relate to ourselves as though we were empty vessels needing to be filled, consumers needing to consume. It means ceasing to move only toward what feels good or familiar, and instead opening to the unbelievably interesting mystery that we are.

POINT FIVE—
AVARICE *and*
NONATTACHMENT

*We must have beginner's mind, free from possessing anything,
a mind that knows everything is in flowing change. Nothing exists except
momentarily in its present form and color. One thing flows into another and
cannot be grasped. Before the rain stops we hear a bird. Even under the heavy
snow we see snowdrops and some new growth.*

—SHUNRYU SUZUKI[1]

We all tend to hold on to what we have. This is a universal characteristic when we are identified with our personality. From the perspective of Point Five, this tendency to clutch at what we have and our reluctance to let it go is one of the most powerful driving forces and hallmarks of our ego. It leads us to be miserly, greedy, and possessive not only of the external objects we possess but also of those we hold near and dear, and at a more fundamental level, of our very sense of who we are. The tenacity with which we cling to things is an enormous force in most people's lives, and for some it is their central preoccupation. The great irony is that the more we cling to things, the less we have them. But before we get there, let's explore the inclination itself.

What we hold on to depends a lot upon our temperament as well as upon our ennea-type and instinctual subtype. Some of us, for instance, tend to hoard our funds and to be niggardly and parsimonious, reluctant to spend anything we have. Others of us hold on to possessions, imbuing them with great value, and being afraid to lose them. Still others of us clutch at our status, power, and importance; while yet again others tend to hold on to their partners for dear life. In these differing objects of our grasping, we can see the self-preservation, social, and sexual instinct focus.

This brings us to the final inner atmosphere of the personality described in the map of the enneagram—the passion of *avarice*. Avarice is defined as an "insatiable or excessive desire for wealth or gain," and is synonymous with greediness.[2] In the language of the enneagram, the passion of avarice refers to our retentiveness, the drive to hold on to what we already have rather than our drive to acquire more. And while the object of our avarice might or might not be material wealth, as we shall see, this passion refers to something much broader than that. This passion, then, underscores and calls our attention to our greediness—our desire to *retain*.

What is being pointed to here is in part our orientation toward stockpiling, laying in of supplies, making sure that we have more than we need. We spoke of conspicuous consumption in the last chapter, and what is being referred to here is part of that dynamic, so prevalent in American culture. The focus here is not so much on accumulating and sampling as many things as possible, which is gluttony; nor is it on devouring them and satiating ourselves, which is lust. In contrast, the impulse here is to *hoard,* not to be stimulated or to be immersed in but simply to possess. Like a squirrel, one of the animals associated with this point, the orientation here is to conserve as many nuts as possible, storing them untasted in our distended cheeks. Our drive to keep, then, is closely related to, but not the same as the passions of Points Eight and Seven, and we see this close relationship in the linkage of these points by the lines of internal flow of the enneagram.

Avarice, as we are seeing, is a holding on to what we have, whether that's something external or internal. It refers to the universal tendency, present when we take ourselves to be our personality, to hang on to what we've got, regardless of whether it brings us pleasure or pain. We discussed in the last chapter the peculiar pleasure we get from the familiar, irrespective of how it feels, and here is represented the tenacity with which we cling to it. This tenacity is implicit in the inertia of the personality, the propensity for our ongoing sense of self to stay intact and our tendency to remain identified with it, which as we saw, is focused upon at Point Nine.

Behind all of this grasping—whether internal or external—is fear. Fear of not having enough of whatever it is that we think we need, and fear of losing what we do have. Deeper still, our avarice is rooted in the fear that we will not be nourished and supported in our lives, that our well-being, not to mention our very survival, is not assured. Ultimately, self-preservation lies at the heart of our tendency to clutch at things, including our sense of self. It is our primary instinct, as we have discussed, out of which the other two refract.

Some of us have few possessions, while others of us accumulate far more than we need. Some of us are by nature generous and giving, having little difficulty parting with what we have if it brings joy or benefit to another. Others of us tend to hang on to whatever we have, giving little and counting what we possess. But this is not the heart of the matter. In either case, appearances notwithstanding, there is a more fundamental avarice at the core, having little to do with our relationship to external possessions.

As we are seeing, this avarice has to do with hanging on, albeit unconsciously, to our sense of self. This is our central attachment, far surpassing in strength and power, as well as effect upon our sense of reality, any clinging to material objects or other people. Because of this centrality, this is where our understanding needs to be focused if we want to experience life beyond our familiar identity and the holographic universe that it generates, which we call ourselves and our lives.

Moving around the enneagram, we can see that what each of the types tends to hold on to the most is, again, not a particular set of external possessions but rather a particular felt sense of self—an internal self-image. In tandem with it, what is also held on to by each type is an image of how they would like to be—an ego ideal. Our ego ideal always operates in counterpoint to our self-image, driving our attempts to mitigate the deficient and painful sense of self at the core of our identity.

Nines tend to hold on to a belief and felt sense that they are unimportant, insignificant, and undeserving of attention, while at the same time clinging to an ego ideal of being loving and benevolent. Ones hold on to a belief and felt sense that they are imperfect, not good enough or just simply not enough, and hold on to the ego ideal of striving to become and behave like a good person. Twos hold on to the belief and experience of themselves as rejectible, while trying to manipulate themselves to be different, and hold on to the ego ideal of being a lovable person. Threes hold on to the belief and felt sense that they must do everything to maintain their world, and hold on to the ego ideal of being accomplished and successful. Fours hold on to the belief and experience of themselves as abandoned and flawed, and cling to the ego ideal of being sensitive, original, creative, and unique. Fives, as we will explore in more depth, hold on to the belief and felt sense of themselves as isolated and cut off, ultimately separate, and hold on to the ego ideal of being knowledgeable. Sixes hold on to the belief and experience of themselves as weak and vulnerable to attack, while holding on to the ego ideal of being devoted and loyal to a person or a cause. Sevens hold on to the belief and felt sense of themselves as being outside of the natural unfoldment of things—hence the need to map and plan—and hold on to the ego ideal of being okay and having it together. Eights hold on to the belief and experience of themselves as having been wronged and meddled with, and hold on to the ego ideal of being powerful, strong, and unassailable.

This holding on, this avarice, is the central passion for Ennea-type Fives, forming the core of their suffering. In Fives, it is a generalized and characteristic retentiveness or stinginess, a "holding back and holding in," as Naranjo describes it.[3] The avarice itself might involve a grasping of money and possessions, or it may arise in a particular Five as retentiveness around the knowledge they possess or their status. More globally than that, however, this hoarding tendency flavors and describes a Five's inner atmosphere, which is reflected in the clutching of these things. It is an internal contractedness and a holding on to and holding back of oneself.

Those familiar with the enneagram know that the Five style is one of pulling back and of hiding; a defensive withdrawal from complete engage-

ment in life, with others and, at the core, with themselves. It is a shrink-
ing back, a drawing away from involvement when viewed from one angle;
and a holding on to oneself, one's energy, and one's resources when seen
from another vantage point. It might best be characterized as a conserving
mentality, safeguarding and preserving what one has. It arises from the
delusion at the core of the Five personality structure that we are ultimately
separate, which we will explore more fully later on. As Almaas says,

> We have seen that objectively there is no such thing as a separate self; so
> when we experience ourselves as separate, we are deluded. The actual real-
> ity is that we are not separate, but the contrary conviction is so powerful
> that we constantly experience ourselves as separate. The belief completely de-
> termines your experience. The sense of being like a fortress, with impenetra-
> ble walls around you that separate you from everything else, is your actual
> experience.
>
> The delusion here is not that you are an individual, but that you are an
> isolated individual, with boundaries that separate you from everything else.
> This is the delusion at the heart of the Five ennea-type. . . . [4]

Fives tend to be very sensitive, wiry, and sometimes seem as if their
nerve endings were exposed. They often feel thin-skinned and delicate,
fragile rather than robust. And they can be emotionally dry and depleted
of vitality, lacking substantiality and vibrancy. The one follows the other.
They often seem reserved and withholding. They are especially sensitive
to intrusion, and prone to be very private, safeguarding and protecting
their solitude. It is here that they feel safe, with a minimum of input from
others. While some Fives seem quite gregarious on the surface, a part of
them always feels withdrawn, kept for themselves alone. Too much expo-
sure seems threatening, and to defend themselves from it, they pull back.

Their withdrawal, originally a defense mechanism to protect the pre-
ciousness of their souls, ends up cutting them off not only from outside
impingement but also from their very aliveness. They seem to live in their
own inner world, which to them may feel quite rich and deep, seemingly
without the need to experience that dimensionality interpersonally. But

this is a bit of a red herring, since their withdrawal, like any psychic process, can never simply be from the outside world without also being from some aspect of their inner world.

Fives tend to be observers both of life and of themselves, looking on from a safe distance. In this sense they are scouts, surveying the terrain both without and within rather than fully traversing it. While many teachers and writers of the enneagram say that Fives are intellectuals, this is not always the case. What is more to the point is this characteristic of garnering foreknowledge of the territory that lies before them. And this includes within themselves. Their defense of pulling away from what threatens externally inevitably ends up cutting them off from themselves—as well as from their aliveness, vitality, substantiality, and fullness. Rather than fully inhabiting their bodies and their emotional life, they end up observing them. But the view from outside distorts what is seen. It is only when we fully engage with ourselves, fully enter into ourselves, that we can begin to have any experiential understanding of our actual experience. Otherwise, what we experience is reified—a disembodied mental representation of what is going on within us.

Self-contained and self-sufficient, Fives tend to feel isolated and disconnected, and so like one marooned on a desert island, they hold on to what they have out of the fear that their resources will run out. As Naranjo says of this passion,

> *This is a fearful grasping, implying a fantasy that letting go would result in catastrophic depletion. Behind the hoarding impulse there is, we may say, an experience of impending impoverishment.*[5]

One of the fear types, their solution to existential anxiety is this holding on and holding back. Implicit in this fear of depletion is a sense of being fundamentally cut off from any source of nourishment and the juice of life, so there is no anticipation or hope of replenishment. Their ultimate fear is of a painful sense of deficiency, a desiccated inner emptiness, a parched and dry barrenness, based on their basic assumption that they are ultimately separate. While our bodies, like all physical forms, are discrete, our nature—as all the spiritual traditions attest—is one thing, arising uniquely in each of these forms. A Five's ultimate estrangement is from this experience of connection and interconnection with all that exists, and this cut-offness in circular fashion creates the very deficiency he or she is so afraid of.

Distancing themselves from their own needs, they seem to get by with quite little compared to other types, and often are afraid of possessing too much or of being encumbered by commitments that might weigh them down. They like to travel lightly through life, limiting what they take in and what they give out, out of fear that their needs will not be filled and that too much will be demanded of them. Their fear, then, ends up limiting their freedom, keeping them tethered to this drive—and it is indeed a drive—not to be encumbered.

But you don't have to be a Five to hold back and hold on. It is part of the nature of the personality, and so is a universal characteristic whenever we are identified with our ego structure. This only makes sense: if we believe that we are ultimately cut off, ultimately isolated—which is the core belief at the heart of the ego—all we can do is clutch at what we have. The specter of our provisions running out and being faced with an intolerable and what feels like life-threatening depletion looms large at the center of our personality, regardless of our type, striking fear into our hearts and making us grasp on to what we have. To be identified with our personality, then, is to be avaricious.

Another way of describing avarice is as attachment. Attachment is the ego's characteristic of attempting to secure and hold on to things. When using the term *attachment* in this context, we are not using it in the psychological sense of forming deep bonds with others but rather in the sense of clinging to things, which is in many respects its opposite. There is little in the psychological literature about attachment in the sense in which we are using that term because it is so foundational to the personality itself. However, there is extensive focus upon it in spiritual understanding.

Exploring this passion takes us deep into spirituality—specifically, it takes us into the heart of Buddhist understanding, since it was central to the Buddha's fundamental insight, formulated in his Four Noble Truths. The first of his Noble Truths is the truth of suffering, that pain is part of human life. The second Noble Truth is about the cause of our suffering. In the words of Buddhist meditation teacher Joseph Goldstein,

> *What is it that binds us to suffering and this wheel of sorrow? The Buddha saw that bondage is in our own minds, it is the bondage of attachment. We are on this wheel of pain because we cling to it, and we cling to it out of ignorance. . . .*
>
> *The second noble truth of the Buddha's enlightenment is the cause of suffering: desire and attachment. Desire for sense pleasure, cherishing views and opinions, the belief that rites, rituals and ceremonies are going to bring a relief to suffering, and the very strong attachment we have to the concept of self. No one makes us hold on. There is no force or power outside of ourselves which keeps us bound to the wheel of life and death. It is just the clinging in our own minds.*[6]

In the Buddha's teaching, then, attachment is seen to be the source of our suffering. In a world that is constantly in flux, in which all forms arise and eventually fall away, the Buddha taught that clinging to any form—pleasant or unpleasant—sets us up for some kind of distress. When we are attached to anything, we aggressively attempt to get it and then we fear its loss once we have acquired it.

As we see, the Buddha lists four primary drives underlying our attachment. The first is our desire for sense pleasure—our proclivity to seek pleasant experiences, whether physical, emotional, or mental, believing that they will end our discontent, our ennui, and our suffering. We have discussed this extensively in the last chapter.

The second, cherishing views and opinions, encompasses holding on to our reactions, our positions, and our preconceptions. Rather than experiencing reality as it is, to the extent that we are identified with our personality we filter what we experience through the veils of our conditioning. Attachment to our beliefs resides at the core of the ego. Clinging to our beliefs about the nature of reality and of ourselves is the basis of all of the nine ego-types, blinding us from seeing and experiencing reality as it is. Each of the enneatypes is based upon a fixed belief—a fixation—about how things are, as we have seen, and it is this fixation that is the basis of the behavioral and emotional patterns of each type. Letting go of our fixation means seeing things as they really are. As Goldstein says of this second great attachment,

> In the Sutra of the Third Zen Patriarch, it says, "Do not seek the truth. Only cease to cherish opinions." If we let go of this attachment, the whole Dharma will be revealed. Everything will be there. We have to let go of our preconceived ideas of how things are, of how we would like things to be.[7]

The third variety of attachment, the belief that rituals will relieve our suffering, is on the face of it not so relevant today as it was in the Buddha's time. Historically, Buddhism was somewhat of a reaction and antidote to the rites and worshipping central to Hinduism as well as to indigenous shamanistic and magical practices in the various cultures of Asia. In Tibet, for instance, Buddhism subsumed and incorporated the ancient Bon religion, creating a unique hybrid. However, that said, if we take the meaning of this attachment to ritual to include our clinging to the form of whatever religious or spiritual practice we engage in, we can easily see its relevance today. The form itself will not free us, nor will our identification with it.

If our mind is all over the place, caught up in replaying the past or anticipating the future, our meditation practice will be fruitless regardless of how many hours we sit. If we are attached to our particular practice as the only one or the best one, or if we use it to shore up our sense of self, it becomes a hinderance. Our very identification with being someone on the Path is a very deep attachment that all spiritual seekers need to eventually work through to become truly liberated. Form without substance becomes emptiness, no matter how profound the truth is underlying that form.

The fourth attachment to our sense of self is perhaps the most problematic for us Westerners to comprehend, and there are many different understandings of what it means in the various schools of Buddhism. It is likely that the Buddha's emphasis on no-self was in part a reaction to the excessive reification of Hinduism, and it certainly addresses the illusion of our ultimately separate entityhood, which we have discussed earlier. This notion of no-self is problematic for many of us because we do have the ongoing experience of being an individual and of having a sense of self, the sense that what we are experiencing is happening here, within what we call ourselves, and that this self has a personal history that we remember well.

On the surface of things, this idea of no-self seems to fly in the face of the very Western notion of soul, of being a particular locus of awareness and experience. If we look more closely, however, we see that while the Buddha emphasized that we have no lasting entityhood, even the earliest Buddhists, the Theravadans, saw that our consciousness is like a continuously moving stream, and the reality of that stream cannot be questioned. In the Mahamudra teaching, this stream of consciousness becomes transformed into what is referred to as the illusory body when enlightenment is attained.* The Buddha, then, was turning our attention to the illusion of being a permanent and enduring entity and challenging the delusion at the core of this type, that of being an isolated individual, without necessarily denying that our soul exists.

How, then, do we work through our attachment, our avarice? The logical solution, at least on the face of things, seems to be not being attached to anything. But this all too frequently becomes simply another variety of attachment: the drive *not* to have. Freedom from desire and attachment is something quite different. One of the things that we find if we look at our experience up close is that it is the standing apart from our experience that is at the heart of our attachment to it.

On the face of it, this may sound wildly paradoxical, but when we look closely at our direct experience, we see that there is a pulling away from what is going on inside of us, an aversion based on our fear of pain and desire for pleasure. We view our experience from a remove, however slight, based upon our prejudice about it, and this is what in fact perpetuates what we are attempting to get away from. We maintain our illusory world, both inner and outer, by not fully experiencing it.

One of the basic laws of consciousness is that what is not ultimately real in our experience will open up to reveal something deeper under experiential inquiry. We begin, then, with where we are—not where we think we should be or wish that we were but with the raw reality of our

---

* For a more thorough discussion of Buddhism and the concept of the soul, see Almaas's book, *The Inner Journey Home* (Boston & London: Shambhala Publications, Inc., 2004), pp. 505–15.

own direct experience. This is our journey, this is our own personal path. There is none other. As we open to it, deeper and deeper levels of the truth of our experience naturally unfold within our consciousness.

The way through our attachment, then, is full engagement. What we think we are experiencing when viewed from a distance changes when we deeply enter into it. We see this mirrored in the following quote from Philip Kapleau, recently deceased *roshi* in the Zen tradition of Buddhism:

> *That our sufferings are rooted in a selfish grasping and in fears and terrors which spring from our ignorance of the true nature of life and death becomes clear to anyone compelled by zazen to confront himself nakedly. But zazen makes equally plain that what we term "suffering" is our evaluation of pain from which we stand apart, that pain when courageously accepted is a means to liberation in that it frees our natural sympathies and compassion even as it enables us to experience pleasure and joy in a new depth and purity.*[8]

We see that our experience is a constantly changing stream, as the Buddhists tell us. We never have the same experience twice. Change is the constant, and when we truly know this experientially, we understand that there is no point in trying to fix or hold on to anything. The dynamism of our consciousness, the transitoriness of all experience, reflects the impermanence of all of the forms that exist in the world around us. Like our soul, all of manifestation is also akin to a constantly moving river, undulating, shifting, and changing.

The ground beneath our feet is in motion: the earth is circling the sun, moving at a speed of eighteen and a half miles per second, over a thousand miles an hour; and our entire solar system, in turn, is moving at one hundred forty miles per second, or about half a million miles per hour, as it circles the core of the Milky Way, the galaxy we are part of. Approximately twenty miles beneath the surface of the earth, things get very fluid. We live on a thin crust that appears to be quite static, while beneath this is a mass of seething movement. Despite how solid and unchanging mountains and continents seem, we know that everything shifts over time. Our moment-to-moment experience is that process of ceaseless change occurring in our own microcosm, electrifyingly quickly.

And there is nothing we can do to change that, no matter how much we would like to hang on to some wonderful experience or to do away with an unpleasant one. It is also not skillful. As Goldstein says,

> As we look at moments of unsatisfactoriness and pain and at moments of pleasure and joy, we can see how we relate to each of them and what really brings us happiness. If we hold on to things and they're changing, does that bring us happiness? Or if we want things to be a particular way, if we want our mind always to be calm or silent or our body always to have certain kinds of feelings, can we do that? Has anybody been able to make a mental or physical state endure forever? We start to see and feel how it is our very wanting to be calm, our need to be free, our spiritual desires, our subtle fear of the actual present that keeps us in conflict, in chains. It is not a matter of finally getting some spiritual state or ideal, but rather of coming back to the center of our being, here and now.
>
> . . . The truth of our being is simply this process of flowing change. Everything is impermanent. Nothing is worth grasping because nothing lasts. It is all empty, without self, like clouds moving through the sky. Knowing that nothing is secure, that there is no solid place on which to stand, we can let go, let be, and come to rest. We discover the depths of what it means to let go. For as much as we grasp and hold the body and senses, the feeling, the memory, ideas, reactions, and observation, so much do we make a separate "self," and so much do we suffer through this attachment.[9]

Not only do we create our sense of self through our attachment but in chicken-and-egg fashion, our holding on is driven by our beliefs about who and what we are. Believing ourselves to be separate from the fabric that makes up everything, we have no choice but to cling and grasp at things in order to survive. Believing our nature to be our physical self, we fear anything that threatens our bodily survival and do all we can to ensure that our organism will endure. This is what is at the heart of our avarice.

From another angle, we grasp at things and try to fix them to give ourselves a sense of permanence, since deep down we know that even that most constant thing, our body, will someday cease to exist. Intuiting our impermanence, in other words, we try to stem the tide of change, since inevitably that change involves cessation—the death of this form. We grasp after something solid and permanent to give us a sense of constancy in this endless sea of transitoriness. We have no alternative but to cling until we make peace with the fact that, like the earth, we may look solid and unchanging on the surface, but at the core change is our nature.

One face of our ultimate nature—who we fundamentally are—is this form, this manifestation, this unique soul. Our very existence is that ultimate nature taking form via our body and our soul. And all of manifestation, as we have seen, partakes of constant change. Existence and transitoriness are implicit one in the other.

The other face of our True Nature is focused on in the Buddha's truth of the nonexistence of the self. From this vantage point, all that exists also does not exist. It is here that we are faced with the mind-bending paradox that our deepest nature can neither be said to exist nor to not exist. The Absolute, the core of the core of us, is beyond the concepts of existence and nonexistence, cessation and birth, since these polarities require each other; and in the Absolute, all disappears.

When we know this, know this throughout the fabric of our consciousness, our avarice ends and we are free to open up. No longer clinging to our sense of self, we experience the virtue of this point: *nonattachment*. No longer holding on to this separate thing with its drive to survive, we are free to exist or not to exist—and to experience both at the same time. This is liberation. And out of this liberation, we are open to the tide moving in and out, to filling and emptying, to ceasing and generating.

Ichazo uses the word *detachment* as the virtue of this point, but with its connotation of distancing, which is more characteristic of egoic life than of liberation, the word *nonattachment* comes closer to what this virtue is all about. He defines this virtue as follows:

> It is the precise understanding of the body's needs. A detached being takes in exactly what he needs and lets everything else go. Detachment is the position which allows the energy of life to flow easily through the body.

A little translation and amplification is useful here. What Ichazo is describing is a realistic sense of one's *actual* needs—not our needs when experienced through the illusory filter of the separate self with its survival anxiety—and an openness to what actually fills those needs. This, of course, requires knowing ourselves to be something other than exclusively our bodies. The real question is what does our soul really need, and are we receptive to what truly nourishes it or not.

Answering this riddle calls for a dramatic shift in our orientation toward ourselves. It necessitates, ultimately and ironically, moving beyond our personality's self-referentiality, opening to what is beyond the confines of our skin, which paradoxically is what makes up what is within that containment of our body and what makes up everything else.

We get there by fully inhabiting our souls, as alluded to earlier. We have seen that the personality is perpetuated by our aversion to and withdrawal from direct immersion in our experience. This contraction, implicit in our soul and our body when shaped by our ego, is fear based. We are afraid of the contents of our experience, afraid to be fully swept up in the current of our inner movements, afraid that what we feel will overwhelm us or swallow us up. There is truth to this, but not in the way we think. What will be affected and will disappear is our familiar sense of things.

If our personality is characterized by withdrawal, then it only makes sense that working through our personality necessitates diving into what is going on within us. The argument typically arises at this juncture that our problem is that we are *too* engaged with our experience, but if we look closely, we see that this is really not the case. The contents of our consciousness keep repeating like a tape loop because we are not opening fully to them. Fully entering into our experience is not the same thing as emoting or acting out. Even then we are not fully inhabiting our experience, although it is often a start. We are simply being run by it.

Whether it is acted on or not, there is always some pulling away based on wanting the fear or pain or whatever difficulty we are experiencing to go away, or based on a judgment that what we are experiencing should be different or isn't all right. Even our positive experiences aren't fully entered into, out of our fear of fully opening our hearts to them. Instead, we tend to hold on to the experiences without their fully touching our soul. We experience everything through our judgments of good and bad, our positions and assumptions, and remain cut off from it all.

When we do this, we cannot really explore the contents of our consciousness in an impartial, objective way, a way in which we uncover our underlying convictions that tend to be wildly out of date. Most of them originated when we were quite young, and so are based on a child's assumptions and are no longer current or accurate. Even though these beliefs still feel convincing, they need to be made conscious so that we can explore what is still giving life to them, rather than assuming they are valid and being run by them.

What is needed, then, is twofold: becoming present to what is going on within our hearts, minds, and bodies, and experientially inquiring into what we find. Being present with our immediate experience and observing it is often not enough for the structures of the personality to relax and allow our soul to deepen. Many forms of inner work are oriented toward doing just this, but for most of us, this is not enough. Once we are deeply in touch with ourselves, what do we do with the content that we find? Sitting it out, as those of us who have spent years meditating know perhaps all too well, does not fully transform this content in most of us.

Nor is it enough to simply attempt to let that content go. We are caught up with it, identified with it, and so it is very difficult to just drop it, as many spiritual practices attempt to do. If we are identified with a belief or a feeling, which means that we take it to be the truth, one way we attempt to pry it out of our grip is by moving away from it—detaching ourselves and pulling away, in other words. This is the attempt we make when we are counseled to disidentify from something. We might for a time be able to successfully pull away from it—to not experience a particular thought or feeling—but our identification with it has only gone into hiding. In some cases, this approach works, but for the majority of us, when we try to disidentify by pulling away, we are simply supporting the orientation of the personality itself. We are supporting its holding on and holding back—its avarice—and so for most people, this is self-defeating and leads to a spiritual cul-de-sac.

Nor is this the most effective way of working through our personality structure in such a way that our fundamental identification shifts from the ego to Being. This comes down to the question of what we do with our mind, since our beliefs about reality are primary, forming the underpinning for our emotional states, our affective atmosphere, our perceptions of others and the world around us, and even our relationship and experience of our own body, as we have seen. We may know that the content of our mind shapes our reality and obscures our vision, our perception of what lies beyond it, but trying to drop our mind, to overcome it, or get rid of it is simply the ego trying to get rid of itself. Especially for Westerners, rather than attempting to let go of our mind, using it in a way that supports our unfoldment is the most effective way through.

Effective use of the mind in the service of transformation means using it to inquire into the contents of our consciousness, not in a disembodied way but in conjunction with being fully present to our here-and-now experience so that we are engaging it with the totality of ourselves—with our minds, our hearts, and our bodies. As we dive into our ongoing experience with an attitude of curiosity, we can begin to question the assumptions underlying our beliefs and emotional states. Such inquiry is what leads to true nonattachment.

Paradoxically, then, it is our wholehearted engagement with ourselves that takes us beyond our inner confines, beyond the prison walls of our conditioned sense of reality. This engagement is in fact an opening to ourselves, and this vulnerability and intimacy relaxes our gripping and clutching at ourselves. It is this openness that produces and in turn embodies and expresses nonattachment.

Nonattachment allows a precise understanding of our nature. And when we know our nature, what we truly are, we are open to the flow of life, which includes its other face—death. When we drop our self-containment, we open to the undulation of everything, we open to the dynamism that embodies the will to be, and in the same instance, who we have taken ourselves to be ceases.

All barriers are gone and we know ourselves to be part of that blackest of oceans, with its endless change on the surface, and its luminous and mysterious cessation at its depth. It is only then, when we understand that we are not separate from the ground of Being—that what we *are* is the ground of Being—that our impoverished attitude ends. When we see and know this directly, we realize that there is nothing to protect and nothing to hoard. We realize that we are part of the fabric of everything—that great Everything that is both existence and nonexistence in the same instant.

This is the start of a real life, a life that encompasses coming into being as well as cessation, or more accurately, a life expressing form and emptiness completely united, of ebb and flow, emptying and being filled, movement and stillness.

This is also the beginning of true generosity, which is the expression of nonattachment. In the words of Chögyam Trungpa, describing the Buddhist concept of *shunyata,* or the empty face of True Nature,

> Shunyata *literally means "openness" or "emptiness." Shunyata is basically understanding nonexistence. When you begin realizing nonexistence, then you can afford to be more compassionate, more giving. A problem is that usually we would like to hold on to our territory and fixate on that particular ground. Once we begin to fixate on that ground, we have no way to give. Understanding shunyata means that we begin to realize that there is no ground to get, that we are ultimately free, nonaggressive, open. We realize that we are actually nonexistent ourselves. We are not—no, rather. Then we can give. We have lots to gain and nothing to lose at that point. It is very basic.*[10]

When we know this side of our nature, we are open to receive and to give. We know that there is nothing to be attached to, nothing to hold on to or to hold back, because what we are is this openness. In the words of Sharon Salzberg,

> *Generosity has such power because it is characterized by the inner quality of letting go or relinquishing. Being able to let go, to give up, to renounce, to give generously—these capacities spring from the same source within us. When we practice generosity, we open to all of these liberating qualities simultaneously. They carry us to a profound knowing of freedom, and they also are the loving expression of that same freedom.*
>
> *The Buddha said that no true spiritual life is possible without a generous heart.*[11]

When we know our nature to be something that we cannot attach to, something that simply *is,* our soul can at long last fully relax, let go, and open up. Giving and receiving become the same thing. It is only then that we are able to truly take in, when there is no one who receives and no one who pulls away from anything. It is only then that we can fully open to and know the beauty and the richness that surround us in this world of form, which in turn expresses and embodies the effulgence and the generosity that is our deepest nature. It is only then that we are filled in an everlasting way with all of the treasures of reality.

—⁓— Having explored the passions and virtues of the fear corner of the enneagram, we have seen how fear is central to our experience when we are identified with our personality and believe we are our body. We explored this in its purest form when discussing the passion of fear at Point Six, and we have seen how our fear of pain—the issue highlighted by the passion of gluttony at Point Seven—causes us to grasp after pleasure and distraction. At Point Five we have seen that fear drives our avarice, our clinging to what we have, and we have explored how each of these differentiations of fear form formidable obstacles to our unfoldment.

We have also seen how facing our fear and questioning the assumptions that sustain it is a supreme act of courage—the virtue of Point Six—in action. As we soberly enter into and inhabit the totality of our experience—the virtue of Point Seven—our fear of pain gradually diminishes, replaced by our relief in making full contact with ourselves and with our love of the truth of our experience. And finally, we have seen how fully entering into ourselves paradoxically unwinds our frightening assumption that we are isolated individuals who must hang on to what we have, opening our consciousness to participation in the inclusiveness and generosity of reality.

AFTERWORD

———◇◇◇———

So I will just draw your attention to a couple of things here and there: that's all.
I will offer a few points of orientation, because the signs have become rusty
and covered over through lack of use. But you will have to make the journey on
your own. And that's the beauty of it. It exists for you alone.
—PETER KINGSLEY[1]

Our exploration of the passions and the virtues comes to
an end, but ideally your understanding and conscious living of them is only just beginning. Much of our focus has
been on the passions themselves rather than on the virtues. The reason, I hope, is obvious by now: understanding the passions within ourselves unlocks the virtues. The
virtues are a natural expression of our self-existing nature,
and so all we have to do is explore, shed the light of understanding on, and open up through inquiry what stands
between us and that nature in order for the virtues to
manifest in our consciousness.

It is easy to say that this is all we have to do. While
the task is really quite simple and straightforward, it is at
once incredibly difficult. It is not something we can do
with our minds alone. You can read this book and take in
a lot of useful and interesting information, but if it stays
only conceptual, the reality that is your potential will remain only an idea to you as well. All of the insights in the
world do not transform us if they remain only intellectual, and this is the limit that many people reach in talking about their issues, whether in psychotherapy or in

spiritual work. Unless your insights are experiential ones that illuminate your soul and shed light upon your ignorance, transformation of the actual substance of your consciousness—your soul—does not happen. It is this direct and immediate understanding about the state of your soul, felt down to your marrow, that expands your consciousness—nothing else.

And you must be ruthless to do this. Unearthing the passions within your own soul requires brutal honesty with yourself. It demands being willing to see yourself exactly as you are, which is often not easy to do. This is because the passions themselves stand in our way, convincing us we don't need to look in the first place and obscuring what we see when we do look. Our inertia and our self-deception, our pride and our fear that we can't bear what we see all block our path—and I'm touching on just a few of the passions. Learning to see ourselves clearly is itself the heart of this process, and being willing to see ourselves as we are is only possible with infinite self-acceptance and kindness toward ourselves. You must forsake your judgments and have the utmost compassion for yourself, knowing that this is just the way things are in the world of ego.

When you do this sincerely, when you face your reality as it is without any blinders, and you bring the full weight of the intelligence of your soul to bear on the conundrums represented by the passions, then you stand a good chance of getting in touch with the virtues in time. This means getting in touch with them in the only way that matters—through your own transformation, through the changes and openings that you, personally, experience. Neither the passions nor the virtues have any inherent value unless your work with them helps you grow. That is what the map of the enneagram is for—helping you to develop.

This is indeed a process. Developing the necessary qualities needed for this journey takes time, just as our whole exploration of the passions takes time even if we have the requisite determination, truthfulness, and compassion. This is because there are layers and layers of subtleties of the passions within ourselves. We open up one level of them only to find another revealing itself in the recesses of our hearts. As long as our personality is operative, the passions are present, so this should come as no surprise.

This book, then, is a chart of this journey that we can each take. On this journey, there are places that we all must visit, places that we invari-

ably all pass through. This is what the enneagram maps out for us. This is
its gift and its value for us. This is not a rapid journey but one for which
we need enormous patience. We cannot rush the process, no matter how
good a map we have. We must remember that our soul has its own tim-
ing, the time it takes to really see ourselves objectively and digest our insights, which can't be hurried, and which is always individual.

And even though there are common ports of call along the way, this
is a journey that each of us must make on our own. While many of
the places that we pass through are collective—ones that we all must
encounter—nonetheless we each must pass through them within our own
self. We must traverse them in the aloneness of our own soul. We may have
guides for the journey, and in fact almost all of us need them since the territory is so slippery and elusive, so full of hidden pitfalls and abysses. But
no matter how much guidance we get, in the end it is our own personal
journey.

This journey necessitates a great deal of hard work and discipline,
since facing ourselves goes against the grain of our conditioning and, at
least initially, is never easy. It calls upon us to embrace our inner reality,
and to do so with courage and realism. It requires that we experience ourselves fully and intimately, with infinite sincerity and truthfulness, profound vulnerability and openness of heart. It requires nothing less than
the virtues themselves. When we align our consciousness with the attitudes that are the virtues, our process opens up. When we stay caught up
in the passions, the territory we travel through stays the same, repeating
endless variations of the same scenery, while the soundtrack just keeps replaying the same old song. As we become skilled in traveling our inner
landscape, the virtues themselves are informing our soul.

And this is a peculiar journey, full of paradoxes and unlike any other,
since on this odyssey, we don't arrive anywhere. There is nowhere to get to
except right here. The traveling itself transforms the landscape. Before we
know it, everything looks and feels different and we are changed, even
though the terrain is all the same.

This is not a journey for everyone, nor is it a trek that anyone is forced
to make. In fact, you can't be commandeered into it. You have to choose
to do it. And you have to undertake it wholeheartedly if you are going to

get anywhere—even though that turns out to be where you started. You certainly don't have to make this trip; life in many ways can seem easier if we don't. But if you are one of those who cannot rest without exploring, if you have always had a particular homesickness that nothing in life resolves, if you can't remain cozily asleep in the familiar and the known of your life and must set out on the daring adventure of discovering yourself, it is my sincere hope that this book has given you some signposts that will be useful in your travels.

NOTES

—◦◦◦—

CHAPTER 1.
THE ENNEAGRAM, THE SOUL,
THE PASSIONS AND THE VIRTUES

1. Plotinus, *Enneads* (Cambridge, Mass., and London: Harvard University Press, 1984), bk. II, treatise iii, sec. 7.
2. Claudio Naranjo, *Character and Neurosis: An Integrative View* (Nevada City, Calif.: Gateways/IDHHB, 1994), 29.
3. Ibid., 24.
4. Ibid., 25.
5. Ibid., 24.
6. Ibid., 28.
7. J. G. Bennett, *Enneagram Studies* (York Beach, Me.: Samuel Weiser, 1983), 2.
8. Ibid., 2–3.
9. Michael S. Schneider, *A Beginner's Guide to Constructing the Universe* (New York: HarperCollins, 1994), 223.
10. Claudio Naranjo, *Ennea-type Structures: Self-Analysis for the Seeker* (Nevada City, Calif.: Gateways/IDHHB, 1990), 7.
11. Ibid., 8–9.

CHAPTER 2.
POINT NINE—LAZINESS AND ACTION

1. P. D. Ouspensky, *In Search of the Miraculous: Fragments of an Unknown Teaching* (New York: Harcourt Brace Jovanovich, 1949), 219.

2. Naranjo, *Character and Neurosis* (Nevada City, Calif.: Gateways/IDHHB, 1994), 255.

3. Ibid., 2.

4. A. H. Almaas, *Facets of Unity: The Enneagram of Holy Ideas* (Berkeley: Diamond Books, 1998), 44–45.

5. Naranjo, *Character and Neurosis,* 246.

6. Ouspensky, *In Search of the Miraculous: Fragments of an Unknown Teaching,* 121.

7. This and all following definitions of the passions and virtues by Oscar Ichazo are from unpublished teaching notes of the Arica Institute.

CHAPTER 3.

POINT EIGHT—LUST AND INNOCENCE

1. King James Version of the Holy Bible.

2. Sigmund Freud, "The Ego and the Id" (1915), *Standard Edition of the Complete Psychological Works of Sigmund Freud,* edited by James Strachey (London: Hogarth Press and the Institute of Psychoanalysis, 1953–74), vol. 19, 26.

3. Claudio Naranjo, *Character and Neurosis: An Integrative View* (Nevada City, Calif.: Gateways/IDHHB, 1994), 28.

4. Virginia Woolf, *The Waves* (New York: Harcourt Brace Jovanovich, 1931), 289–90.

5. Jay R. Greenberg and Stephen A. Mitchell, *Object Relations in Psychoanalytic Theory* (Cambridge, Mass., and London: Harvard University Press, 1983), 26, 57.

6. Calvin S. Hall, *Primer of Freudian Psychology* (New York: New American Library, 1979), 27.

7. Freud, *New Introductory Lectures on Psychoanalysis* (New York and London: W. W. Norton, 1933), 91.

8. Freud, "The Ego and the Id," (1923) *Standard Edition,* vol. 19, 25.

9. Freud, *New Introductory Lectures on Psychoanalysis,* 100. [Italics mine.]

10. W. R. D. Fairbairn, *Psychoanalytic Studies of the Personality* (London and New York: Routledge, 1990), 106.

11. Gopi Krishna, with psychological commentary by James Hillman, *Kundalini: The Evolutionary Energy in Man* (Boulder: Shambhala, 1970), 68.

12. Naranjo, *Character and Neurosis,* 140.

13. Ibid., 140–41.

CHAPTER 4.

POINT ONE—ANGER AND SERENITY

1. Chien-chih Seng-ts'an, translated by Richard B. Clarke, *Hsin-hsin Ming: Verses on the Faith-Mind* (Buffalo, N.Y.: White Pine Press, 1973), n.p.

2. Claudio Naranjo, *Character and Neurosis: An Integrative View* (Nevada City, Calif.: Gateways/IDHHB, 1994), 40.

3. A. H. Almaas, *Facets of Unity: The Enneagram of Holy Ideas* (Berkeley: Diamond Books, 1998), 151.

4. Calvin Hall, *A Primer of Freudian Psychology* (New York: New American Library, Inc., 1954), 34.

5. Freud, "Civilization and Its Discontents," (1930) *Standard Edition,* vol. 21, 128–29.

6. Ibid., 136.

7. Ibid., 134.

8. Ibid., 110.

CHAPTER 5.

POINT THREE—DECEIT AND VERACITY

1. Lao Tzu, *Tao Te Ching: The Definitive Edition,* translation and commentary by Jonathan Star (New York: Tarcher/Putnam, 2001), verse 32, 45.

2. Claudio Naranjo, *Character and Neurosis: An Integrative View* (Nevada City, Calif.: Gateways/IDHHB, 1994), 201.

3. A. H. Almaas, *Facets of Unity: The Enneagram of Holy Ideas* (Berkeley: Diamond Books, 1998), 272.

4. Ibid., 260.

5. Almaas, *Diamond Heart Book Three: Being and the Meaning of Life* (Berkeley: Diamond Books, 1990) 72–73.

6. Ibid., 73.

CHAPTER 6.

POINT TWO—PRIDE AND HUMILITY

1. James Fadiman and Robert Frager, editors, *Essential Sufism* (Edison, N.J.: Castle Books, 1998), 177.

2. Claudio Naranjo, *Character and Neurosis: An Integrative View* (Nevada City, Calif.: Gateways/IDHHB, 1994), 176.

3. Ibid., 176.

4. Ibid.

5. Ibid., 175.

6. Ibid., 191.

7. Karen Horney, *Neurosis and Human Growth: The Struggle Toward Self-realization* (New York: W. W. Norton, 1950), 90.

8. Ibid., 91.

9. Ibid., 87.

10. Ibid., 96.

11. Chögyam Trungpa, *Cutting Through Spiritual Materialism* (Berkeley: Shambhala, 1973), 13.

12. Ibid., 15.

13. Carl G. Jung, *The Portable Jung,* edited by Joseph Campbell (Princeton: Princeton University Press, 1971), 87.

14. Jack Kornfield, *A Path with Heart* (New York: Bantam Books, 1993), 129.

15. Mariana Caplan, *Halfway Up the Mountain* (Prescott, Ariz.: Holm Press, 1999), 187.

16. *Webster's Third New International Dictionary* (Springfield, Mass.: Merriam-Webster, 1993), s.v. *humility.*

17. Jacob Needleman, *The American Soul: Rediscovering the Wisdom of the Founders* (New York: Tarcher/Putnam, 2002), 95.

18. Benjamin Franklin, *The Autobiography of Benjamin Franklin* (New York: Penguin/Putnam, 2001), 49.

19. Walter Isaacson, *Benjamin Franklin: An American Life* (New York: Simon & Schuster, 2003), 92.

CHAPTER 7.
POINT FOUR—ENVY AND EQUANIMITY

1. Nyanaponika Thera, "The Four Sublime States: Contemplations on Love, Compassion, Sympathetic Joy and Equanimity," *The Wheel Publication,* no. 6 (Kandy, Sri Lanka: Buddhist Publication Society, 1958).

2. St. John of the Cross, *Dark Night of the Soul,* translated by E. Allison Peers (New York: Image Books, 1959), 58–59.

3. Peter Salovey, editor, *The Psychology of Jealousy and Envy* (New York: Guilford Press, 1991), 272.

4. *Merriam-Webster's Collegiate Dictionary and Thesaurus,* s.v. *envy.*

5. Melanie Klein, *Envy and Gratitude and Other Works, 1946–1963* (New York: Free Press, 1975), 181.

6. Ibid., 189.

7. Ibid., 183.

8. Claudio Naranjo, *Character and Neurosis: An Integrative View* (Nevada City, Calif.: Gateways/IDHHB, 1994), 97.

9. Ibid., 96–97.

10. Ibid., 117.

11. Ann and Barry Ulanov, *Cinderella and Her Sisters: The Envied and the Envying* (Einsiedeln, Switz.: Daimon Verlag, 1998), 45.

12. Ibid., 46.

13. Ibid., 177.

14. Harold Boris, *Envy* (Northvale, N.J., and London: Jason Aronson, 1994), xv.

15. Ulanov, *Cinderella and Her Sisters,* 69.

16. Ibid., 100–1.

17. Sharon Salzberg, *Lovingkindness: The Revolutionary Art of Happiness* (Boston and London: Shambhala, 2002), 138–39.

18. Joseph Goldstein and Jack Kornfield, *Seeking the Heart of Wisdom: The Path of Insight Meditation* (Boston and London: Shambhala, 1987), 75.

19. Ulanov, *Cinderella and Her Sisters*, 153.

CHAPTER 8.

POINT SIX—FEAR AND COURAGE

1. Jean-Yves Leloup, translator, *The Gospel of Mary Magdalene* (Rochester, Vt.: Inner Traditions, 2002), 27.

2. A. H. Almaas, *Facets of Unity: The Enneagram of Holy Ideas* (Berkeley: Diamond Books, 1998), 243.

3. Claudio Naranjo, *Character and Neurosis: An Integrative View* (Nevada City, Calif.: Gateways/IDHHB, 1994), 223.

4. Ibid., 227.

5. Sigmund Freud, *Inhibitions, Symptoms and Anxiety* (New York and London: W. W. Norton, 1959), 100.

6. Ibid., 101.

7. Ibid., 103.

8. Sigmund Freud, *New Introductory Lectures in Psycho-Analysis* (New York and London: W. W. Norton, 1965), 110.

9. Jay R. Greenberg and Stephen Mitchell, *Object Relations in Psychoanalytic Theory* (Cambridge, Mass., and London, 1983), 93.

10. Ibid., 99.

CHAPTER 9.

POINT SEVEN—GLUTTONY AND SOBRIETY

1. Stephen Mitchell, editor, *The Enlightened Mind: An Anthology of Sacred Prose* (New York: HarperPerennial, 1991), 77.

2. *Webster's Third New International Dictionary* (Springfield, Mass.: Merriam-Webster, 1993), s.v. *gluttony*.

3. Claudio Naranjo, *Character and Neurosis: An Integrative View* (Nevada City, Calif.: Gateways/IDHHB, 1994), 151.

4. St. John of the Cross, translated by E. Allison Peers, *Dark Night of the Soul* (New York: Image Books, 1959), 54.

5. Ibid., 57.

6. Sigmund Freud, "Formulations on the Two Principles of Mental Functioning" (1911), *Standard Edition of the Complete Psychological Works of Sigmund Freud*, edited by James

Strachey (London: Hogarth Press and the Institute of Psychoanalysis, 1953–74), vol. 12, 218.

7. Freud, "The Economic Problem of Masochism," vol. 19 of the *Standard Edition*, 1924, 160.

8. Freud, "Formulations on the Two Principles of Mental Functioning," vol. 12 of the *Standard Edition*, 1911, 200.

9. Jay R. Greenberg and Stephen Mitchell, *Object Relations in Psychoanalytic Theory* (Cambridge, Mass., and London: Harvard University Press, 1983), 400.

10. Ibid., 405–6.

11. *Webster's Third New International Dictionary*, s.v. *sober.*

CHAPTER 10.
POINT FIVE—AVARICE AND NONATTACHMENT

1. Shunryu Suzuki, *Zen Mind, Beginner's Mind* (New York and Tokyo: Weatherhill, 1970), 138.

2. *Webster's Third New International Dictionary* (Springfield, Mass.: Merriam-Webster, 1993), s.v. *avarice.*

3. Claudio Naranjo, *Character and Neurosis: An Integrative View* (Nevada City, Calif.: Gateways/IDHHB, 1994), 66.

4. A. H. Almaas, *Facets of Unity: The Enneagram of Holy Ideas* (Berkeley: Diamond Books, 1998), 102.

5. Naranjo, *Character and Neurosis,* 66.

6. Joseph Goldstein, *The Experience of Insight: A Natural Unfolding* (Santa Cruz, Calif.: Unity Press, 1976), 88–90.

7. Ibid., 89.

8. Philip Kapleau, editor, *The Three Pillars of Zen: Teaching, Practice, and Enlightenment* (Boston: Beacon Press, 1967), 16.

9. Joseph Goldstein and Jack Kornfield, *Seeking the Heart of Wisdom: The Path of Insight Meditation* (Boston and London: Shambhala, 1987), 56.

10. Chögyam Trungpa, edited by Carolyn Rose Gimian, *The Essential Chögyam Trungpa* (Boston and London: Shambhala, 1999), 118.

11. Sharon Salzberg, *Lovingkindness: The Revolutionary Art of Happiness* (Boston and London: Shambhala, 2002), 154–55.

AFTERWORD

1. Peter Kingsley, *Reality* (Inverness, Calif.: Golden Sufi Center, 2003), 159.

BIBLIOGRAPHY

Almaas, A. H. *Diamond Heart Books 1–4*. Berkeley: Diamond Books, 1987–97.

———. *The Elixir of Enlightenment*. York Beach, Me.: Samuel Weiser, 1984.

———. *Essence*. York Beach, Me.: Samuel Weiser, 1986.

———. *Facets of Unity*. Berkeley: Diamond Books, 1998.

———. *The Inner Journey Home*. Boston and London: Shambhala, 2004.

———. *The Pearl Beyond Price*. Berkeley: Diamond Books, 1988.

———. *The Point of Existence*. Berkeley: Diamond Books, 1996.

———. *Spacecruiser Inquiry*. Boston and London: Shambhala, 2002.

———. *The Void*. Berkeley: Diamond Books, 1986.

Bennett, J. G. *Enneagram Studies*. York Beach, Me.: Samuel Weiser, 1983.

Bettelheim, Bruno. *Freud and Man's Soul*. New York: Vintage Books, 1982.

Blanck, G., and R. Blanck. *Ego Psychology: Theory and Practice*. New York: Columbia University Press, 1974.

Boris, Harold. *Envy*. Northvale, N.J., and London: Jason Aronson, 1994.

Caplan, Mariana. *Halfway Up the Mountain*. Prescott, Ariz.: Holm Press, 1999.

Fadiman, James, and Robert Frager. *Essential Sufism*. Edison, N.J.: Castle Books, 1998

Fairbairn, W.R.D. *Psychoanalytic Studies of the Personality*. London and New York: Routledge, 1990.

Franklin, Benjamin. *The Autobiography of Benjamin Franklin*. New York: Penguin/Putnam, 2001.

Freud, Sigmund. *Inhibitions, Symptoms and Anxiety*. New York and London: W. W. Norton, 1959.

————. *New Introductory Lectures in Psycho-Analysis.* New York and London: W. W. Norton, 1965.

————. *The Standard Edition of the Complete Works of Sigmund Freud.* New York: W. W. Norton, 1949.

Goldstein, Joseph. *The Experience of Insight: A Natural Unfolding.* Santa Cruz, Calif.: Unity Press, 1976.

Goldstein, Joseph, and Jack Kornfield. *Seeking the Heart of Wisdom: The Path of Insight Meditation.* Boston and London: Shambhala, 1987.

Greenberg, Jay R., and Stephen A. Mitchell. *Object Relations in Psychoanalytic Theory.* Cambridge, Mass.: Harvard University Press, 1983.

Hall, Calvin. *A Primer of Freudian Psychology.* New York: New American Library, 1979.

Horney, Karen. *Neurosis and Human Growth: The Struggle Toward Self-Realization.* New York: W. W. Norton, 1950.

Isaacson, Walter. *Benjamin Franklin: An American Life.* New York: Simon & Schuster, 2003.

Jung, Carl G. *The Portable Jung.* Edited by Joseph Campbell. Princeton: Princeton University Press, 1971.

Kaplan, Louise J. *Oneness and Separateness: From Infant to Individual.* New York: Simon & Schuster, 1978.

Kapleau, Philip, editor. *The Three Pillars of Zen: Teaching, Practice, and Enlightenment.* Boston: Beacon Press, 1967.

Kingsley, Peter. *Reality.* Inverness, Calif.: Golden Sufi Center, 2003.

Klein, Melanie. *Envy and Gratitude and Other Works, 1946–1963.* New York: Free Press, 1975.

Kornfield, Jack. *A Path with Heart: A Guide Through the Perils and Promises of Spiritual Life.* New York: Bantam Books, 1993.

Krishna, Gopi. *Kundalini: The Evolutionary Energy in Man.* Boulder: Shambhala, 1970.

Laloup, Jean-Yves, translator. *The Gospel of Mary Magdalene.* Rochester, Vt.: Inner Traditions, 2002.

Mahler, Margaret, Fred Pine, and Anni Bergman. *The Psychological Birth of the Human Infant.* New York: Basic Books, 1975.

Maitri, Sandra. *The Spiritual Dimension of the Enneagram: Nine Faces of the Soul.* New York: Tarcher/ Penguin, 2000.

Merriam-Webster's Collegiate Dictionary. Springfield, Mass.: Merriam-Webster Publishers, 1993.

Mitchell, Stephen, editor. *The Enlightened Heart: An Anthology of Sacred Poetry.* New York: HarperPerennial, 1989.

Mitchell, Stephen A., and Margaret J. Black. *Freud and Beyond.* New York: Basic Books, 1995.

Moore, James. *Gurdjieff: The Anatomy of a Myth.* Rockport, Mass.: Element, 1991.

Naranjo, Claudio. *Character and Neurosis: An Integrative View.* Nevada City, Calif.: Gateways/IDHHB, 1994.

———. *Ennea-type Structures: Self-Analysis for the Seeker.* Nevada City, Calif.: Gateways/IDHHB, 1990.

Needleman, Jacob. *The American Soul: Rediscovering the Wisdom of the Founders.* New York: Jeremy Tarcher/Penguin, 2002.

The New English Bible. Oxford and Cambridge, U.K.: Oxford University Press, 1961.

Ouspensky, P. D. *In Search of the Miraculous: Fragments of an Unknown Teaching.* New York: Harcourt Brace Jovanovich, 1949.

Salovey, Peter, editor. *The Psychology of Jealousy and Envy.* New York: Guildford Press, 1991.

Salzberg, Sharon. *Lovingkindness: The Revolutionary Art of Happiness.* Boston and London: Shambhala, 2002.

Schneider, Michael S. *A Beginner's Guide to Constructing the Universe.* New York: HarperCollins, 1994.

Seng-T'san. *The Hsin Hsin Ming: Verses on the Faith Mind.* Translated by Richard B. Clark. New York: White Pine Press, 2001.

St. John of the Cross. *Dark Night of the Soul.* Translated by E. Allison Peers. New York: Image Books, 1959.

Suzuki, Shunryu. *Zen Mind, Beginner's Mind.* New York and Tokyo: Weatherhill, 1970.

Tarnas, Richard. *The Passion of the Western Mind: Understanding the Ideas That Have Shaped Our World View.* New York: Ballantine Books, 1991.

Trungpa, Chögyam. *Cutting Through Spiritual Materialism.* Berkeley: Shambhala, 1973.

———. *The Essential Chögyam Trungpa.* Edited by Carolyn Rose Gimian. Boston and London: Shambhala, 1999.

Tzu, Lao. *Tao Te Ching: The Definitive Edition.* Translation and commentary by Jonathan Star. New York: Tarcher/Penguin, 2001.

Ulanov, Ann and Barry. *Cinderella and Her Sisters: The Envied and the Envying.* Einsiedeln, Switz.: Daimon-Verlag, 1998.

Webster's Third New International Dictionary. Springfield, Mass.: Merriam-Webster Publishers, 1993.

Woolf, Virginia. *The Waves.* New York: Harcourt Brace Jovanovich, 1931.

INDEX

ABOUT THE AUTHOR

Sandra Maitri has worked with the enneagram for three and a half decades since studying with Claudio Naranjo in the first group in which it was taught in the United States. As one of the principal teachers of the Diamond Approach to Inner Realization, the work founded by Hammeed Ali (A. H. Almaas), she teaches the enneagram within the larger context of spiritual unfoldment. She leads groups in the San Francisco Bay Area, the United Kingdom, and Europe. She lives, writes, and paints in Marin County, California.